Living Beauty

Celebrating Faith
Explorations in Latino Spirituality and Theology
Series Editor: Virgilio Elizondo

This series will present seminal, insightful, and inspirational works drawing on the experiences of Christians in the Latino traditions. Books in this series will explore topics such as the roots of a Mexican-American understanding of God's presence in the life of the people, the perduring influence of the Guadalupe event, the spirituality of immigrants, and the role of popular religion in teaching and living the faith.

Living Beauty

The Art of Liturgy

Alejandro Garcia-Rivera and
Thomas Scirghi

ROWMAN & LITTLEFIELD PUBLISHERS, INC.
Lanham • Boulder • New York • Toronto • Plymouth, UK

ROWMAN & LITTLEFIELD PUBLISHERS, INC.

Published in the United States of America
by Rowman & Littlefield Publishers, Inc.
A wholly owned subsidiary of The Rowman & Littlefield Publishing Group, Inc.
4501 Forbes Boulevard, Suite 200, Lanham, Maryland 20706
www.rowmanlittlefield.com

Estover Road
Plymouth PL6 7PY
United Kingdom

British Library Cataloguing in Publication Information Available

Library of Congress Cataloging-in-Publication Data:

García-Rivera, Alex.
  Living beauty : the art of liturgy / Alex García-Rivera and Thomas Scirghi.
     p. cm.
  ISBN-13: 978-0-7425-5216-6 (cloth : alk. paper)
  ISBN-10: 0-7425-5216-0 (cloth : alk. paper)
  ISBN-13: 978-0-7425-5217-3 (pbk. : alk. paper)
  ISBN-10: 0-7425-5217-9 (pbk. : alk. paper)
  1. Liturgics. 2. Public worship. I. Scirghi, Thomas J. II. Title.
  BV176.3.G37 2008
  264'.02001—dc22

                                                              2007014070

Printed in the United States of America

∞™ The paper used in this publication meets the minimum requirements of
American National Standard for Information Sciences—Permanence of Paper
for Printed Library Materials, ANSI/NISO Z39.48-1992.

✛
Contents

✝

Acknowledgments

There are many kind souls who helped make this book possible. We would like to thank our students and guest lecturers in our liturgical aesthetics class. They were the first to be exposed to this material and to help us shape the contents. We are also grateful to the Hermeneutics seminar of the North American Academy of Liturgy, the theologians attending the Second International Theological Aesthetics conference, and the faculty of the Jesuit School of Theology at Berkeley for inviting us to present material from the book and providing encouraging and critical feedback. We would also like to thank architect James Goring for his helpful comments on part of this material.

Thomas Scirghi would especially like to thank the School of Theology and Ministry at Seattle University for inviting him to present "This Blessed Mess" to their faculty and students. He is indebted to the Cathedral Parish of Christ the Light, Oakland, California who inspired the first chapter and more. Even more special have been the discussions that took place at the East Bay "Theology on Tap" program, Newman Hall of the Holy Spirit, and the catechetical class at San Quentin prison. Their lively discussion on selections from the book have enriched the material.

Alejandro Garcia-Rivera would especially like to thank Michael Fish and the Camaldolese monks at Incarnation monastery at Berkeley and New Camaldoli Hermitage at Big Sur who were exposed to much of the material in the book and gave kind and critical discussion of many of its themes and ideas. He is especially grateful to architect Craig Hartman, Fellow of the AIA, of Skidmore, Owings & Merrill, San Francisco, California and chief architect for the Cathedral Christ the Light of Oakland for his lectures to our students. He is indebted to Professor Mary McGann of the Franciscan School of Theology at Berkeley who read the chapter on theodramatics and gave very helpful advice. He is also indebted to the Courtney Murray group on North American philosophy that meets in July every summer at Berkeley. Their kind comments and helpful discussions of many of the chapters in this book have truly made this work a community affair.

Indeed, we both feel this work is the work of a community, a community of the Beautiful.

Introduction

Alejandro Garcia-Rivera

A LIVING BEAUTY

I stood in awe. The Cathedral of Metz that had stood for hundreds of years now loomed before me. I had come to Metz to give a talk on Latin American theology and was looking forward to seeing my first European Gothic cathedral. I had come expecting to see something ancient and monumental. Yet before me, as I walked in, a breath-taking work of beauty captivated my eyes. A very much alive and contemporary stained glass window created by the Jewish artist Marc Chagall alerted me that I was not standing in a museum. This cathedral was alive in beauty! Yet more of the cathedral's beauty began to reveal itself. Next to the Chagall, a sober and restrained Gothic window gave muted witness to a time of great sensibility to the dignity of the One who comes to meet us. In contrast to the Gothic, a Renaissance window explodes with color and unrestrained lines and forms. I had not expected this. This cathedral was not an ancient museum filled with beautiful things. It had a life and that life was beautiful in itself.

The windows told me this cathedral was alive. It had changed and adapted as the centuries passed within its walls. Yet, instead of growing old and weathered, it had become a place of beauty, a beauty, as Saint Augustine said, ever-ancient and ever-new. The cathedral was beautiful not merely for containing beautiful artworks though it was filled with these. Her beauty was more elusive. It lay in a life that took place century after century within her walls. It became perfectly clear to me. The beauty of the Cathedral of Metz was not the experience of a beautiful thing but a

1

shot of life itself, a life thoroughly laced in beauty. I stood in the presence of a Living Beauty. As such, it is not the kind of beauty philosophers and art critics write about. Of course, the Chagall window can be described by a philosophical aesthetics or by the tools of art criticism. Its ability to give life, however, and to give it precisely through its beauty, of this contemporary aesthetics and art criticism know very little. What sort of beauty is this, then? And where does it come from?

A TALE OF TWO ALTARS

The answer to these questions, I realized, must be found in the peculiar sign of almost all pre-Vatican II churches. This church had two altars. One altar stood pressed against the Eastern wall of the cathedral. A priest celebrating mass there would have been lost in the cavernous space of the nave. Indeed, it appeared to be this way by design. This altar was meant to be a kind of horizon, a place where heaven and earth meet. This horizon was located at what could be characterized as the "head" of the cathedral. When viewed from above the floor plan of the cathedral has the form of a cross. The pre-Vatican II altar is located where Jesus' head would have hung in agony.

The other altar, in contrast, was found on the centerline of the nave, near the intersection of the "arms" and the "body" of the cross. This intersection could be characterized as the "heart" of the cathedral. It is located on the cross shape near where Jesus' heart would have beaten until the last breath would be offered to the Father. The two describe a tale, a tale of two altars. It is a tale that, in a sense, has yet to be told in its entirety. For in the contrast between "head" and "heart" lies the meaning of the vision of the great council of Vatican II. Over forty years have passed since the council closed, and it is becoming distant enough that its teachings are being revisited by all sorts of groups in the Church. Perhaps the teaching that is receiving the greatest revisit is that on the liturgy, *Sacrosanctum Concilium*. What prompted the writing of this book is the danger that much of this revisiting will result in a judgment of *Sacrosanctum Concilium* rather than an assessment.

That such a judgment has already happened can be garnered in the way the tale of two altars is often told. One such tale speaks of the altars as a "before" and "after" story. Either one altar represented all that was wrong with the Church before Vatican II and the other all that was right after the council. Of course, the other variation of the tale is that one altar represents all that is wrong with the Church after Vatican II and the other all that was right before. Indeed, a brief exploration through the Internet reveals a great deal of discussion of reforming the "reform" of Vatican II. But what is the true meaning of the two altars? Can the before and after story adequately describe the meaning and the implications of *Sacrosanctum Concilium*? Father Scirghi and I argue that it is not. An assessment of *Sacrosanctum Concilium*, we argue, reveals that the ground of the Council's vision of the liturgy was a profound aesthetics, an aesthetics that unfortunately was intuited but not developed.

The tale of two altars, as we see it, is a tale of horizons, a tale where Life and Beauty, Heaven and Earth, meal and sacrifice, praise and lament, indeed head and heart meet. The tale of two altars is not a "before" and "after" story but a story of living continuity, a place where a memory comes alive and gives life, and life abundantly through a Beauty that takes form in the Liturgy. Such living form is a new creation, a new form of life crafting a way of holy living in the active hallowing of God's name. Yet while such a tale is a tale of continuity, the second altar gives the key to the meaning of the tale. This heart as revealed in the teachings of Vatican II is also the heart of the world.[1] The liturgy is not merely for those who would gaze at the agonized face of the crucified Christ but also for the world itself. When John gives us the moving imagery that connects Jesus' crucifixion and the liturgy, the blood and water that flows from his side, he reveals, as well, the sense of the second altar.

Christ's sacrifice is a "lifting up" for the entire world to see. In the Church's liturgy, a kind of living imagination exists. It is the imagination of a great Beauty that gives life abundantly. It is an imagination that "lifts up" the carnal both in the sense of giving flesh life but also of giving ordinary materials great Beauty. Such an imagination, an imagination that lifts up the Christ for the world to see, is the anagogical imagination of all true art and beauty. It is also the neglected and overlooked dimension of the second altar. This dimension has implications for liturgical theology. It suggests that a liturgical theology that takes account of the second altar may find its proper foundation not in history or Scripture or tradition or dogma or ritual but in aesthetics. For a liturgy given not so much for the sake of the Church but for the sake of the world must attract the world to what is lifted up. In other words, it must be something of great Beauty.

This was Vatican II's greatest gift to help the Church enter the twenty-first century of its life. This book was written that the consciousness of such gift may not be lost in hasty judgments. More importantly, it was written that such a gift, like a true gift, may continue to give in the generations to come. That gift is not only the revelation that within church walls lies the beating heart of the world within the beating heart of the risen Christ but also that the Liturgy is the gift of one heart to another heart, a gift of great Beauty, indeed, a Living Beauty.

A TALE OF TWO VOICES

I suppose it is appropriate that a book written to elucidate a tale of two altars would be written in two voices, Father Scirghi's voice and my own voice. As such, it raises the question of method and calls to explain the unique approach to this book resulting from many decisions and judgments that signal, we think, changes in the way theology is done and written. This book was born in a fruitful conversation between Father Scirghi and me. The conversation centered around a question we posed to one another: what would an aesthetics of the liturgy look like? Behind our question was the document by the U.S. bishops called *Built of Living Stones*.[2] The document has much to praise it for its treatment of the arts within the liturgy. We were greatly encouraged that the Church was officially renewing its interest in the role of the arts in the liturgical life of the Church.

At the same time the document raised for both of us serious questions about its adequacy. The great insight of *Built of Living Stones* was that the liturgy took place with the help of living forms, forms come alive through the arts, indeed, forms made of "living stones." Yet this great insight seemed to us not to be as profound as it could be. Are the arts merely an "environment" for the celebration of the liturgy? Are the arts merely a "support"? Or is there a deeper connection between the liturgy and the arts? Father Scirghi and I came to the conclusion that there was. It was a conclusion made by two scholars in different fields. Father Scirghi's field is liturgical theology and mine systematic theology. To others outside our fields, such distinctions appear petty and insubstantial but liturgical theology has an approach very different from systematic theology.

Liturgical theology is, at once, a theology that can be highly speculative but also very pastoral. It needs to be so. It studies a practice that is a theology. Systematic theology, on the other hand, can be highly speculative, especially my specialty, fundamental theology. Fundamental theology is a branch of systematic theology that tries to ask questions such as: What is theology? What are its sources? What makes theology possible? My interest in fundamental theology, on the other hand, comes from trying to understand a practice. I wanted to understand the theology behind Hispanic popular religion. Indeed, a fundamental question in Latin American theology has been where an authentic Latin American theology can be found. That question, the consensus indicates, is to be found in the poetry, music, and rites of popular religion.

In *Built of Living Stones*, Father Scirghi and I found a common interest but two different voices, two ways of articulating the great mystery that wove the liturgy and the arts together. Through a happy inspiration, we decided to teach a class on this topic together. In the spring of 2005, Father Scirghi and I offered a doctoral seminar on what we called a Liturgical

Aesthetics. The class was designed around some key ideas that we believed gave a deeper sense of the relationship between the liturgy and the arts and lectures given by top artists in different fields, literature, dance, music, architecture, and drama. We were pleasantly surprised by the vitality of the class and the quality of the response of the students and guest lectures. The class gave further shape to the ideas proposed in this book. And so a decision was made. We would write a book on a liturgical aesthetics, even if it would be a book with two voices.

A CHANGING FIELD

The decision to write *Living Beauty* presented us with an issue that at first glance appeared to be merely a practical choice but later turned out to be of deeper import. Should we write the book with one voice or two? The "one voice" approach was tempting. It would smooth the flow of ideas and arguments coming from both of us. It would give the reader the sense of a unified work that might be more satisfying. The "two voices" approach, on the other hand, would make more difficult a continued flow of thoughts. It might "chop" up the unity of the book and put the integrity of our proposal in jeopardy. In other words, we had every reason to choose the one voice approach over the two voices approach. Yet, after much discussion and reflection, Father Scirghi and I decided that *Living Beauty* would be a tale told in two voices.

What convinced us was the realization that the forces and interests that brought us together, that had conspired and inspired us to tackle such a project were part of a significant shift occurring in theology. Theology has rapidly become an inter-disciplinary enterprise in a fundamental way. The days when a theologian could write a Christology without having to go outside the field of theology are rapidly waning. Instead, theology finds itself increasingly wandering into other fields of study for its sources. Sociology, cultural studies, the natural sciences, literary criticism all have become almost standard partners in theological investigations. Such inter-disciplinarity, however, is more than reading the fruits of another's work over their shoulder. It is increasingly demanding the theologian be as expert in that field as the field reasonably demands. In other words, theology itself is becoming "many voices."

It became clear to Fr. Scirghi and me that *Living Beauty* was a project within this new way of doing theology. The real issue became not whether to write with two voices or one but, rather, how to write well in two voices. Somehow, we had to find a way where the voices of fundamental theology and liturgical theology each spoke with their own clarity yet gave a satisfying unity. Putting it this way, we realized that the challenge was to write in a truly catholic style. By this we mean "catholic" in its original etymological sense, "kata holos," the many according to the whole, which we understand in its aesthetic sense of "unity in variety."[3] We would write *Living Beauty* by allowing each of our voices its own clarity and style but we would strive to make these two-voices intertwine toward a whole. Whether we succeeded will be left for the reader to judge, but successful or not, our attempt, we believe, is the most reasonable approach to the challenges theology faces today.

Having said this, the problem of writing in such an aesthetic catholic style still had to be faced. How do two theologians from relatively very different fields and with very different styles begin to write a kata holos with two voices? Our solution, we believe, is not the only one but it has proved to be satisfying to both of us. We decided that each chapter would be written in two voices but on the same topic. To maximize both clarity and unity for each chapter, we followed this procedure. Each of us would write a chapter alone, and then we would read what the other had written. Later, we would meet at Berkeley's Brewed Awakening (over a cup of espresso and sometimes a cranberry scone) to critically analyze each other's work. We then revised the chapters only to return to Brewed Awakening once again for another round of analysis and espresso. This process turned out to be highly enjoyable and extremely helpful. We both felt a new style was taking shape. Finally, when all the chapters were written we both sat down with all the chapters before us and looked at the entire work as a whole. Our goal at this stage was to make sure that a consciousness about the project as a whole was present in all our writings. This raised another issue: what is this whole, this unity, which would give aesthetic satisfaction to the book's variety?

It was obvious that we had not written a whole in the sense of a systematics. *Living Beauty* does not propose a systematic liturgical theology. Neither had we written a whole in the sense of pieces coming together to form a bigger single piece. The whole we had written was more elusive. What we have proposed turns out to be a whole in the sense of a style, a way of thinking about and living the liturgy in such a way that it gives not only meaningful direction to liturgical decisions and judgments but cultivates a liturgical way of life. Such a whole is part process and part *telos*. Its unity is found in the unified struggle to achieve a kind of ideal, an ideal not in the sense of a normative idea but in the sense of a desired state of life. It is, in this sense, a dramatic whole. What ties our two voices together in *Living Beauty*, we believe, is the unity provided in our common struggle to come to terms with what we deeply felt to be the *telos* of Jesus' command: do this in memory of me, a *Living Beauty*. Thus, *Living Beauty* is not simply the articulation of an ideal but the articulation of a new form of life achieved in the process of attempting to live it.

In this sense the *holos* of *Living Beauty* is the whole that a good drama provides. A dramatic whole differs from other kinds of unity in that the aesthetic satisfaction of a good drama lies not in its unity as such but whether its unity provided some insight into the human condition. Such a whole is characterized by five marks: breadth, coherence, a personal touch, the sense of the need of salvation, and insight into the way of that salvation. A good dramatic whole covers a great deal of issues yet gives coherence to such variety. As such, it corresponds to the definition of beauty as unity-in-variety. A dramatic aesthetic unity, however, adds three other elements. First, such unity-in-variety must touch us personally. It must move our hearts. Second, a good drama raises in us the sense that all is not right with my life and the life of others. All the elements of a drama move toward that purpose, the sense of a great need, a conflict to be resolved not simply on the stage but in the balcony as well. Finally, a good drama is not mere conflict. It is conflict that brings insight and understanding into the human condition. A good drama does not resolve conflict but gives a sense of what it might take to resolve it. A good drama raises the sense of the need of salvation and gives us insight into the way of that salvation.

Though *Living Beauty* is not a drama, we believe it possesses a kind of dramatic unity. Our two voices, we believe find their unity not only in the breadth and coherence we give each of the issues raised but also, we hope, our writing will touch the reader personally. Moreover, *Living Beauty* was written to emphasize the soteriological dimension of the liturgy. Liturgy saves and it does so by helping us come to terms with our need of salvation and showing us insight into the way of that salvation. These five marks have shaped the tale told by our two voices. Thus, *Living Beauty* has been the work of a new methodology. The new method, we propose, reflects a change in the way theology has been done. Theology, increasingly, will require more than one voice. This means more than an edited volume of individual pieces. Rather, it means the creative collaboration of two (or more) minds and hearts providing a coherent, touching, work of breadth that is both acutely critical of past work but at the same time gives great hope.

WHAT IS A LITURGICAL AESTHETICS?

So what is a liturgical aesthetics? First, it is an attempt to understand the very nature of liturgy itself. A liturgical aesthetics gives an account of the nature of the liturgy. As such, it is less than a liturgical theology. It does not attempt to give a systematic account of a theology embedded in the liturgical rites. *Living Beauty* will not give a theology of the Eucharist or a

theology of the sacraments. Nonetheless, a liturgical aesthetics in elucidating the nature of the liturgy may provide guidance to those who
would write a liturgical theology. Second, a liturgical aesthetics is an approach to liturgical practice. It attempts to give guidance as to how the
liturgy ought to be enacted and incorporated in the life of the faithful.
Such guidance is fundamental in nature. By this we mean that a liturgical
aesthetics offers principles by which to make practical decisions for enacting the liturgy rather than a collection of how-tos or actual proposals
for enactment. A liturgical aesthetics in elucidating the nature of the
liturgy also elucidates the means that affect the liturgy. While this defi-
nitely implies that a liturgical aesthetics illuminates the role of the arts in
the liturgy, the principles it offers for enacting the liturgy are broader than
the arts.[4]

   Living Beauty, then, attempts to give a fundamental theology of the
liturgy. It attempts to answer the question: What drives the liturgy? What
is its nature? It differs from other attempts to understand the nature of the
liturgy by its approach. While others have tried to find the source of the
dynamics of the liturgy through historical, biblical, and sociological perspectives, we attempt to answer the fundamental questions above
through the perspective of the Beautiful, an aesthetics. What follows from
such an approach, we hope, is a basis from which a liturgical theology
based on the beautiful may emerge and a set of principles that may revi-
talize our liturgical practice.

A LITURGICAL AESTHETICS

Living Beauty was inspired in great part by the work of the great Swiss
theologian Hans Urs von Balthasar. In *Glory of the Lord*, von Balthasar
proposed a theological aesthetics.[5] A theological aesthetics has as its
guiding principle that Beauty is the key to understanding Christian
faith. Such Beauty is found in the depth of the forms of this world. Or as
Hopkins so well put it: "The world is charged with the grandeur of
God." Another way to put it is that von Balthasar sees in the forms of
this world the beauty of the icon. The depth of these forms reveals a radiance that is the glory of the Lord. Von Balthasar's bold proposal inspired a small group of theologians to develop further the ideas and implications of a theological aesthetics. At one of our conferences on
theological aesthetics, the suggestion was made by Nicholas Wolsterstoff that the arts in the liturgy would not be served well by a philosophical aesthetics. A philosophical aesthetics, he believes, is still
guided by what he called "The Grand Narrative of Aesthetics," which
began in the eighteenth century.[6] This Grand Narrative tells us that the

beautiful consists of disinterested, perceptual contemplation of works of art. Liturgical art does not fit the "grand narrative." Wolsterstoff proposed that a theological aesthetics of the liturgy might be the only way to understand such art.

Wolsterstoff's proposal happily coincided with the talks that Fr. Scirghi and I had been having on the relationship between the liturgy and the arts. We decided then to try to write what we now call a liturgical aesthetics. The use of von Balthasar's theological aesthetics came to mind as a way to begin a liturgical aesthetics. Unfortunately, von Balthasar's formulation of a theological aesthetics insofar as it resembles a theology of the icon does not grasp the dynamism of the liturgy. The arts in the liturgy serve such dynamism. It is for this reason that they do not lend themselves to "disinterested, perceptual contemplation." Indeed, not von Balthasar's theological aesthetics but his Theo-Drama appears more congenial to a liturgical aesthetics.

Von Balthasar not only wrote a theological aesthetics, he also wrote what he called a Theo-Drama.[7] I believe it is his best work. If a theological aesthetics roughly corresponds to the transcendental that is the Beautiful, the Theo-Drama corresponds to that of the Good. Nonetheless, von Balthasar warns us that these are rough correspondences, he sees the Theo-Drama as part of his aesthetics as well. I would go further. I believe drama ought to be considered the heart of all aesthetics. What other artistic form is capable of supporting all the arts without losing its integrity? Drama includes visual arts, dance, music, sculpture, architecture, indeed all the arts, yet can identify itself as an integral art form with its own constraints and sensibilities. Moreover, I believe all true religious art has a dramatic dimension. Religious art, as I have written elsewhere, is not only art to "look-at" but art that is "lived-with."[8] The tale of two altars now offers us another category.

The life that is the gift of the liturgy presents itself as a new aesthetic category. I would characterize this category as an experience of "life-abundant." This new aesthetic category reflects the soteriological dimension of the liturgy. It is a dimension that we feel has been woefully neglected in much liturgical theology. Yet this dimension, if it is to be considered from the point of view of the beautiful, ought not to be considered as a kind of rescue from human folly or human wickedness. And while salvation can be understood as communion with God and with each other, such communion is intrinsically a sharing of life. Life, it seems to us, is the crucial category that gives salvation its deep Christian meaning. Yet even a category such as life can be viewed from an aesthetics. Let us suggest that Jesus' statement of his mission defines that aesthetics: "I came that they may have life and have it abundantly." The liturgical aesthetics proposed in *Living Beauty* attempts to develop this category.

AN OUTLINE OF LIVING BEAUTY

Living Beauty begins its exploration of the nature of the liturgy with the tale of two altars. It revisits the crucial liturgical document of Vatican II, *Sacrosanctum Concilium*, and asks what its original inspiration was. That answer takes us to an exploration of the initial proposal given by Odo Casel that the liturgy was an encounter with divine Mystery. In the first chapter, Fr. Scirghi and I explore the nature of that mystery. Fr. Scirghi begins his exploration with the insightful phrase: "this blessed mess." He alerts us to a disturbing shift in liturgical practice toward an undue concern with rubrical purity. In contrast, he offers us the tale "Elves and the Shoemaker," a tale of the nature of true giving and gratitude. True gifts engender gracious response. Such response, as the fairy tale suggests, is a kind of labor, a labor of gratitude. Such labor calls for creativity and, thus, cannot be associated with an attitude that squelches freedom in act or thought. By its very nature, the labor of gratitude is messy.

I continue Fr. Scirghi's reflections by arguing that a blessed mess comes out of the heart of the Mystery of Christian worship. It is a sensible Mystery. In *A Sensible Mystery*, I attempt a *ressourcement* of the influential and fruitful insight of Odo Casel's *Kultmysterium*.[9] Casel's shifting the emphasis of the Eucharistic rite from receiving a sacrament to an encounter with Mystery influenced in no small way the key liturgical document of Vatican II, *Sacrosanctum Concilium*. Unfortunately, Casel's understanding of mystery was undermined by two other influential understandings of mystery as articulated by the great Jesuit theologian Karl Rahner and the French philosopher Jean-Luc Marion. These two understandings of mystery, I argue, have profound iconoclastic tendencies. As such, they undermine the aesthetic underpinnings of the Mystery of Christian worship. This Mystery is a Sensible Mystery in that it is experienced as *affectus* not only by the individual but by the Church as a whole. Such experience takes form in the arts, the true form of a blessed mess.

Having established the aesthetic roots of the liturgy in the encounter with a Sensible Mystery, *Living Beauty* continues in the next two chapters by interpreting as an aesthetics what *Sacrosanctum Concilium* proposed as the two defining aims of the liturgy: the sanctification of humanity and the glorifying of God. These chapters are heavily indebted to the North American philosophical tradition. We found in this tradition of thought a marvelous complement to von Balthasar. The North American philosophical tradition has its roots in a deep and prolonged encounter of British empirical thought, German Romanticism, and Medieval Scholasticism. Charles Peirce, for example, based much of his logic from his study of Duns Scotus. If von Balthasar brings into our discussion a rich synthesis of Patristic aesthetic thought, then the North American philosophers,

Jonathan Edwards, Charles Peirce, Josiah Royce, and Charles Hartshorne, bring an alternate Modernism that is sympathetic to the Scholastic tradition. They bring in a rich discussion of aesthetics different but complementary to von Balthasar's aesthetics. If von Balthasar's aesthetics is based on an aesthetics of Being, an aesthetics of the icon, then the North American philosophical aesthetic tradition give us an aesthetics of Becoming, an aesthetics of experience. This mix of a Patristic-based and Scholastic-inspired aesthetics forms the ground for the key aesthetic proposals that follow.[10]

Fr. Scirghi continues the implications of a blessed mess by exploring an ancient topic, the idea of the *habitus*. By *habitus*, Fr. Scirghi refers to more than a routine habit. He means the development of a higher disposition toward embodying experience. From this notion, he goes on to describe the liturgical *habitus* as a higher disposition toward worship. As such, the *habitus* also becomes a sensibility, a sixth sense toward a Sensible Mystery. He goes on to introduce what is one of the key proposals in our book for a liturgical aesthetics, the unitive revelatory experience. Fr. Scirghi explores this experience in his reflections on the role of music in the liturgy. My section, "In Whom We Live and Move and Have Our Being," attempts to ground even further the aesthetics of a unitive revelatory experience. Inspired by Hartshorne's brilliant study of birdsong, in which he proposes an aesthetics of moderation, I develop three aesthetic principles of a liturgical aesthetics based on such an aesthetics. A living aesthetics, like the aesthetics of birdsong, can be characterized by the moderate position along an axis depicting extremes. These three aesthetic axes include order, intensity of feeling, and creativity. With these three axes, I believe, the foundation of a living aesthetics of Church Song can guide the application of the arts in response to a Sensible Mystery.

Yet such an aesthetics is "living" because it is more than a disinterested perceptual contemplation of Beauty. It is "living" because it is a unitive experience into a Mystery that reveals itself as Beauty. And in that unitive revelation something else is revealed. Such Beauty is Life itself. An aesthetics of a unitive, revelatory experience of a Sensible Mystery is a new form of life and that life is characterized by the liturgical *habitus* of holiness. This is the aesthetic meaning of *Sacrosanctum Concilium*'s insight that the liturgy exists for the sanctification of humanity.

Such sanctification, however, cannot be disjointed from its corollary, the glorifying of God that is *Sacrosanctum Concilium*'s second insight into the liturgy. The next chapter attempts to give an aesthetics of this insight. Fr. Scirghi sees it as making something beautiful for God. His reflection of the building of the Tabernacle as depicted in the Scriptures offers a strong apology for the arts in the liturgy. The arts, Fr. Scirghi tells us, are more than a decoration or an environment for the liturgical rites. They are the heart of what it means to glorify God for glorifying God also means making something beautiful for God. But what is it that is made and is, indeed, beautiful?

My section, "The Glory of the Lord," attempts to answer this question. I begin by studying the rabbinic understanding of the Divine Imagination, the *Yetzer*, and correlating it to our human capacity for such imagination, our *capax Dei*. Such correlation results in what I call the anagogical imagination. Such imagination suggests a new look at one of the aesthetic principles developed in the previous chapter, the aesthetic axis of creativity. Creativity, after all, requires imagination but the anagogical imagination has a salvific dimension. It is the dimension that is sung in Mary's hymn, the *Magnificat*: "the mighty shall be humbled in the imagination of their hearts and the poor shall be lifted up." In other words, the aesthetic axis of creativity has a temporal dimension that is best described as drama. It is here where the aesthetics of Being and the aesthetics of Becoming truly merge and provide a marvelous vision of Beauty. A living aesthetics is drama-like oriented toward an aesthetic understanding of justice. For in the "lifting up" the lowly and "laying low" the mighty, God's glory reveals itself as a life-giving Beauty. Such justice is geared toward building a Community of Life and Beauty. What is it that is made beautiful for God? We argue: It is the Community of the Beautiful, the Body of Christ, which includes not only humanity but the sun and the wind, the stars and the dew and the rain.

At this point, Fr. Scirghi and I thought we had laid down the fundamental aesthetic principles for a liturgical aesthetics. When we presented our project to members of the Liturgical Hermeneutics seminar of the North American Academy of Liturgy, someone raised the question of lament in the liturgy. Our book was all about praise and thanksgiving and not a single word on the nature of lament was mentioned. The following discussion made it clear that another chapter needed to be included in this book, a chapter that not only deals squarely with the role lament plays in the liturgy but also does so as an aesthetics. We were pleasantly surprised that the chapter that came out of this discussion has become for us one of the strongest in the book.

Fr. Scirghi immediately saw that the issue of lament is addressed in the liturgy's rite of dismissal. *Ite Missa Est* means more than "The Mass is finished." It also means "Go and do likewise." In the dismissal, Fr. Scirghi argues that the liturgy is not quite over. We are to share the fruits of our liturgical experience with a troubled world. Such sharing amounts to the *diakonia* that is meant to be part of the liturgical tradition. Fr. Scirghi retells the story of Emmaus in a moving reflection that reveals a three-part structure to the liturgy: the Word, meal, and dismissal. It is in the dismissal where the Church's *diakonia* is most clearly seen as a continuation of the liturgy. In the dismissal we are sent to continue Jesus' ministry in which the hungry are fed and the good news is told. As such, liturgical theology is more than the *lex orandi* and a *lex credendi*. It is also a *lex agendi*. Such *lex agendi* is our response that continues the liturgy's action even when the rite is over. It answers the question: what shall the community do with the gift that it has been given? The *lex agendi* answers: go and share Christ's memory not only through words but as a way of life.

Thus, Fr. Scirghi introduces a new aesthetic dimension in the liturgy's concern for justice: "fruitfulness." The Constitution on the Sacred Liturgy does not mention justice but it founds an aesthetic understanding of justice which, in Fr. Scirghi's estimation, is grasped by the notion of being fruitful. Such reflection becomes an inspiration for my section where I take up Fr. Scirghi's suggestion that there exists an aesthetic understanding of justice and that that understanding is best understood as being fruitful.

In "Do This in Memory of Me," I also ask the question of the aesthetic foundation of justice. To do this, I explore the story of Cain and Abel. In this story, the first lament is uttered. And it is uttered by God. What is lamented? I argue that it is the loss of the joy that Abel's life could bring. Indeed, I propose that an aesthetic understanding of justice may be found as that which leads to a joy of life. Such joy reveals the fruits of justice. It is life abundant. Indeed, I argue, life abundant is not only the fruit of justice. It is the aesthetic meaning of the Christian doctrine of salvation. Life abundant, however, means tackling the sorrows of the world. And this means lament is part of the Living Beauty that is revealed in the liturgy. Can the world's misery be beautiful? This is the deepest and most profound claim of the liturgy. This claim is found in the liturgy's profound theodicy, the *Felix Culpa* proclaimed in the Easter Vigil.[11] Such claim ought to be the first sign that lament is taken up in the liturgy in a profound way.

But how can suffering, even agony, be beautiful? I argue that there is one artistic form in which suffering and conflict founds its beauty: drama. In "Do This in Memory of Me," the dramatic dimension proposed in the aesthetic axis of creativity now receives full treatment by the addition of von Balthasar's best aesthetic thought, the Theo-Drama. When Jesus commanded us to "do this in memory of me," he was asking us to put on a very special kind of play. I am not speaking of a theatrical performance. I am speaking of a drama-like orientation that is the only adequate way to appropriate Jesus' wish. To enact Jesus' memory is to enact it dramatically. Such enactment goes beyond a dramatic performance and, even, von Balthasar's proposal of a Theo-Drama. In this section, I attempt to find a middle way between these two and suggest what I call a theodramatics.

A theodramatics uses dramatic techniques to explore in the liturgy what von Balthasar called the dramatic horizon. These horizons are the place where heaven and earth encounter each other. In other words, it is the place where one encounters a Sensible Mystery. Unlike an ordinary horizon, a dramatic horizon does not recede from us as we approach it. On the contrary, a dramatic horizon by its very aesthetic force draws us into it and makes us become part of it. It is the same principle in which an audience grasped by the action on the stage now becomes part of the action. Dramatic horizons offer insight and understanding (but no final answers) into the meaning of existence. They do so, however, not from the immanent action of the drama but from a background that radiates out of the action. Von Balthasar offered three candidates as dramatic horizons: death, the struggle for the Good, and judgment. I offer one more: the struggle for the Role.

These horizons are principles that found a theodramatics. I discuss them in greater length in the section. Dramatic horizons can help shape the form of the liturgy. A liturgy ought to be shaped in such a way that one or more of these horizons become immanent in the enactment. Dramatic horizons allow lament a meaningful part in the enactment of the liturgy. They reveal what may seem startling. True praise and thanksgiving is founded upon the lament against the loss of joy that injustice steals. They also reveal the aesthetic dimension of salvation. Jesus' sacrifice becomes a banquet for in his sacrifice death becomes a life abundant. A theodramatics of Jesus' command attempts to make both the sacrifice and the banquet a living force that shapes, in turn, the lives of those that come to experience it.

A FINAL WORD

Living Beauty is by all reckonings an ambitious project. Attempting a truly fundamental liturgical aesthetics is bound to be plagued by omissions and inconsistencies if not by the nature of its scope but also by the lack of a precedent that could have been used as a guide. In this, we are aware that part of the value of our project may lie in the inadequacies it leaves for others to address. One of these we have already mentioned. For an aesthetics, there is little reference to the arts. We plan to address this insufficiency in a later book. Our apology for leaving such an inadequacy is simply that this work is not meant as a systematics but a prolegomena of a liturgical aesthetics. We hoped to propose a few basic principles that uncover the intrinsic relationship between Beauty and the Liturgy. Before we could go on to the arts per se, this step had to be taken first.

Another motivation for going ahead with an insufficient aesthetics is the urgency we feel to propose it. There are changes coming to the liturgy uninformed by a liturgical aesthetics. Such changes, we fear, may diminish the vitality and power of the liturgical celebration. Our sense of urgency was also fueled by the other realization. The liturgy needs revitalization. It has stagnated, we believe, because liturgical studies failed to take a more serious look at the aesthetics and the role of the arts in the liturgy. Our deepest hope is not that *Living Beauty* becomes the last word on a liturgical aesthetics but that it becomes a beginning to finding out together such an aesthetics. To the extent that *Living Beauty* starts a fruitful conversation about bringing back the sense of Beauty into the liturgy, then it was worth bringing it into print insufficient and inadequate as it is. We, thus, place our work into the reader's hand hoping that compassion and a mutual passion for the liturgy may overlook the inadequacies found in this first attempt at a liturgical aesthetics.

NOTES

1. Much of this reflection comes from a previous work: Alejandro Garcia-Rivera, "A Tale of Two Altars: The Pilgrim Church of Vatican II," in *Pilgrimage; Concilium*, ed. Charles Duquoc and Virgil Elizondo, vol. 4 (Maryknoll, N.Y.: Orbis Books, 1996), 123–135.

2. Catholic Church, *Built of Living Stones Art, Architecture, and Worship* (Washington, D.C.: United States Catholic Conference, 2000).

3. The oldest theological sense of beauty is "unity in variety." Tatarkiewicz called it the "great theory of Beauty." Wladyslaw Tatarkiewicz, "The Great Theory of Beauty & Its Decline," *Journal of Aesthetics and Art Criticism* 31, no. 2 (1972): 165–179.

4. *Living Beauty* was written to help us understand better the role of the arts in the liturgy. As we began, we had planned to include a section precisely on the arts. As the book progressed, we discovered that the principles we were laying down had many more implications in its aesthetics than the arts. Nevertheless, without a discussion of the arts in the liturgy, a liturgical aesthetics is not complete. Indeed, *Living Beauty* is half-finished. Father Scirghi and I plan a second volume dedicated to the role of the arts. This volume will build on the aesthetic principles proposed in *Living Beauty*.

5. Hans Urs von Balthasar, *The Glory of the Lord: A Theological Aesthetics*, translated by Erasmo Leiva-Merikakis Riches and edited by Joseph Fessio and John Riches (San Francisco, Calif.: Ignatius Press, 1983–1989), 7 vols.

6. Nicholas Wolsterstoff, "The Grand Narrative of Aesthetics and Religious Art," Paper presented at the First International Theological Aesthetics Conference (Bonaventure, New York: St. Bonaventure University, May 19, 2004).

7. Hans Urs von Balthasar, *Theo-Drama: Theological Dramatic Theory*, translated by Graham Harrison (San Francisco, Calif.: Ignatius Press, 1988–1998), 5 vols.

8. Religious art is used in processions or at home. It is touched, kissed, carried in cars, taken on pilgrimages, indeed made public in many creative ways. Religious art is art that shares in the life of the one who comtemplates it. It is more

than a presence to be contemplated; it is a presence that accompanies. It is art that is "lived-with" not only "looked-at." I argue this more fully in a forthcoming article "On a List of New Aesthetic Categories," which is part of a yet untitled book edited by Oleg Byrchov and to be published by Ashgate in 2007.

9. By *ressourcement*, I refer to a pre-Vatican II movement by Catholic theologians to recover theology's Patristic heritage overshadowed by a massive and unwieldy scholasticism. The strategy of *ressourcement* included more than reading the Patristic sources in order to make them influential again. It also attempted to revisit the issues they raised so as to gain new insights. It was not only a re-reading of Patristic thought, but a reading anew. With this strategy in mind, I re-read Casel's *Mystery of Christian Worship* with the intention to understand anew the nature of the Mystery that encounters us in the liturgy.

10. Von Balthasar's major works include treatises on Origen and Gregory of Nyssa. Indeed, many Eastern Orthodox theologians consider von Balthasar "one of their own." Charles Peirce was an avid student of Duns Scotus. He used insights from Scotus to critique Kant's transcendental logic and Locke's empiricism. In this, I believe he brought an alternate Modernism insofar as it was a dialogue with Modernity based in sympathy for Scholastic thought as opposed to a Modernism based on a hostility to that intellectual tradition.

11. John Hick thought that the *Felix Culpa* tradition was the most philosophically astute understanding of evil ever proposed in Western philosophy; Josiah Royce made it the basis of his philosophy. Cf. John Hick, *Evil and the God of Love* (London: Macmillan, 1966).

REFERENCES

Catholic Church. *Built of Living Stones Art, Architecture, and Worship.* Washington, D.C.: United States Catholic Conference, 2000.

García-Rivera, Alejandro. "A Tale of Two Altars: The Pilgrim Church of Vatican II." *Pilgrimage; Concilium.* Edited by Charles Duquoc and Virgil Elizondo. Vol. 4. Maryknoll, N.Y.: Orbis Books, 1996, 123–135.

CHAPTER 1

This Blessed Mess

Thomas Scirghi

After the celebration of the Triduum one year, I realized more than ever that messiness is a part of good liturgy. Consider the following scenario. On Holy Thursday, after the Gospel reading of Jesus washing the feet of his disciples,[1] an elderly bishop removes his chasuble, replaces it with a towel, drops to his knees and shuffles slowly along the sanctuary floor, washing the feet of twelve members of the congregation. The one we normally look up to as a leader stoops lower than us, assuming the role of a servant. On Good Friday, a large and heavy wooden cross is passed over the heads of the congregation. In this variation of a traditional veneration, the worshipers all participate, struggling to reach the cross, lowering it for the children, raising it higher to avoid hitting the tall people. For a moment each person gets to not only touch, but also carry the cross, as if the whole congregation takes on the role of Simon of Cyrene. Then on Saturday night, we sit in a darkened church. The worshipers hold candle tapers and pass the flame from the new light—the Easter Candle—among each other, careful not to let the wax drip or to burn a neighbor. At the Gloria, the lights of the church are turned on suddenly as we stand to sing. The burst of light has a blinding, disorienting effect, suggesting the moment of resurrection. Later in the liturgy the neophytes are washed in the baptismal pool. This same water of salvation spills over the font onto the sanctuary floor. A server grabs a towel to mop it up lest someone slip and fall. After the bath the oils of anointing are poured and smeared onto the heads of the candidates for baptism and the gooey scented chrism drips down their faces. In the background, the smoke of incense rises, clouding the sanctuary, causing some to cough. At least this is the way it is done in one parish. Here the messiness of good liturgy proves refreshing. The symbols are used generously and lavishly. All the while the human quality is never lost, that is, here we never forget that worship is an embodied exercise.

As I discuss this messiness of liturgy it will help to make a distinction. Here "messy" falls between the notions of "sloppy" and "pristine." By sloppiness I think of poorly prepared liturgy. Little thought or care is given to the preparation of the worship space, or to the movement of the ministers throughout the service. The readings were merely glanced over without deriving a feel for the author's intent or a concern for how the assembly will hear the Scripture. The vestments and vessels are of poor quality, and the symbols cheaply used. The attitude here could be summed up as: "Let's not make a big deal out of this." To the other extreme is pristine, a condition of being pure, uncorrupted and unspoiled, literally, found in its original condition. Pristine service is what you would find in a fast food restaurant. It is antiseptically clean and efficiently managed with the goal of feeding as many people as possible in the shortest amount of time.

Messiness lies somewhere between these two conditions. It is found at a family feast, where the table is set with the good china. The menu has been planned in advance and the meal presented with pride. In the comfort of one's own home people are more relaxed, talking a little louder and moving about with greater freedom than they would in a restaurant. Plates are passed but not always to the right. A whole loaf of bread sits on the table waiting to be broken and passed. And with the guests serving themselves it is likely that some food will fall from the serving dishes, crumbs will scatter about, and a drop of wine will stain the tablecloth. The family feast lacks the pristine quality and the efficiency of a fast food eatery, but would we have it any other way?

A PRISTINE RUBRIC?

Am I making too much of this? In the Roman Catholic Church it seems we are moving toward a more pristine approach to liturgy. A new instruction concerns the careful attention to the Communion wine, perhaps too careful. This "instruction" from the Vatican's Congregation for Divine Worship and the Discipline of the Sacrament changes the way Catholics handle the wine in the liturgy. It reads: "The pouring of the Blood of Christ after the consecration from one vessel to another is completely to be avoided, lest anything should happen that would be to the *detriment* of so great a mystery."[2] According to this particular instruction, when more than one cup is used for Communion wine, the extra cups should be brought up to the altar at the time of the preparation of the gifts, and the wine poured into them at that time. Until now the custom has been to bring forward a flagon, or pitcher, filled with wine. Some of the wine would be poured into one cup, while the rest would remain in the flagon on the altar table.[3] The single cup on the table serves as a symbol of the unity of the assembly. The priest consecrates all the wine on the table during the Eucharistic Prayer. Then, just before Communion, an acolyte brings more cups to the table and pours the consecrated wine into them. These cups will be distributed among the faithful. The Vatican Congregation sees a problem here. Suppose some of the now consecrated wine spills onto the table? Is that not, in their words, "to the detriment of so great a mystery," literally, a damaging of the mystery? One way to avoid this "detriment," as recommended by the instruction, is to bring all the cups that will be used for Communion to the table at the time of the preparation of the gifts and pour wine into them from the flagon, then remove the empty flagon from the altar. The difference of course is that if some of the wine spills before it is consecrated it is not so bad as spilling the "precious blood" after the consecration. Note that there is no mention of the bread since it is presumed that the church is using wafer hosts, so there is no problem of spilling crumbs. To be clear, this argument does not mean to challenge the belief in the real presence of Christ in the celebration of the Eucharist. As stated in *Sacrosanctum Concilium* (no. 7), we know the presence of Christ in our worship in a four-fold way. "He is present in the sacrifice of the Mass, not only in the person of His minister . . . but especially under the Eucharistic species. . . . He is present in His word. . . . (And) He is present . . . when the Church prays and sings," that is, in the assembly.[4] So the intention here is not to demean in any way the real presence of Christ in Eucharistic worship.

The concern here comes from the conflicting values raised by this new instruction. Note that, often in liturgical disputes, it is a matter of which values should be given priority. Here the conflicting values are those of unity and purity. On the one hand, the presence of the one cup on the altar table signifies the unity of the congregation; we drink from one cup, the cup of our salvation. On the other hand, the presence of several cups, as recommended by this instruction, emphasizes purity. Nothing should spill, the table remains clean and, most importantly, the integrity of the "precious blood" is maintained. A problem here is that, in some cases, by placing a priority on purity we may lose the aesthetic appreciation of the celebration. An obsession with purity challenges our aesthetic sense since purity can lead to a concern for efficiency. It was this same concern for purity that led to the removal of the cup from the congregation during the Middle Ages. For Martin Luther, this was the first "captivity" of the Eucharist, citing the mandate from Jesus "Drink from it all of you."[5] At that time due to an excessive concern for purity, and the problem with bread crumbs and spilled wine, the bread was reduced to hosts and the cup removed from the people. After all, if Jesus were *in* the bread, one would have to worry about all those crumbs that come from using fresh bread. Hosts helped to alleviate this situation. Also wine can be spilled. At this time the doctrine of "concomitance" was developed, claiming that the Lord is equally present under both species of bread and wine thus it is not necessary to drink from the cup.[6] The revised reception of Communion created a more efficient liturgy.

AN OBSESSION WITH PURITY

Earlier I mentioned an "obsession" with purity. This may seem to be a strong word, but consider the following language used in the current *General Instruction of the Roman Missal.* "The sacred vessels are *purified* by the priest, the deacon, or an instituted acolyte after Communion or after Mass. . . . The *purification* of the chalice is done with water alone or with wine and water, which is then drunk by whoever does the *purification.* The paten is usually wiped clean with the *purificator.*"[7] This is the language of the rubrics. But do we really mean to "purify" the vessels? The word "purify" is defined as "to purge or rid of impurities or pollution; to free from ceremonial uncleanness; to free from incorrect or corrupting elements."[8] Isn't this so-called purification more a matter of *cleaning* the vessels? Of course it makes good sense, both practically and aesthetically, to wash the Communion vessels after they have been used. It displays the proper respect for the vessels used in the liturgy, as well as a concern for those who use them. It is the same care we would take for a family feast. But this is more a matter of cleaning than of "purification."[9]

A scholar of the Old Testament, Fr. Michael Guinan, OFM, explains that we only purify something when it has been defiled.[10] Throughout the Hebrew Scriptures we find various rituals whose purpose was to restore people to life either within the religious community or with their relationship with God.[11] For example, we read in the Book of Numbers, "The Lord said to Moses: take the Levites from among the Israelites and purify them. This is what you shall do to them to purify them. Sprinkle them with the water of remissions; then have them shave their whole bodies and wash their clothes, and so purify themselves."[12] Also in the story of Maccabees we read of the purification of the temple sanctuary after it had been defiled by Antiochus Epiphanes, King of the Greeks. After the military victory by Judas Maccabeus and his army, he proclaims: "Now that our enemies have been crushed, let us go up to purify the sanctuary and rededicate it. . . . (Judas) chose blameless priests, devoted to the law; these purified the sanctuary and carried away the stones of the Abomination to an unclean place."[13] When the Old Testament speaks of "purification" it is always within the context of defilement. Likewise for Jesus when he criticizes the tradition of the elders and their code of purity: "For from the heart come evil thoughts. . . . These are what defile a person, but to eat with unwashed hands does not defile."[14]

An overemphasis on purity points to a more general obsession with the rubrics of the liturgy. As Albert Rouet argues, an obsession with rubrics can turn the liturgical celebration into an action divorced from its environment, making it a theater of abstractions.[15] Such an obsession reduces the liturgy from a symbol to an allegory. According to Rouet, allegory is based on a direct correspondence between a literal sense and a hidden sense. The allegory is an equation with no adaptation. A scrupulous obedience to rubrics will lead to a rational materialism, suggesting that what is legally executed will have an immediate significance. Such liturgies are rubrically perfect but humanly deadly because their performance leaves no place for the present, that is, this particular people, these human circumstances, this moment in time. Too tight a connection with the almighty erases the immediacy of the present resulting in a deadly distance from the present and a forgetfulness of the body and human circumstances.[16] It could lead to what Walter Brueggemann calls "the exaggerated God," that is, an objectification of God to such a degree that nothing else matters besides the omnipotent, omniscient, and omnipresent God. In the world of the exaggerated God the needs and suffering of people become insignificant.[17] Symbol is different from allegory. From the Greek word, *sumballein*, meaning "to throw together," a symbol joins together two realities that are different, distinct, and separate. This joining together requires a third reality that holds the elements in communion and binds them together. The "messiness" of good liturgy, when applied to the elements of the Eucharist, calls attention to the point that the wine manifests the Blood of Christ and at the same time is not identical with the Blood of Christ that poured from His side on Calvary. For in the traditional theory of transubstantiation the Roman Catholic Church claims that, through the action of the Holy Spirit and the consecratory prayer of the priest, the wine is transformed into the Blood of Christ while maintaining the appearance of wine. Or, in the language of Aristotelian metaphysics, the "substance" of the wine is changed while the "accidents" remain. Hence we receive Christ while we see, smell and taste wine. It is our faith-filled action in response to the Lord's command, "Do this in memory of me," that is the "third reality," which holds together Christian faith and these elements of bread and wine.

An overemphasis of the rubrics and of allegory could distract the worshipers from the dynamic of the meal. Jesus offered Himself to His

followers within the celebration of a family meal. Within the context of the
Jewish community the meal was a sacred event; the household was a do-
mestic house of worship. With the traditional Hebrew breaking of bread
before the meal (a gesture of gratitude to God for their food) and the
blessing of the cup of wine after the meal (an expression of gratitude for
their land) the Jewish family gratefully acknowledged God's presence
and favor. Also, as is widely known, the "breaking of bread," that is, the
sharing of a meal with someone, held much significance, for this indicated
a bond of camaraderie. In the Gospel of Luke, for example, Jesus regularly
reveals some aspect of His mission through a series of ten meals.[18] Consequently, the real presence of Christ in the celebration of the Eucharist is
understood appropriately in a symbolic way rather than as an allegory.
More than a direct correspondence between rubrics and the result, the
Church has focused on the dynamic activity of worship. Rubrics are necessary but not sufficient for good worship. Rubrics, like the rules of a
game, are helpful for guiding us along and showing us the way to worship. But good liturgy also requires the proper disposition. Recall St.
Paul's criticism of the Corinthians for their sloppy celebration of the Eucharist.[19] He does not comment on their following of the rubrics; we can
assume that part was done correctly. Rather his concern is with their treatment of one another, and how some of the community go hungry while
others gorge themselves. The dynamic of the meal with its inherent intimacy was lost on them. Their Eucharistic meal had become a dinner party
for a select few. The problem for the community at Corinth was that they
attempted to worship the sacred in a secular manner.

THE EUCHARIST AS A LABOR OF GRATITUDE

The Lord chose to celebrate with His disciples within the context of a
meal. This is the way in which they would commemorate Him, honoring
His command: "Do this in memory of me." We who heed this command
need to allow for the embodied interaction—the human dynamic—which
is part of every meal. To state the matter simply, surely Jesus would have
anticipated crumbs and stains as He broke the bread and passed it, and
then passed around the cup. Was it His concern that nothing be spilled?

An overemphasis on purity could be construed as a limitation of our
embodied participation. Roman Catholics have experienced this in the
past, for example, by having the host placed on their tongues rather than
taking it in their own hands. For this is one of the reasons it was thought
that the priest's hands are consecrated; he alone may touch the "sacred
species." A problem here is that we may come to focus more on what we
are doing through the priest as opposed to what the Lord is doing here

and now. Since this is our Eucharist, that is, our "thanksgiving," we begin by recognizing what the Lord has done for us. In return we respond in the way He showed us through the Lord's Supper.

This sacred meal retells the story of the gift Christ gave to humanity, and how we are to respond to it. To illustrate this notion of the reception of a gift and the grateful response, it would help to review an old fairy tale by The Brothers Grimm, "The Shoemaker and the Elves."

A shoemaker is down on his luck and has only enough leather to sew a single pair of shoes. He cuts the leather out and goes to bed, planning to sew the shoes in the morning. During the night, two naked elves come and make the shoes. The shoemaker is speechless with astonishment when he finds them. Not a stitch is out of place! The shoes are such a masterpiece that the first customer to appear in the morning pays handsomely for them, and the cobbler has enough money to buy leather for two pairs of shoes. That night he cuts the leather out and goes to bed. Again in the morning the shoes are made, and again they sell for such a price as to afford the leather for four pairs of shoes. In this way the shoemaker soon prospers. One evening, not long before Christmas, the cobbler suggests to his wife that they stay up and see who has been helping them. They leave a candle burning, hide behind some coats, and, at midnight, see the elves come in and set to work. In the morning the wife says to the shoemaker, "The little men have made us rich and we should show our gratitude for this. They are running about with nothing on and might freeze! I will make them each a shirt, coat, jacket, trousers and a pair of stockings. Why don't you make them each a pair of little shoes?" The cobbler willingly agrees, and one night when the clothes are finished, he lays them out on the bench in place of the leather. He and his wife hide behind the coats to watch. The elves are surprised and pleased to find the clothes. They put them on and sing "We're sleek, we're fine, we're out the door. We shan't be cobblers anymore!" and they dance around the room and away. They never return, but everything continues to go well with the shoemaker and he prospers at whatever he takes in hand.

Lewis Hyde analyzes this tale in his book *The Gift*.[20] Hyde distinguishes between "work" and "labor." He describes "work" as an activity performed for the purpose of completing a task, usually within a specified time frame and often for compensation, for example, someone washing the dishes, a farm hand picking corn, or a doctor tending to his patients. Also, work is an intended activity that is accomplished through the will. In contrast "labor" has no limits on time. It may be intended but only for laying the groundwork. "Labor has its own schedule. Things get done, but we often have the odd sense that we didn't do them."[21] Hyde adds that because labor sets its own pace it is usually accompanied by leisure and sleep. He connects this understanding of labor with an appreciation of the Sabbath and that, for Christians, Sunday was set aside for no work.[22] The Sabbath was designed to provide us with leisure, not in the sense of simply sitting around idly, but a leisure time that is necessary for creativity. In fact, the Greek word *schole*, from which we derive "scholar" and "school," means leisure. Leisure is necessary for scholars to reflect upon what they have learned. This reflection process is important as the human mind is not merely a machine absorbing information; an individual must leave time to comprehend what has been learned. This is an organic process, rather than mechanical. However, with the rise of industrialism and the substitution of machines for human work, society at large tends to follow a mechanical model, forsaking the need for rest and reflection. As Hyde notes, "machines don't need a Sunday."[23]

The tale of the "Shoemaker and the Elves" illustrates the role of leisure within the creative process. The shoemaker has laid the groundwork by cutting out the leather pieces that he will work with the next day. He then retires for the evening with his wife. During their sleep the elves intrude to fashion the shoes masterfully for him. The shoemaker, upon rising, recognizes the quality and reaps the profit for their work. He and his wife also recognize the gift they have received and respond in kind to the elves.

As with all fairy tales, this story defies a logical adherence to the discovery of truth. There is no causal relationship at work here but an openness of the reader/listener to the opportunity for discovery. Also there is an element of surprise, the bestowing of an unanticipated gift. This story carries a moral for the celebration of liturgy. A strict adherence to rubrics may reduce the liturgy to a mechanical exercise. Once again, rubrics are necessary. They are like the dutiful actions of the shoemaker who prepares his work the night before with his talent and in his poverty he prepares his worktable. Then in his rest something miraculous happens. Similarly we prepare the Lord's table, bringing the gifts of bread and wine, the "fruits of the earth and of the vine and work of human hands." We then ask the Lord to intervene, transforming them into a sacred meal. The rubrics are helpful if they serve to enhance our participation in the Eucharistic celebration and direct us more deeply into the mystery of the Eucharist. However, the rubrics will be a hindrance if they distract us from participating in this mystery.

THE INTIMACY OF A MEAL UNDONE BY EFFICIENCY

For modern society, the loss of the inherent intimacy within the sharing of a meal is due in great part to the re-orientation of the meal toward a notion of efficiency. The re-orientation of the meal can turn us into, what

Wendell Berry calls, "industrial eaters." In his essay "The Pleasures of Eating,"[24] Berry laments that for "industrial eaters" the places where they eat have come to resemble filling stations. These consumers seem to have decided that life is not very interesting and have lowered their satisfactions to that which is minimal, perfunctory, and fast. Industrial eating, like industrial sex, has become a degraded, poor, and paltry thing.[25]

Some parishes in business districts offer a lunch time Mass with an option for Communion after Mass for those who do not have time for the whole liturgy but want to receive Communion nonetheless. Have we reduced the Eucharistic banquet to a snack? Also, just by the fact that most parishes use hosts—little round wafers of wheat, rather than real bread—contributes to an attitude of convenience and efficiency. The advantage to using hosts rather than bread is that they avoid the messiness of crumbs, and they are easier to store and preserve in the tabernacle. Here again we can ask, has the value of purity (efficiency) prevailed over that of unity, that is, the one bread broken for the community?

We find some tension between these values even within the *General Instruction of the Roman Missal*. There are two specific instructions that describe the Eucharistic bread. Number 320 specifies that the bread must be made only from wheat, that it must be baked recently, and be unleavened. Clearly the commonly used hosts fit this description. However, this description is then qualified by the next instruction (no. 321), which explains: "The meaning of the sign demands that the material for the Eucharistic celebration truly have the appearance of food. . . . [Thus the bread should] be made in such a way that the priest . . . is able . . . to break it into parts for distribution to at least some of the faithful." The instruction makes clear that while small hosts are not ruled out, we should recall that it is the action of the fraction, or breaking of the bread, that gave its name to the Eucharist in apostolic times. The early Christians were known as those who broke bread together. And this action will bring out more clearly the force and importance of the sign of unity of all in the one bread, and of the sign of charity by the fact that the one bread is distributed among the faithful.[26]

THIS MERCIFUL MESS: CELEBRATING SIN AND SALVATION

The "mess" of the liturgy, as discussed earlier, refers to the condition of humanity, a recognition that we come to the house of the Lord as "saved sinners," with soiled hands and broken hearts, yet inspired and hopeful. We enter Church on any given Sunday steeped in secular culture yet aspiring to the transcendent. We worship with the heavenly court in the here and now. Consequently the beginning of the liturgy presents a problem: how do we get the congregation from the street into the Church? The liturgy of the Eucharist, like all sacramental worship, provides us with a liminal experience, that is, the crossing of a threshold by which we move from one state to another. According to Rouet, worship differs from the rhythm of society where extraordinary things seem banal. Worship signifies another reality found in the depth of human history, a reality that lies beneath the surface of things.[27] In worship we move out of *chronos*, or chronological time, and into *kairos*, or meaning-filled time, a point at which the present moment "becomes meaningful in relationship to a past and future."[28]

In preparing liturgy we need to pay attention to this transition: how we cross the threshold. Cardinal Roger Mahony of Los Angeles comments that the Sunday liturgy actually begins at home, with one's personal preparation for coming to the church.[29] This remote preparation is reminiscent of the practice found in the early church with its prayers upon rising to greet the new day, along with prayers for washing and dressing. This early morning prayer helped to foster the proper disposition for worship. A popular analogy could be found with the home game of a college football team. Fans descend upon the stadium, many of whom are clad in the colors and insignia of the home team. Tailgate parties precede the kick-off. The stalwart fans do not simply walk into the stadium on game day; the preparation begins at home, continues in the parking lot, and proceeds into the stadium. Another comparison with liturgy is the theater. However, theater moves from the stage outward to the audience. In contrast, liturgical action comes from the outside in order to move closer to supernatural mystery.[30] To be clear, the purpose of liturgy is a response to the presence of God; God has taken the initiative in calling out to humanity. Human beings respond as they are moved to open themselves to God. Liturgy allows the faithful to be immersed in mystery. Its celebrations are a movement, advancing toward a mystery.

When the assembly has gathered, they are called to prayer. After the presider's greeting, the faithful call upon the mercy of God with a six-fold litany. There is some confusion here as this "Penitential Rite" is paradoxical. We acknowledge our sinfulness while celebrating God's abundant mercy, all in this brief litany.[31] This rite speaks primarily of a celebration of a merciful God. Consider just one set of the invocations found in the *Sacramentary*. "You were sent to heal the contrite. You came to call sinners. You plead for us at the right hand of the Father." Again, the initiative has been taken by God, the One who calls humanity out of the darkness of sin and into the light of salvation. In the glow of God's mercy Christians recognize their sinfulness. Thus the individual's breast beating of contrition should give way to praising an all-merciful God. In prayer we acknowledge that we are truly beholden to this Lord and we say so publicly. To be sure, we come in need of God's mercy. On Sunday we approach the sanctuary in all humility, called by God from a world all too busy to hear. We try to approach with a sense of old-fashioned "fear of the Lord" (read "awe"), as taught by Sirach: "The beginning of wisdom is fear of the Lord, which is formed with the faithful in the womb."[32] In wisdom and awe, we come before God, aware of our humble beginning, responding in faith to the divine mystery, our eternal destiny. This penitential rite follows from the custom of sacrificial cultures and includes a purification process. According to Catherine Pickstock, arriving at an altar is never simply a temporal-spatial journey, but requires a preparation of oneself, that is, a process of purification.[33] "Thus, liturgy is not only a difficult language, but it is an expectant work, the hope that there might be a liturgy."[34] Even in the great hymn of praise, "Gloria in excelsis Deo," we admit our sinfulness and plead for mercy:

Lord God, Lamb of God
You take away the sin of the world:
have mercy on us.
You are seated at the right hand of the Father:
receive our prayer.

The reason for rejoicing comes from the realization that His removal of our sins has already been accomplished: "You take away the sin of the world." Hence purification and proper worship is possible.

This purification rite carries through to the liturgy of the Word. As the deacon or priest prepares to read the Scripture, he prays that he may worthily proclaim the Gospel. For the deacon, he asks for the priest's blessing who prays: "The Lord be in your heart and on your lips that you may worthily proclaim his Gospel." In the absence of a deacon, the priest prays: "Almighty God, cleanse my heart and my lips that I may worthily proclaim your Gospel." Then at the end of the Gospel reading the deacon or priest adds ("inaudibly"): "May the words of the Gospel wipe away our sins." Pickstock explains that our exaltation in praise of God is indistinguishable from our preparatory purification, since the condition for admission into the divine presence is to admit that we require purging. In this way we offer ourselves to God. Once we have made this admission we discover that we are already within the place of purity. The marvelous meaning of God's mercy is that Christ has made our sinful condition itself the place in which we encounter Him. In the mess of our sinfulness we put on Christ's own purity. Metaphorically speaking, Christ is the great physician and healer. As a patient meets the doctor in the midst of his illness, so too, the sinner meets the divine healer in the midst of his sin. The penitential rite, then, does present us with a paradox; we recognize the darkness of sinfulness in the light of God's abundant mercy. As St. Paul writes to the Romans, "It is precisely in this that God proves his love for us: that while we were still sinners, Christ died for us."[35] Moreover, according to Pickstock, this ritual purification prepares us for the Eucharist. It is only through the purification of the congregation that we can refer to the "precious blood" as mentioned earlier. This is a traditional term for the sacramental wine. That it is precious implies a relationship, that is, it is precious to me. Literally, it is something held in high esteem, an object of great desirability. Because the blood of the Lamb was shed for our sins, we hold this cup of salvation to be precious.[36]

THE AWKWARD SILENCE

In crossing the threshold from the street to the sanctuary we are aware that the liturgy is counter-cultural. One way this is shown is in the use of silence. For Americans, especially, silence can be deadly. Consider the fact that with commercial radio, when no one is speaking or playing music, producers call that silence "dead air." In a system where time is money, silence kills profits. Surely an unplanned gap of quiet time is bad for radio. But is this a metaphor for our culture as well? It seems that many people operate on the same principle: they dread silence. It can seem to be a waste of time. Radio, television, and the iPod provide white noise—news or music—that keeps us moving to the rhythm of society. Sitting in silence, either alone or with someone, can cause people to feel awkward. Silence can be "messy" when it is perceived to be a loss of control. With a business mindset we will try to use time most efficiently; how much work can we manage in the shortest amount of time?

Sacred silence is one way by which we cross the threshold from the secular to the sacred, leaving behind *chronos* and entering into *kairos*. Sacred silence allows us to be present to the invisible Spirit of God: "Be still and know that I am God." It is also necessary if we are to be present to one another, a visible sign of Christ in our midst. Moreover, silence is necessary for speech. Silence is the womb from which words are formed, that is, significant words, those words that reveal and transform.[37] We do not simply rattle off our prayers by rote memory. The liturgical prayers should guide our thoughts, moving us from the mundane to the divine. So it is not simply a matter of what we say— the words, the thoughts and images evoked, the meter and prose—but how we say it, prayerfully, thoughtfully, wholeheartedly. Once we have settled into a prayerful state we are disposed to listening to hear the Word of God. This silence, along with the recognition of our sinfulness, is discomforting; they are somewhat messy.

CONCLUSION

I will conclude this section with an image from St. Paul's Chapel that is part of Trinity Episcopalian Church, in lower Manhattan. This colonial style chapel dates back to the late seventeenth century. In fact, George Washington celebrated his inauguration there and this is the church where he worshiped. His pew is sectioned off like a museum piece. The chapel stands just one block from where the World Trade Center stood. After September 11, 2001, the church was transformed into a mission center. For the nine months of the rescue and recovery operation, volunteers from the congregation and around the city provided food, clothing, medicine, and shelter for the hundreds who worked at Ground Zero. These workers slept in the pews and on mattresses along the walls of the chapel. St. Paul's became a haven for the hungry, the weak, and those in need of spiritual healing. According to one member of the staff, the chapel became a "chaotic hotel of radical hospitality." Even George Washington's pew was pressed into service. It was used as a podiatrist's station where volunteer doctors cared for the feet of the rescue workers. (A footwashing of sorts?) In June of 2002 the operation ended and the parish community of St. Paul's set out to restore the chapel. They painted the walls and today they look like new. But when it came to restoring the pews they paused. These white benches were marked from the workers who sat in them for their meals, and slept there as well. Their heavy workboots and toolbelts scraped the white painted wood, leaving large brown scratch marks. The community decided to leave the pews as they were. This is what you see today. These marks mar the pristine appearance of the chapel and serve as a reminder of the ministry this church performed, and how this community was transformed. This mess becomes a sign of hope. This blessed mess.

NOTES

1. John 13:1-20. All scriptural citations are from *The Catholic Study Bible: New American Bible*, ed. Donald Senior et al. (New York: Oxford University Press, 1990).
2. Francis Cardinal Arrinze, "Redemptionis Sacramentum: On Certain Matters to Be Observed or to Be Avoided Regarding the Most Holy Eucharist," *Congregation for Divine Worship and the Discipline of the Sacrament*, March 25, 2004, no. 106. (Emphasis mine.)
3. Catholic Church, National Conference of Catholic Bishops, Bishops' Committee on the Liturgy. *Environment and Art in Catholic Worship* (Washington, D.C.: National Conference of Catholic Bishops, 1978), 47.

4. "The Constitution on the Sacred Liturgy," in *The Documents of Vatican II*, ed. Walter M. Abbott (New York: Herder and Herder Association Press, 1966).

5. Martin Luther, "The Babylonian Captivity of the Church (1520)," Philadelphia, translated by Albert T. W. Steinhauser, in *Works of Martin Luther: With Introductions and Notes*, vol. 2 (Philadelphia: Muhlenberg Press, 1943).

6. Matthew 26:27. See James F. White, *The Sacraments in Protestant Practice and Faith* (Nashville, Tenn.: Abingdon Press, 1999), 93–94.

7. United States Conference of Catholic Bishops, Committee on the Liturgy, *The General Instruction of the Roman Missal* (Washington, D.C.: United States Conference of Catholic Bishops, Committee on the Liturgy, 2003), no. 279. (Emphasis mine.) There are several other references to purifying, cf. nn. 248, 271, 286, 306, 304.

8. *Webster's New World College Dictionary* (New York: Webster's New World Dictionaries, 4th ed.).

9. A comparison could be made to the Scripture as well. Until the recent modern translations of the Bible it was common to hear the Bible read in an antiquated English, for example, using "thee, thy and thine" for you, your, and yours. This suggests that there should be a special language when talking about God. Yet the original biblical languages of Hebrew and *koine* Greek were the commonly used languages of the time. There was no "Bible Hebrew" or "Bible Greek." Why should there be a "Bible English"?

10. I am grateful to Fr. Guinan for bringing this idea to my attention.

11. Donald K. McKim, *Westminster Dictionary of Theological Terms*, 1st ed. (Louisville, Ky.: Westminster John Knox Press, 1996), vii.

12. Numbers 8:5–7. The purification of the Levites was necessary for them to be made ritually clean for their special work. Also, the "waters of remission," literally the "water of sin," refers to the remission of sin. *Catholic Study Bible*, 151.

13. 1 Maccabees 4:36, 42–43. Note that this celebration of dedication marks the institution of the feast of Hannukah. *Catholic Study Bible*, 559.

14. Matthew 15:19–20.

15. Albert Rouet, *Liturgy and the Arts* (Collegeville, Minn.: Liturgical Press, 1997), xii.

16. Rouet, *Liturgy and the Arts*, 11.

17. Walter Brueggemann, *Finally Comes the Poet: Daring Speech for Proclamation* (Minneapolis, Minn.: Fortress Press, 1989), 49.

18. Cf. Eugene LaVerdiere, *The Eucharist in the New Testament and the Early Church* (Collegeville, Minn.: Liturgical Press, 1996), xi, 79.

19. 1 Corinthians 11:17–22.

20. Lewis Hyde, *The Gift: Imagination and the Erotic Life of Property* (New York: Vintage Books, 1983), 48–50.

21. Hyde, *The Gift*, 50.

22. For a contemporary discussion on the importance of Sunday as the Sabbath day, see John Paul II, *Dies Domini*, Apostolic Letter, Keeping the Lord's day (1998).

23. Hyde, *The Gift*, 51.

24. Wendell Berry, "The Pleasures of Eating," in *What Are People for?* (San Francisco, Calif.: North Point Press, 1990). Cf. Daniel Green, "Gift of the Land," unpublished work.

25. Berry, "The Pleasures of Eating," 146–148. Cf. Green, "Gift of the Land."

26. United States Conference of Catholic Bishops, *The General Instruction of the Roman Missal*, no. 321.

27. Rouet, *Liturgy and the Arts*, 84.

28. John Melloh, "Theology of Liturgical Time," in *The New Dictionary of Sacramental Worship*, ed. Peter E. Fink (Collegeville, Minn.: Liturgical Press, 1990), 734–736.

29. Roger Cardinal Mahony, *Gather Faithfully Together: Guide for Sunday Mass* (Chicago, Ill.: Liturgy Training Publications, 1997), 13–14.

30. Rouet, *Liturgy and the Arts*, 44. See also Christopher A. Dustin, "The Liturgy of Theory: Lessons on Beauty and Craft," in *Colloquium: Music, Worship, Arts*, ed. M. Fassler and B. Spinks (New Haven, Conn.: Yale Institute of Sacred Music, 2004), 12.

31. Cf. John Francis Baldovin, S.J., *Bread of Life, Cup of Salvation: Understanding the Mass* (Lanham, Md.: Rowman & Littlefield, 2003), 73–74.

32. The Book of Sirach (Ecclasiasticus), 1:12.

33. Catherine Pickstock, *After Writing: On the Liturgical Consummation of Philosophy* (Oxford, UK: Blackwell Publishers, 1998), 186–189.

34. Pickstock, *After Writing*, 186.

35. Romans 5:8.

36. Pickstock, *After Writing*, 186–189.

37. Walter J. Ong, *The Presence of the Word: Some Prolegomena for Cultural and Religious History* (New York: Simon & Schuster, 1970), 2–3.

✝

A Sensible Mystery

Alejandro Garcia-Rivera

Fr. Scirghi raises a question about his concern on the direction the liturgy is taking from "blessed mess" to pristine rubrics: "Am I making too much of this?" This section is, in a sense, an answer to his question. There is a deep and profound sense, I think, to the notion of a "blessed mess." It lies in the very nature of the divine Mystery, which is the heart of Christian worship. This section attempts an assessment of two contemporary understandings of divine Mystery as to their adequacy to be what Odo Casel called The Mystery of Christian Worship. Casel's understanding of divine Mystery was instrumental in the crafting of *Sacrosanctum Concilium*. I believe this understanding has been neglected due to competing understandings of mystery, one modern and the other postmodern, that have left the sensibility of divine Mystery either ambiguous or impossible. A comparison of these three accounts amounts to a ressourcement, a looking anew and reinterpreting, of Casel's understanding of divine Mystery. Mystery emerges in this ressourcement as kin to Scirghi's "blessed mess." The Mystery of Christian worship is a Sensible Mystery. Scirghi's observations about the messiness of liturgy are also observations about a profound mystery.

Casel, for those who may not be familiar with him, was a monk of the German Benedictine monastery, Maria Laach, and editor of the prestigious liturgical journal *Jahrbuch fur Liturgiewissenschaft*. He was one of the most influential writers in the field of liturgical theology in the first half of the last century. His writings on the liturgy expressed discontent with the neo-Scholastic sacramental theology of his time. In response to this discontent, Casel turned to the Patristic writers of an earlier theology where he found inspiration in their references to the mysteries of the liturgy. His 1932 master work, *Kultmysterium*, reflects this Patristic ressourcement with its lyrical and non-systematic tenor.

Yet *Kultmysterium* was to have an influence that many, friend and foe alike, believe led to Vatican II's magisterial document *Sacrosanctum Concilium*. In 1964, for example, none other than Louis Bouyer could write that "the heart of the teaching on the liturgy in the conciliar Constitution is also the heart of Dom Casel's teaching." Pope Benedict XVI said that Casel's *Kultmysterium* was "perhaps the most fruitful theological idea of [the 20th] century." The loftiest praise comes from Aidan Nichols who said that Casel should be accounted "a giant among theologians of the Liturgy and a figure raised up by Providence to salvage from perils the worship of the Church . . . one of the great fathers, I would say the great father of the 20th century liturgical movement."[1]

But how has Casel's rediscovery of mystery magisterially expressed in *Sacrosanctum Concilium* fared into the twenty-first century? Another search on the Internet based on the words "liturgy" and "reform" brings up a surprising number of references to the "reform of the reform" of the liturgy. There is consensus that the Mystery of Christian worship has not been effectively encountered in the thirty-six years since *Sacrosanctum Concilium's* teaching. So what went wrong? Two extreme positions appear to shape an answer to this question. One position holds that Casel was a "confused theologian" and "errant liturgist" that misguided the Second Vatican Council. Casel's notion of mystery implemented in *Sacrosanctum Concilium* brought about a crisis in the liturgy. Thus, the "non-infallible" teachings of *Sacrosanctum Concilium* need to be revoked and replaced.[2] The other, equally extreme, position holds that the teachings of Vatican II have been betrayed by a right-wing restoration movement within the Roman Catholic Church. The discontent with the liturgy has been the reluctance to put into effect the teachings of *Sacrosanctum Concilium*.

Is there a third, more centrist, position? There are actually many. A liturgical aesthetics is one of them. It suggests that contemporary misconceptions of mystery, both theological and philosophical, lie behind the discontent that drives the "reform of the reform." It is the insight of a liturgical aesthetics that contemporary notions of divine Mystery have misconstrued the ineffability of God as a non-sensible reality. Indeed, it is the proposal of a liturgical aesthetics that whatever the shortcomings of liturgical reform have been, they were made possible by a kind of iconoclastic attitude toward the Mystery of Christian worship. This iconoclastic attitude comes in two forms, one subjective and the other, objective.

On the subjective side, there exists an attitude that divine Mystery in the liturgy comes to be experienced through some form of communal experience of the assembly participating in the rite. This attitude encourages a "campfire" approach to liturgical celebration. On the objective side, there exists an attitude that divine Mystery in the liturgy can only be approached as a kind of objective ineffability or liturgical *mysterium tremendum*. Since the divine Mystery is ineffable and objective, only a strict ritual purity can serve as reliable guide in the face of divine Presence. This encourages an overreliance on the rubrics of the rite and an overall pristine approach to the liturgy in general. Both forms are iconoclastic in their own way. The former eschews concrete images in favor of a vague and unthematic communal experience. It prefers social communication over aesthetic experience. It is marked by information in the form of liturgical instructions to be read or instructions spoken from the ambo, "Now we will . . ." It is marked by banal and manipulative techniques that borrow from the arts to achieve social participation. Music, symbols, and performances are used more to manipulate emotion than provide a beautiful sacrifice of praise.

The latter, on the other hand, eschews true images in the form of a liturgical blindness. It emphasizes the objectivity of divine Mystery's ineffability to the point that it finds itself lost without some sort of absolutely objective guide to help it along the way toward this Mystery. It is blind to divine Mystery were it not for the certainty of its rubrics of liturgical tradition. It is marked by a machine-like actualization of the rite, motion without animating breath, a stultifying performance that is not worthy of the name celebration. It is marked by concern over ritual purity rather than ritual celebration. It is marked by hushed silence and reserved behavior more fitting to a funeral wake than to a joyful celebration. While either form of iconoclastic attitude may not exist in the admittedly extreme form I have given them, I believe most have noticed their symptoms at one time or another in our contemporary liturgies.

A liturgical aesthetics is a response to the iconoclasm that threatens the very life of the liturgy in our day. It attempts to identify the source of this iconoclasm and to propose a theology responsive to the nature of divine Mystery. Such a theology must begin with a crucial starting point. Divine Mystery is Beauty itself. It must aim toward a special kind of aesthetics— an account of a true sensibility to such Beauty, in other words, a liturgical aesthetics. In order to do this, a liturgical aesthetics starts by going back to the origins of a contemporary understanding of divine Mystery and asking about its adequacy in regards to the Mystery of Christian worship. A liturgical aesthetics begins with a ressourcement of divine Mystery.

TOWARD A RESSOURCEMENT OF MYSTERY

What is the nature of divine Mystery? Put this way, the question is unanswerable for divine Mystery is by definition, ineffable, hidden, a kind of secret. A better question might be to ask: what is the experience of divine Mystery? This question, at least, has had many answers. Ranging from St. Paul to John Paul, the experience of divine Mystery has had many articulations. What is striking, however, is an uncommon agreement. Divine Mystery is experienced at the same time as beautiful light and ineffable darkness. It is not a question of an ineffability eschewing sensibility or a sensibility that knows nothing of ineffability. It is a sensibility to the ineffable. Divine Mystery, in other words, is a sensible Mystery. Yet it is more. Accounts of the experience of divine Mystery, the report of the mystics, also speak of a marvelous love that weaves together this beautiful light and ineffable darkness. It is what the tradition calls affectus, a term not easily translated into English.[3]

Affectus is, in part, a tender, spontaneous, and gracious love. It is endearing. In Spanish, I would use the word *cariño*. It is that which moves the heart to another heart. Such movement has been experienced by the great mystics as a purified eros exemplified in the biblical love song that is the Song of Songs. It is, however, a love that reveals. Divine affectus reveals the human heart to itself precisely because it orients it to another heart. This movement and orientation is unitive and revelatory. It is what liturgical aesthetics calls a unitive revelatory experience. It reveals not only the many but also the One. More important, it reveals the very nature of Beauty itself, the many now become one. Unitive revelatory experience, in other words, is the experience of the oldest understandings of beauty, unity in diversity.[4] It is also more than that. It is the experience of Pentecost. It is Pentecostal delight. It is also the Pauline vision of the many now become one Body of Christ. Thus, the unitive revelatory experience that is the aesthetics of divine Mystery's affectus serves to distinguish it from other accounts of aesthetic experience and allows another look at the nature of divine Mystery.[5] It allows a ressourcement of Mystery itself.

Ressourcement, of course, refers to that theological movement of a return to the Patristic sources of theology. Theologians like Henri de Lubac and Yves Congar figured prominently in it. As return, it was envisioned as more than a restoration. Theologians went back to the sources to start a new dialogue not to restore an ancient one. As such, the theologians of the Ressourcement brought new life into theological reflection on the mysteries of the Church, which led eventually to the Second Vatican Council. Did such ressourcement, however, actually engage ancient traditions on divine Mystery in order to start a new dialogue? New conversations on mystery did occur but they were conversations engaged with modern philosophy or the new sciences of political and social theory. Perhaps the only true ressourcement on the nature of divine Mystery may be found in Hans Urs von Balthasar's epic work *Herrlichkeit*, known in English as *The Glory of the Lord*.[6] A liturgical aesthetics must attempt such a ressourcement as well. The critical discontent found at all levels of the Church signals a fundamental problem or lack in the conceptualization of the nature of the liturgy itself. This problem or lack will not be solved by playing with the rubrics or citing Conciliar documents. It is more fundamentally a theological problem, a problem having its roots in an inadequate understanding of divine Mystery, or a lack of engaging the mystical tradition toward a new conversation. What follows below is an attempt to do so.

What is divine Mystery, then? Or, more specifically, what is the Mystery of Christian worship? Casel gives us the characteristics of such Mystery:

> In the first place, the mystery [of Christian worship] is defined by a revelation (epiphany) from God; it is settled and prescribed by him; its piety is therefore theocentric. Next, the mystery is not concerned with race nor nation, but with the individual, yet in such a fashion that this individual comes immediately into a community, under a religious authority. The act of separation from the profane, and the solemn initiation, give him a great insight into the new life; its mysticism finds practical application, not in purely individual, interior strivings, but in actions which all share; they lead to vision, not of a quietistic interior sort, but to the real showing of God. In them all the soul's faculties are engaged; the rite is sacred art of great stylistic value: rich drama, deep symbolism hold individual and congregation. It puts the individual into a gripping and upraising circle of divine action, carries him up beyond himself.[7]

Casel describes, in essence, the unitive revelatory experience that belongs to divine Beauty. As such, it sets the ground for a liturgical aesthetics. It is theocentric, in the sense, that the conditions for such an experience come from and point toward God. It is interior in the sense that it is aimed at the individual but it is an interiority that is unitive. It is experienced as a community. It is an active sensibility in the sense that it is more than receiving a vision but leading to one in which "all the soul's faculties are engaged." It is revelatory in both being an epiphany from God but also as giving "great insight into the new life."

Casel goes further. The Mystery of Christian worship is the *mysterium Paschale*: "The pasch of the Lord, his death and exaltation is the mystery of redemption proper." It is, moreover, a "continual, lasting, mystical and yet concrete presence in the Church, from which the power of his blood is to flow daily to give life and healing to the faithful." As such, the Mystery of Christian worship is a "concrete yet Spirit-filled presence and objective in nature."[8] This Paschal sacrifice turned banquet gives the liturgy special form. Casel continues:

> Thus Catholic worship has strong objective lines: they are expressed in its form. Nothing subjective or arbitrary, no personal enthusiasm, momentary ecstasy or expressionism are to mark it; what it seeks are clarity beyond the limits of any single person, roots for a content that is divine and everlasting, a sober peaceful and measured expression of what belongs to it, in forms which give direction to the over-flow of thought and emotion, which put nature and passion within bounds.[9]

Christian worship takes the struggles of both intellect and passion, of ideas and feelings, of joys and sufferings running like electrical currents in our life outside the liturgy and gives them shape, beautiful shape, and, also beautiful expression. The Mystery of Christian worship as the pasch of the Lord means that

> the liturgy is as broad and as deep as the life of Christ and His church, the life they have in the Father. The liturgy is a hymn of love; at one time the bride praises the bridegroom, and then the order is reversed; at others it is they two who praise the Father. [Thus, the liturgy] does not merely teach, it leads to love. In it the word becomes a song of love; and where truth and goodness stand together beauty will not be lacking. In the liturgy God's truth is given form and shape, and so becomes a work of art, not through isolated aestheticism or dilettantism but of its own weight.[10]

Thus Casel brings to a finish his master work. I have quoted extensively for the sake of a genuine ressourcement. I wanted his words to speak anew in the freshness in which he wrote them. For time has clouded Casel's aesthetic sense of mystery.

The Mystery of Christian worship was, for Casel, not only the mysterium Paschale but also the mystery of divine Beauty. Such a liturgical aesthetics of sensibility ought not to surprise us. The Paschal mystery, after all, is the most sensual of all the mysteries. It is a mystery wrapped up in the myriad of sensations and images that make up the call of a people into Israel, a falling away from a profound covenant, the foretelling of a great mystery, the birth of a child in a barn with angels singing and cows bellowing, the sounds and smells of a wedding where water becomes wine, a prolonged agony where drops of sweat become drops of blood, and a heartfelt cry rings out: "Eloi, Eloi, lama sabachtani!" Then follows restless nights of fear and darkness only to awaken to a dawn of delighted surprise and renewed innocence, a life-giving breath given to many by a risen Jesus, a breaking of bread on the road to Emmaus, a spectacular ascension into the heavens, and an equally spectacular descension of little flames of fire, a Pentecostal finale of sound, color, and marvelous sights.

The Paschal mystery is one with such sensuality. It is, above all, a sensible mystery. It is a life-giving mystery. It is a Living Beauty.

Yet somehow the intrinsic connection between the Paschal Mystery and divine Beauty was lost in the years after *Sacrosanctum Concilium* was written. Given the benefit of distance in time, it is possible to look back and see what forces led to this unfortunate break. Time reveals formidable obstacles in contemporary theological (and secular) thought about the nature of Mystery and its experience. Hard-won syntheses of contemporary thought and Christian theology also militate against any easy accounts of aesthetic sensibility. A liturgical aesthetics that would take on a ressourcement of Casel's insights into divine Mystery must face two major challenges.

These two challenges revolve around the (traditional) tense-filled relationship between Mystery's *affectus* and human understanding. The true center of this revolving tension, as I shall argue, is actually the role of human sensibility. One challenge, represented in the thought of Karl Rahner, involves the role of human loving in the transcendental knowing of God's mysterious horizon. The other challenge, represented in the thought of Jean-Luc Marion, involves the role of human understanding in the postmodern re-articulation of Mystery's *affectus* as the pure given-ness of love by the God without being.

These two challenges raise fundamental issues about divine Mystery. How is divine Mystery apprehended? Is it the report of an affective experience caught up in a momentum-toward-mystery? Or is it more than a report, a real experience, the experience of being embraced by the fullness of Form? Is divine Love experienced as pure gift? Then how is one to understand that he or she is loved? Or is it not only gift but also a work, a work of art? Does God's love conform our affectivity as well as gift us with one? If so, what role does human knowing play in this gift that conforms? On such questions a liturgical aesthetics can founder or thrive. As challenges, they reveal the profundity of the thinkers who brought these challenges to public awareness. As challenges, they also point to inadequacies in contemporary understandings of divine Mystery that a liturgical aesthetics may correct. At stake is a revitalization of Christian worship for a deeper understanding of mystery can renew attitudes toward the liturgy that have lost fervor and vision.

The first synthesis a liturgical aesthetics must face is one best represented by the great Jesuit theologian Karl Rahner. Rahner achieved an exquisite synthesis of scholastic theology and modern thought through what is known as transcendental Thomism. Such a synthesis required an anthropological turn, that is, a turn to the dynamic elements of a self as a hearer-of -the-word as opposed to a more static but objective being-in-the-world. Such an approach takes the human self into the heart of mystery and this is Rahner's wonderful contribution. The experience of mystery is not an extraordinary event but intrinsic to our human nature. Rahner sees mystery in terms of an ever-approachable but, nonetheless, unreachable intellectual horizon. Unfortunately, such an intellectual formulation of mystery makes problematic the sensible relationship of divine Beauty and divine Mystery, especially in the important liturgical category of praise.

The second synthesis is that of contemporary mystical theology best represented in the work of Jean-Luc Marion. Marion's major work, *God without Being*, makes a credible synthesis with what is known as postmodern thought.[11] Postmodernity arose, in part, as disenchantment with the intellectual optimism of modernity. Against the confident assumption that the world could be known, it proposes the opposite. Intellectual discourse about the world is intrinsically capricious and, thus, knowledge about the world is problematic. In a brilliant distinction between idol and icon, Marion brings postmodern insights to bear on the idolatries of our day. Idolatry in our day is perpetuated by a culture that offers the not-visable as the spiritual invisible. Culture's idols encourage our gaze to fix on superficial appearances that offer no satisfaction. In this, they pass off as invisible while, in fact, what they offer is the not-visable. Only the icon offers a true experience of the invisible for only there, the icon through a marvelous love gazes at us and not us at the icon. This marvelous love, however, is based on the goodness of Being and not Being itself. Idols are inspired when God is spoken of in terms of Being and not of love. Only a God without Being can be a God of love. This means that God, as such, can only be experienced as pure given-ness.

But what kind of a gift is a pure gift? Can a pure gift be received and understood as gift? I do not believe Marion answers this question. Indeed, I believe Marion opens the door to a profound iconoclasm in the liturgy. In his emphasis on God's love based on the good, Marion introduces the liturgical equivalent of the moral into the celebration of the liturgy. A liturgy marked by a love that knows only the good is marked by a concern for ritual purity and an emphasis on rubrics.

The time has come to respond to these two challenges. I intend to bring other great thinkers on mystery and gift in dialogue with these two great thinkers. The great Jesuit poet Gerard Manley Hopkins and the great writer on gift Lewis Hyde will serve as dialogue partners that offer not simply correction but, more modestly, other considerations into the profound insights of both Rahner and Marion. These new insights constitute my ressourcement of the Mystery of Christian worship.

THE TRANSCENDENTAL HORIZON

Rahner tries to ground mysticism in the everyday. To do so, he takes a thoroughly modern approach. He grounds mystery in the nature of the self. Absolute Mystery, according to Rahner, beckons the self. The self cannot but respond to the beckoning for it is fundamentally oriented toward its call. As such, the self is caught in a momentum-toward-mystery, a journey to an ever-transcending horizon. This intrinsic momentum toward a transcendental horizon finds impulse in the questions raised by our everyday experience. Thus, the self's experience of this transcendent horizon of absolute mystery "is not some extraneous spiritual luxury but the condition for the very possibility of everyday knowing and wanting."[12] Here lies the heart of how Rahner understands mystery. Rahner shifts the question from whether mystery is accessible only to a few to the question of the conditions for such accessibility. These conditions Rahner finds in the very heart of the human subject. As such, Rahner's formulation becomes quite problematic for the notion of a sensible Mystery. This quote from Rahner makes clear the problematic:

> Don't go talking about them, making up theories about them, but simply endure these basic experiences. Then in fact something like a primitive awareness of God can emerge. Then perhaps we cannot say much of it; then what we 'grasp' first of all about God appears to be nothing, to be the absent, the nameless, absorbing and suppressing all that can be expressed and conceived. Consider for example the situations in which man is brought back to this basic experience of God. Somewhere, someone seems to be weeping hopelessly. . . . Someone has the basic experience of being stripped even of his very self. . . . Someone experiences joy. . . . All that man has then to say of this God can never be more than a pointer to this primitive experience of God. If someone says that this is mysticism, then it is in fact mysticism and then this very factor of mysticism belongs to God. But it is not mysticism in the specific sense: it is the obviousness of being encompassed absolutely by God at the moment of a man's whole awakening to mental existence.[13]

Rahner begins with affective experience. He ends with the incomprehensibility of mystery as evidenced by the inability of language to describe it. For Rahner, the experience of mystery is closest to formless and unthematic experience. Affectivity plays a role in so far as it introduces an element of perplexity that leads to the unthematic, pre-reflective condition that is intrinsic to fundamental human nature. At this point, it is not clear in Rahner whether the affectivity that takes one to absolute mystery has any organic connection to that mystery or if it is simply the occasion that begins the process by which the human is taken to a transcendental horizon. It is, I'm afraid, more of the latter than the former. It is the consequence of his starting point in the depiction of absolute mystery as a transcendental horizon.

The God of a transcendental horizon is eminently approachable but never reached; readily accessible but not very intimate; eminently majestic but not very personal. Indeed, it is hard to see how the personal God of Jesus Christ can affect us when represented as a transcendent horizon of absolute mystery. Rahner acknowledges the role affective experience has in raising the questions that lead us to the mystery that is God but tends to disconnect affectivity from the reality that is God.

In this light, it is useful to compare Rahner to another Jesuit, the great poet Gerard Manley Hopkins. Hopkins matured into his marvelous aesthetics of mystery by a revulsion against the florid overabundance of Romantic poetry of which John Keats would be an example. As Hopkins wrote in Spring and Death, "A little sickness in the air/ From too much fragrance everywhere."[14] This is not to say that he was not interested in the sensuous. What bothered him was not sensuality per se but that Romantic aesthetic tendency to revel in it aimlessly. Hopkins found in the "rose-mole" of pinked salmons and the "brinded cows" of England's countryside sensuousness with an aim.

Sensuousness in Nature, Hopkins discovered, tended toward unifying form.[15] Such sensuousness started with the unique individual, the particular, but revealed a tendency toward unity that did not obliterate its starting point. This inspired Hopkins to understand divine Beauty in a brilliant and insightful way. Hopkins saw the sensual awareness of the diverse variety of the particular found in nature converging onto a transcendent unity: God. He did this through his appropriation of the biblical notion of "type" and applying it to the natural beauty he saw in his beloved England. The biblical notion of type is a kind of interpretation that sees an Old Testament person, event, or thing prefigure, parallel, or foreshadow a New Testament person, event, or thing. As such, it is related to the Platonic sense of form but it is quite different for it also carries with it the biblical concern for the unique and particular. Indeed, the particular in its detail is essential to discover the "typical."

The turn to the type rather than to the classical notion of form gives Hopkins the basis for a powerful theological aesthetics of mystery. In the type there exists a satisfying tension between its multitude of denotations and the unifying energy of the type itself. As such, it is another way to articulate the ancient definition of secondary beauty as unity in diversity. When this type, however, happens to be Jesus Christ, the archetype of all Creation "through whom all things were made," we have a theological aesthetics based on the Incarnation.[16] Applying the archetype of Christ to the asymmetric particularities found in nature reveal an "instress" in the reality of the world. This instress creates "inscapes" of great beauty converging onto the divine archetype. Thus, in his 1868 notes on Parmenides, Hopkins could write: "All the world is full of inscapes and chance left free to act falls into an order as well as purpose: looking out of my window I caught it in the random clouds and broken heaps of snow made by the cast of a broom."[17] Herein lies the great difference between these two great Jesuits. While Rahner finds the ambivalence of language a problem in describing absolute mystery, Hopkins finds in such ambivalence the primary condition to engage and experience the divine archetype. While Rahner finds in the perplexity that strong affective experience brings to rational understanding the threshold to absolute mystery, Hopkins finds in the affective experience of the particular, inscapes created by an instress in reality converging onto a mystery he called Pied Beauty. While Rahner takes affective experience to the formless and unthematic in the human condition and, thus, to the threshold of absolute mystery, Hopkins begins with the unthematic but particular in the world of nature in order to take us to the inscapes brought about by the reconciliating instressful energy of the archetype of all Creation.

Ultimately, what is at stake here is the theological significance of the actual experience of love or affectivity in an encounter with divine mystery. For Hopkins, it is Scotus' insight that one can only love the particular that leads him to his inscapes, which draw and connect us to the archetype of their unique and particular beauty.[18] Rahner speaks of the need of affectivity in the encounter with mystery. He tells us that "the actual experience of love is indeed absolutely basic and absolutely indispensable. But despite this fact the experience itself as such can in itself be accepted more profoundly, more purely, and with greater freedom when we achieve a knowledge of its true nature and its implications at the explicitly conscious level."[19] As such, Rahner gives a rather ambivalent relationship between knowing and loving in the experiential encounter with mystery.

On the one hand, he tells us that the affective experience in mystery is "absolutely indispensable." On the other, he seems to locate it on the side of the formless and unthematic experience of the human person. In doing this, he qualifies what he means as absolutely indispensable. There is a purer way to the affective experience. It would be more profound if it took knowledgeable form in human consciousness. In other words, it must be intellectualized! It is not clear in Rahner what the relationship between head and heart is in the affective experience of divine Mystery. One could ask Rahner: Is it head or heart that delights when God's love as mystery is experienced?

I do not think Rahner was able to answer that question. Nonetheless, much can be learned from Rahner's struggle to give both affective experience and the incomprehensibility of divine mystery their due. Perhaps divine Mystery should not be seen as incomprehensible. Put as incomprehensible, divine Mystery can only be understood in a negative way with respect to the intellect. On the other hand, neither should it be understood in a positivistic way with respect to the will. Put as a matter of the will, encounter with divine Mystery means, on the side of the human, an affair of pure will, a will that is willing to enter a formless and fearful abyss. This is simply the incomprehensibility of the intellect mirrored in terms of the will.

The basic problem is that, in Rahner (and the modern thought he was addressing), the philosophical relationship between head and heart is problematic. Rahner knows this and it is his understanding of affective experience in the encounter with divine Mystery that helps him address this problematic. To assume the relationship as problematic, however, is the problem itself. If it is true that we experience head and heart as distinct and, even, as incommensurable with one another, then it is because at a profound and deep level in our soul, they are one. Our experience in the garden of good and evil is, in essence, an experience of falling short of that unity that is already ours. It is an experience of the formless within us but not as fundamental to our nature but, rather, against it.

Hopkins' theological aesthetics helps formulate divine mystery in a different and, I think, more fruitful, way. It is not incomprehensibility that marks divine Mystery but the fullness of form. Indeed, divine Mystery beckons and calls all chaos and darkness to itself creating particular inscapes and "charging the world like shook foil" in its loving embrace of what is dark and partial. Such a view of mystery reveals the heart of God's love. It is not formlessness per se that describes God's loving spirit embracing the formless and giving it form. Such a view allows a renewed understanding of the mystical experience that Pseudo-Dionysius and the author of the "Cloud of Unknowing" tried to articulate. It is an experience not of negativity but *kenosis*. *Kenosis*, understood in the light of Hopkins' instress, is not solely a negative dynamic of self-emptying but also a positive dynamic of embracing the formless, the broken, and the partial. It is *kenosis* understood in the light of the Paschal Mystery, the Mystery of Christian worship.

Divine *Kenosis* seen in both its positive and negative dynamics describes a mystery where forms find their fullness and abundance. Divine Mystery, then, is best described not as a formless incomprehensibility but as an incredibly fertile and creative spirit superabundant in form. Such a view of mystery gives Pentecostal shape to Rahner's transcendental horizon. It sees mystical experience, like Rahner, as present in the ordinary experiences of our lives but present there not as perplexities but as true experiences. It allows not so much for an absolute Mystery but for an infinite, full, and, thus, sensible Mystery.

GOD WITHOUT BEING

The second challenge to the proposal of a sensible Mystery comes from the work of the French philosopher of religion Jean-Luc Marion. Marion has become well-known for his masterly struggle with the nature of divine Mystery in the context of postmodern philosophical thought. He asks the important question: what does the God of Scripture and theology have to do with the God of metaphysics and philosophy? His answer is more subtle than Jerome's. It is not simply that Athens has nothing to do with Jerusalem but, Athens also needs to reconsider its assumptions. It is an important answer, especially today. Philosophers have all but banished God from their sophisticated discussions. Theologians have all but banished philosophy from theirs. What was once a rich and organic marriage is now a bitter divorce. Jean-Luc Marion brings his understanding of divine Mystery to bear on this divorce and achieves a striking and original understanding. God is not being or non-being. God is beyond being itself. God is God without being.

Marion comes to this conclusion after many years of study with his great teacher, the master of postmodern thought Jacques Derrida. In other words, Marion is a thoroughly postmodern philosopher. This means that Marion is sensitive to postmodern suspicions of a bird's eye view of reality. He sees such a bird's-eye view in the traditional philosophy of Being. More alarming, he sees such a view applied to God by theologians. Marion feels that the very nature of God has been compromised by theologies, such as Thomism, that see God as *ipsum esse*, or Being itself. God cannot be conceptualized, Marion insists, and any attempt to do so is idolatrous. Thus, God cannot be conceived in terms of Being. God is beyond such conception. God is God without being.

Marion makes his point by taking elements of postmodern thought and mystical theology and weaving them into a brilliant distinction between "icon" and "idol." Postmodern thought, for example, is fond of the metaphor of gazing at an image reflected countless times in a mirror to describe human understanding. Marion uses a similar metaphor to explore philosophical understanding of God. He applies this metaphor to make a distinction between the icon that provokes vision and the idol that postpones vision. Through this distinction, he comes to conclusions that are startling but profound.

The idol presents itself to human gaze as representing the divine in such a way as to afford understanding of the divine. In Marion's words,

> The idol shows what it sees. It shows that which, indeed, occupies the field of the visible, with neither deceit nor illusion, but which indissolubly invests it only on the basis of vision itself. The idol supplies vision with the image of

what it sees. The idol produces (itself) in actuality (as) that at which vision intentionally aims. It freezes in a figure that which vision aims at a glance. . . . In the future of its aim, at a certain point that nothing could foresee, the aim no longer aims beyond, but rebounds upon a mirror-which otherwise never would have appeared-toward itself; this invisible mirror is called the idol. It is not invisible in that one cannot see it, since to the contrary one sees nothing but it; it is invisible because it masks the end of the aim.[20]

Thus, the idol deceives human spiritual gaze for it offers what it cannot deliver: vision's aim to see the invisible. For in the idol, vision sees only the reflection of an invisible mirror turned upon itself and mistakes the invisible mirror's restless reflections as true vision of the invisible. The

idol therefore appears as a reflection on the individual: an aim towards the visable that, at a certain point of the aim, is inflected upon itself, is inflected upon itself in order to characterize as invisible that at which it can no longer aim. The invisible is defined by the reflection whose defection abandons the visible as not-visable, hence not visible-in short, invisible.[21]

I have taken care to quote Marion extensively because his thought is subtle. In his writing, one can detect the influence of postmodern thought's metaphor of untraceable reflections upon mirrors. One also detects, however, a masterful exposition of the form idolatry has taken in the age of the Internet, global communications, and marketing strategies.

Idolatry, in our day, can be seen in Marion's terms. It is spiritual experience offered as the not-visable rather than an experience of the invisible. It is the spirituality of the seeker rather than the dweller or, rather, a seeker that does not intend to ever be a dweller. The not-visable is an insidious form of idolatry in our day. It is easily achieved by modern technologies and, therefore, quite easily manipulates human longing for spiritual food. The idol in our day emerges from a technological way of life in which a "traditional, contextual" substance such as cream becomes an "opaque" commodity such as Cool Whip through a "concealed and intricate machinery of techniques and therapies." Such is the stuff of idols today. The not-visable devices in our society are social mechanisms that conceal deep social structures even while revealing convincing surface appearances. The effect of this is atrophy in our ability to sense God's presence; indeed, even to enjoy God's absence.[22]

Thus, true encounter with divine Mystery becomes even more difficult in our day. Powerful social forces increased in power by a technological way of life in society today offer themselves as true encounter with the invisible. They play on humanity's deepest longings to experience the spiritual in a new and, unfortunately, demonic way. It is not hard to see that Marion has brilliantly exposed the malaise that threatens spiritual life today. It is not a lack of spiritual fervor but its deflection into a spiritually fruitless play of visions easily manipulated by powerful social forces. If Marion is correct, then liturgy stands at a prophetic threshold today. Liturgy can expose the idol of the not-visable with an experience of divine Mystery, a Mystery of the invisible truly made visible. It must do so, however, in a new way. If in modernity, the issue was whether the invisible made visible was an illusion of superstitious premodern thought, then, in postmodernity, the issue is whether the visible is truly the invisible it purports to be. It is this issue that liturgy must take up if it is to render divine Mystery. Gregorian chant and incense will not do it. Liturgy must offer a new experience of the invisible such that the not-visable is exposed for what it is. Marion offers a possible avenue for a renewed liturgy in his insightful account of the icon.

The icon is not a vision of the divine but, rather, provokes one. It summons sight by letting the invisible radiate and infiltrate the visible without reducing the visible to the invisible. As Marion puts it,

> The icon regards us-it concerns us, in that it allows the intention of the invisible to occur visibly . . . he who sees it sees in it a face whose invisible intention is envisaging him. The icon opens in a face, where man's sight envisages nothing, but goes back infinitely from the visible to the invisible by the grace of the visible itself: instead of the invisible mirror, which sent the human gaze back to itself alone and censured the invisable, the icon opens in a face that gazes at our gazes in order to summon them to its depth. . . . The icon alone offers an open face, because it opens in itself the visible onto the invisible, by offering its spectacle to be transgressed-not to be seen, but to be venerated. The reference from the perceived visible to the invisible person summons one to travel through the (invisible) mirror, and to enter, so to speak, into the eyes of the icon-if the eyes have that strange property of transforming the visible and the invisible into each other.[23]

In this breathtakingly beautiful account of the icon, Marion, I think, correctly identifies the antidote not only to the idolatry of our day but to the discontent with our liturgy. The iconic element of the liturgy has been diminished or, even, missing. Liturgy, in the wake of Vatican II, became at the same time more and more concerned with words rather than with images and enabling participation by the assembly in the liturgy.

These two directions are not in themselves undesirable and, perfectly reasonable in light of the lack of these elements in the pre-Vatican II liturgy. Nonetheless, it was not foreseen how easily postmodern society co-opts and manipulates these fine aims into something less than divine mystery. The "cream" of Christian worship becomes "Cool Whip" at the hands of liturgical committees that do not look very deeply into the nature of the Mystery of Christian worship. Liturgy, in these hands, takes on the form of a commodity rather than divine Mystery. Liturgy becomes something to be consumed rather than encounter and communion with divine Mystery. Indeed, little veneration takes place in our liturgies anymore. But what is the antidote? What needs to happen for the liturgy to be a place where encounter and communion with divine Mystery take place?

Unfortunately, it is not clear whether Marion's brilliant and beautiful distinction between icon and idol can answer this question. Behind Marion's icon and idol lies an analysis of the relationship between the human mind and the nature of things-in-themselves. Can we ever know someone as they truly are, if our minds always conceptualize that someone? The intrinsic nature of our knowing by conceptualizing means that the someone that is known can easily be mistaken for the concepts in our minds. Since concepts can be easily influenced and manipulated by other forces than the reality that is conceived, they lend themselves to the superficial. The antidote is to recognize that concepts are a second step in understanding. Reality first is given to our understanding, then we conceive it. Reality, in other words, is a donum not a datum. And reality itself is given to us by God.

This notion of gift is taken up by Marion to offer us an understanding of God. In order to break out from the idol to the icon, God must be understood as pure given-ness. This means that conceptual understanding is an obstacle in understanding God. God must be understood as the inconceivable and unthinkable. Our gaze can never become fixed on God. It is in trying to conceptualize God that the idol is born. Indeed, the only way to approach God is through the icon for it is not we who gaze at the icon, but the icon who gazes at us. The icon, then, is the medium of gift and such a gift, freely given, in being given cannot be determined by the one who receives it. It springs from a well that is beyond our conceptual understanding and control. How is this pure given-ness received or experienced?

Marion has a ready answer. It is agape. Marion identifies God's pure given-ness in the profound definition given in 1 John 4:8: God is Love (agape). Marion follows his brilliant exposition into deep waters. God's love as the free gift of agape is now applied to the liturgy. He offers a devastating critique of present understandings of God's presence in the Eucharist. In doing so, Marion, I believe, also takes his philosophical theology to the threshold of an unrelenting iconoclasm, but, at least, a very instructive iconoclasm for it is an iconoclasm that reveals the foundation for a liturgical aesthetics, the intrinsic relationships between love and sensibility.

Marion asks a fundamental question of the meaning of real presence in the Eucharistic bread and wine:

> Can the Eucharistic presence of Christ as consecrated bread and wine deter-
> mine, starting from itself and itself alone, the conditions for its reality, the di-
> mensions of its temporality and the dispositions of its approach? Does eu-
> charistic presence suffice for its own comprehension?[24]

To answer the question, he insists that the question of presence must be
measured "against the fullness of gift." This leads to the conclusion that
the presence does not refer merely to the "here and now" of the present
but there is a fuller meaning of the temporality of Eucharistic presence in
its nature as gift. Christ's gift in the Eucharist is not received merely in the
"here and now" of the present but also as memorial (the past is included
in the present) and as eschatological (the future is included in the present).

As memorial it is no mere recalling to memory of a past event. It "relies
on an event whose past has not disappeared in our day." Thus, "far from
the past being defined as a nonpresent, or as accomplished actuality, it orders through its irreducibly anterior and definitively accomplished 'deal'
a today, that without it, would remain insignificant, indifferent, in a world
null and void-unreal." As eschatological, the Eucharistic gift is "a question not only of a future period waiting to be unveiled" but also as a "call
that asks for, and, in a sense, hastens the return of Christ." As such, it is
not "a question of a simple nonpresence that it would remain to bring, finally, to presence." It is, indeed, epekstasis, a straining "towards that
which is coming to it."[25]

Marion believes that this fuller understanding of presence has been lost
in a view that sees Eucharistic presence measured by how much attention
the human community gives it. In other words,

> A double dependency henceforth affects the eucharistic presence. Because
> the gift of "God" in it depends on human consciousness, and because the lat-
> ter thinks time on the basis of the present, the gift of "God" still depends on
> the present of consciousness-on attention.[26]

Marion, I think, has put his finger on that malady of most contemporary
liturgy: its wordiness and self-consciousness. *Sacrosanctum Concilium*'s ex-
hortation for active involvement in the liturgy got interpreted as a kind of
self-consciousness of the assembly of the liturgy's action. Such self-
consciousness encourages a kind of wordiness better suited for communication and information than to mystery. Much worse, it encourages the
identification of the Eucharistic presence with the immediate, self-
consciousness of the collective self that is the assembly.

How, then, can the fuller experience of Eucharistic presence become a
reality? Marion believes that this can take place only if "the eucharistic
present itself is distinguished from me and from the consciousness that I

have of myself (that we have of ourselves) on its occasion."[27] But how can this take place, concretely? Here Marion reveals his philosophical limitations. His answer is not very helpful. It is more like a philosophical principle than a practical answer. There is, however, something problematic about Marion's formulation of gift and presence that goes beyond the divide between theory and practice. What role does Jesus' command—"Do this in memory of me"—play in his understanding of consciousness and presence, indeed, of gift? If Eucharist is pure gift, then how can it be reconciled as gift with a command to put together the very gift that one is to receive? Marion, I believe, places the emphasis of gift purely on the side of God's doing. While this is true inasmuch as a gift has to be given, gift is also about the dynamics of receiving.

Fr. Scirghi recounted earlier the marvelous story known as "The Shoemaker and the Elves" that is also a parable about giving. I would also like to refer to it. The story of the elves and the shoemaker is the story of the gifted person. "It describes the time between the initial stirrings of a gift (when it is potentially ours) and the releasing of a gift (when it is actually ours). In this case the gift is the man's talent, carried by the elves."[28] It reveals two striking characteristics of true gifts: they have the capacity to transform the recipient and they are meant to be passed along. This means that there exists a certain dynamics to receiving a gift.

A true gift transforms the one who receives it. Or, put another way, the gift offers a transformative future to the one who receives the gift. It does not do this immediately. There is a process in which the one who receives the gift, like the shoemaker, must first be stirred to develop the gift that is given. This process is the labor of gratitude. It is a labor that tries to match the labor of the one who gave the gift. As such, gifts also teach the recipient how to give. Gifts, in other words, are meant to be passed along. This becomes clear in the case of the shoemaker. The shoemaker finds the ability to receive the gift of the elves only by deciding to stay awake at night to watch the elves. It is then that the gift becomes actualized. As Hyde comments,

> In this story the clothes realize the gift (that is, they make it real, they make it a thing). Note that the shoemaker makes his first pair of shoes (within the tale) in order to dress the elves. It's the last act in his labor of gratitude. Now he's a changed man. . . . The shoes he makes are a return gift which simultaneously accomplishes his own transformation and frees the elves. This is why I say that the end of the labor of gratitude is similarity with the gift of its donor.[29]

The story of the elves and the shoemaker reveals for Hyde the meaning of gift. It also reveals for us what may be some inadequacies in Marion's formulation of the Eucharistic gift.

Like Hyde, Marion believes there are dynamics to receiving a gift. The Eucharistic gift in being received "depends on charity, aims at the ecclesiastical body, and is amenable to a mystical reality."[30] But these are simply effects. Marion does not want to delve in the dynamics of reception or, at least, is unclear about them. He does not seem to appreciate what Hyde calls the labor of gratitude. I believe that Marion mistakes the unconditional nature of the Eucharistic gift for the fullness of gift. The fullness of gift continues into the receiving of it. If true gift is to be appreciated it must be followed into the dynamics of its reception. This is why a liturgical aesthetics is needed.

We do this (the Eucharist) in memory of Him not simply to remember Christ's passion but also to pass along the gift of Himself. We do this as a labor of gratitude. We do this as an act of veneration but, in the sense, of a staying alert to learn how a gift is made. We do this in order to accept a future transformative not only of ourselves but of the entire creation. We do this in gratitude and appreciation for the gift that is given in the making. We do this in the sense of a dramatics, a putting on a play on the stage of human failings, so that Christ's gift can truly be received as a gift for us, in Him, with Him, and through Him in the unity of the Holy Spirit.

I'm afraid that Marion's portrayal of the Eucharistic gift as pure givenness obliterates the very conditions that make gift a gift. It takes away the basis to understand and appreciate that which is given. As such, Marion's understanding of gift can lead to a profound iconoclasm in the liturgy in which neither beauty nor the arts have a real home. Ultimately, it comes down to how Marion envisions God's love. For him it is agape but it is agape inspired by the good not the beautiful. He agrees with Denys that the "good fosters and inspires agape."[31] As such, Marion's agape seems to have little in common with the affectus of divine Mystery.

If affectus is fostered by what endears, Marion's agape is fostered by what is good. These different motivations corresponding to the differences between affectus and agape have certain consequences for a liturgy celebrating the Eucharist. A liturgy based on an Eucharistic gift brought by a love inspired by the good rather than by what is endearingly beautiful encourages the liturgical equivalent of the moral: ritual purity with a corresponding pristine attention to the rubrics. The messiness of a workshop of gratitude, a place of labor for the creative development of gift, the preparation of the gift received so that they may be passed on, all this becomes liturgically immoral to a love that knows only the good.

This may be Marion's most serious shortcoming. In his reaction to the reductionism that conceptual understanding brings to our notion of God, he is, in the end, suspicious of all that glitters, even, I'm afraid, the radiance of divine Beauty. It is a radiance that comes from an unimaginable depth but it is a radiance meant to shine from inside the gifts that the labor of our gratitude has made in response to its Beauty. Christ's life, death, and resurrection not only are a gift made present in the Eucharist; they also teach us to give, thus, "Do this in memory of me."

A SENSIBLE MYSTERY

I have explored the thought of two great thinkers on mystery to not only understand the challenges to a contemporary understanding of mystery but also light the way toward a renewed understanding or, rather, a ressourcement of Casel's insight into the Mystery of Christian worship. Casel saw the depth of divine Mystery in the pasch of the Lord. As such, understanding divine Mystery begins with understanding a new form of life, the "life of Christ and His church, the life they have in the Father." Rahner and Marion understand divine Mystery from a different point of view. What must be understood is either Mystery's incomprehensibility or absolute distance to human experience. Both have good reasons to start there. Rahner concentrated on the relationship between the True and the nature of divine Mystery. His reflections allowed theology to have a fruitful (and prophetic) dialogue with Modernity's absolute claims to truth. Marion concentrated on the relationship between the Good and divine Mystery. His reflections allow theology to have a fruitful (and prophetic) dialogue with Postmodernity's absolute claims on the ethical demands of the "other." Such starting points, however, lead to a reduction in the understanding of the Mystery of Christian worship.

As Casel clearly saw, the Mystery of Christian worship was not only about the True or the Good but a "song of love" where "truth and goodness stand together" and "beauty will not be lacking." In the liturgy, "God's truth is given form and shape, and so becomes a work of art." Not the True or the Good but the Beautiful (both as being received and as being made) is Casel's starting point in his understanding of divine Mystery. This ought to alert the theologian that a theology of the liturgy that takes Casel's insights into divine Mystery seriously that the Beautiful requires a different starting point than the True or the Good. If understanding divine Mystery as absolute Truth begins with an account of human knowing and understanding divine Mystery as absolute Good begins with an account of human willing, then understanding divine Mystery as Beauty begins with an account of human sensibility.

This, I believe, is the key to a ressourcement of Casel's Mystery of Christian worship. It is a double ressourcement because it requires not only a rethinking of the experience of Mystery in the liturgy but also a rethinking of the experience of the beautiful in its origins in the divine. Both of these tasks are the tasks of a liturgical aesthetics and they revolve around an account of human sensibility. The great Swiss theologian Hans Urs von Balthasar saw this clearly. The heart of the question for von Balthasar was the location where divine Mystery and the human meet. For Rahner, it was the human herself. For Marion, it was divine Mystery itself. For von Balthasar, it was the Being of the cosmos. Von Balthasar beginning with this starting point developed what he called a theological aesthetics. Locating the place of encounter between divine Mystery and the human in the cosmos has the virtue of making one begin not with human understanding or human willing but with human sensibility. Creation as place of encounter emphasizes the role of the senses over the role of the mind or the will.

It is von Balthasar's argument in *Glory of the Lord* that the senses have been undervalued in theological reflection due to an overemphasis or misunderstanding of the apophatic dimension of divine Mystery. The remedy, according to von Balthasar, is to understand anew the relationship between faith and the senses. Faith seen solely as an intellectual act that knows nothing of the sensible becomes a sort of illuminationism. On the other hand, faith overwhelmed by sensual experience becomes mere sentiment. Von Balthasar suggests that faith is formed in encountering the form of all forms, which is the Form that is Christ. As Stephen Fields puts it:

> Accordingly, Balthasar grounds anthropology in a notion of faith that stresses the end or object of its activity (fides quae) rather than its activity as such (fides qua). Faith elevates human nature because it reveals the divine object to sensation as formal evidence. This evidence, although sensibly mediated, is not intrinsically sensate. Since faith-inspired sensation opens the way to an experience of God, it follows that faith constitutes an analogous notion of experience. By reforming sensation according to its own form, faith allows the divine to be perceived according to the sensory forms of experience. "Religious" experience thus becomes a dimension of sensory experience; it shares in its forms while not being limited to them.[32]

Thus, faith, in von Balthasar's aesthetics, opens up the human to a kind of sensuousness that goes beyond the sensateness of the physical senses. Faith not only has an active component (it forms), its fides qua. It also has a passive component (it is formed), its fides quae. Faith is formed by its object that is the heart of divine Mystery. In being formed it also forms its experience. In other words, faith is a kind of sense organ, a sensibility to divine Mystery. In this von Balthasar gives a helpful direction. Perhaps it is in the understanding of faith that the relationship between the senses and divine Mystery can be fruitfully approached.

Faith, after all, has been referred to as a sense, a kind of "seeing," in a long and ancient Christian tradition. For von Balthasar, faith has an active role in shaping human experience. It also has its own sensibility to form. Faith is not only formed by divine Mystery but it forms its experience as well. These two dimensions of faith are intrinsically interrelated as a sensibility. Faith is more than a "deposit." It is a marvelous sensibility. Here lies faith's essential contribution to a liturgical aesthetics. To restrict aesthetic experience solely to the physical senses both diminishes the senses and the capacity of human sensibility. We are not only imago Dei. We are also filled with divine Breath. It is not only the intellect that mirrors God's divine nature. It is also the heart.

Thus, the human is made with a marvelous capax Dei capable of experiencing divine Mystery not simply, as Rahner would have it, as a transcendental horizon but, rather, in a self-transcending sensibility. The human is capable of experiencing divine Mystery not simply, as Marion would have it, as an acknowledgment of divine transcendent origins but also a felt intimacy with such transcendence. The key to the role of the senses in divine Mystery is how the Mystery forms faith toward a self-transcending sensibility to divine Beauty. Faith shaped by divine Mystery can "see" the "hidden reality" of ordinary experience not by going "beyond what the senses perceive" but by calling the ordinary senses to a higher sensibility. It is the heart of the liturgy's Credo for it is only through a sensibility shaped by divine Mystery that the Church can meaningfully say: We Believe. It is the liturgy's primary sensibility, which, in turn, ennobles and makes possible the power of the arts in the liturgy.

Thus faith becomes the "sixth sense" of the liturgy. As such, it has both an active and passive element. It is formed by what it senses but also forms its experience of it. Faith as being formed but also as formative of experience recounts Hyde's story of the elves and the shoemaker. Faith "sees" God's grace and love shaping its sensibility but also takes part in what Hyde calls the "labor of gratitude" to become part of faith's sensibility. In other words, the sixth sense of the liturgy is a sensibility toward gift both in receiving it and in passing it on. It is the heart of praise. It is the foundation for the liturgy's doxa.

More important is the refinement in the understanding of God's love in the Paschal Mystery that a heightened view of human sensibility affords. Von Balthasar perhaps describes it best in his reflection on the imagery of the bride and bridegroom in the Song of Songs:

> Here agape and erôs, the Glory of God and beauty of the soul are united: the glowing heart of the mystery of Christ is pure beauty, if it is true that all revelation, all faith, all suffering and death, takes place for the sake of the marriage feast of the Lamb, where creaturely and Christian truth and goodness is transfigured in the eschatological glory.[33]

Von Balthasar here points to the radiant dimension of God's love, divine Beauty, the source of Mystery's affectus. His image of the bride and bridegroom makes one think of Bernini's sculpture *The Ecstasy of Saint Teresa*. Bernini in this work reveals a complex and mysterious kind of love. It is consensual, cordial, transfiguring, erotic, unitive, agapaic, revelatory, and, of course, delightful. Mystery's affectus is Teresa's ecstasy. It is, I would propose, what a liturgical aesthetics identifies as the heart of the Mystery of Christian worship.

This is not to say that the ordinary experience of worship by an individual can be depicted like Bernini's *The Ecstasy of Saint Teresa*. It does mean that Bernini's depiction of ecstasy is experienced by individuals as a community of worship. This is the thrust, I believe, of Casel's insight into the Mystery of Christian worship. If divine Mystery is at the heart of Christian worship, so is divine affectus and this complex, mysterious love is experienced as ecstasy not simply by the individual but by the Church as the assembly gathered around divine Mystery. This ecstasy is easy to detect in liturgical worship. It takes form in the human arts. Ecstatic union in the liturgy is not a mere psychological event of an individual or a "campfire" communal experience but an event of communion and community among individuals. It is a unitive, revelatory experience.

It is also delight but not simply the ecstatic delight of a private individual but the delight of a community of individuals. As delight, it reveals a marvelous sensible communion, the mysterious touch of God's affectus transfiguring the assembly into the Body of Christ alive through the epiclesis of the Holy Spirit. As such, ecstasy manifests itself in Christian worship in the space, movement, drama, color, smells, and sounds of the liturgy. In other words, the arts in Christian worship are the sensuousness of Mystery and the medium of liturgical mystical ecstasy. As such, the arts are more than an "environment" for worship or the "accidents" of liturgy. They are intrinsic to the nature of liturgy itself. You can test this hypothesis anytime. Try to imagine a meaningful liturgy devoid of any artistic expression.

The intrinsic relationship of the arts to liturgy reveals, in turn, the nature of divine Mystery. It is Beauty itself. Moreover, it is Beauty alive for it is a Beauty that shines from within the life of Christ and his Church. It is a Living Beauty. A Living Beauty is not merely the beauty of a painting hanging mutely on a museum wall. It is the Living Beauty of artistic expression. Where Beauty is alive, so is the "labor of gratitude" that are the arts and the necessity of artistic expression. The need of the arts in liturgy reveals that the heart of the Mystery of Christian worship is an experience of a Living Beauty. Such Beauty means that an account of the arts in the liturgy must be more than the account of the arts in ordinary aesthetic experience. The dimension of divine Mystery in the Living Beauty of the liturgy gives the arts a heightened, ennobled role. They express a divine Mystery issuing forth as a unitive, revelatory living experience of delight where eros and agape become one in the beholding and being beheld by divine Beauty.

Understanding such experience with its affective and revelatory elements makes it easier to understand the element of beauty in divine Mystery. It is the Pentecostal element of rapture, of beating, living hearts drawn into the revelatory love of a divine Heart that bestows a delightful communion that is Life itself. Thus, divine Mystery's Beauty manifests itself in the transfiguring ecstasy of the intertwining of many loves to a greater love in a Pentecostal unity of a true joie de vivre, a true joy of Life. It is Living delight. It is, indeed, a Living Beauty. While the Church has many mysteries, it is this Mystery, the Mystery of a Pentecostal or Living Beauty that is the very nature of the Church's liturgy. Such beauty, to be understood, requires a special approach, a special kind of aesthetics. It requires a liturgical aesthetics. For, in the final analysis, the aesthetics of divine Beauty is the aesthetics of divine Mystery. This amounts to a ressourcement of Casel's understanding of divine Mystery. The Mystery of Christian worship, in other words, is a sensible Mystery. It is as Fr. Scirghi so aptly saw a "blessed mess."

NOTES

1. Hugh Gilbert, OSB, *Odo Casel: Prophet and Mystagogue.* mywebpages.com cast.net/enpeters/liturgy&sacraments_casel.htm (accessed June 1, 2005).

2. See, for example, Klaus Gamber, *The Reform of the Roman Liturgy: Its Problems and Background* (San Juan Capistrano, Calif.: Una Voce Press, 1993), xvi.

3. Turner Comments on Gallus' commentary on the Song of Songs as the text that influenced the author of the "Cloud of Unknowing." Cloud borrows from Gallus' commentary and shifts from the intellectualism of Denys to a voluntarism of love. In "Cloud," desire is the *unum necessarium.* Such voluntarism tends toward the absence of God as opposed to the presence of God. Gallus implies that the intellect is not capable of self-negation; it must come from somewhere else. In Gallus, affectus replaces *intellectus* and we have a dialectic between knowing and love. Denys Turner, *The Darkness of God: Negativity in Christian Mysticism* (Cambridge: Cambridge University Press, 1995), x, 189.

4. The most influential scholar proposing this view is the great historian of aesthetics Wladyslaw Tatarkiewicz. His influential argument is found in Wladyslaw Tatarkiewicz, "The Great Theory of Beauty & Its Decline," *Journal of Aesthetics and Art Criticism* 31, no. 2 (1972): 165–179.

5. I am referring to philosophical aesthetics. The elements of love, union, and the revelatory are not usually found in most modern philosophical aesthetic theories.

6. Von Balthasar's *opus magnus* has been translated into English and consists of seven volumes. See Hans Urs von Balthasar, *The Glory of the Lord: A Theological Aesthetics*, translated by Erasmo Leiva-Merikakis and edited by Joseph Fessio and John Riches (San Francisco, Calif.: Crossroad Publications, 1983–1989), 7 vols.

7. Odo Casel, *The Mystery of Christian Worship, and Other Writings* (Westminster, Md.: Newman Press, 1962), 54.

8. Casel, *Mystery of Christian Worship*, 58.

9. Casel, *Mystery of Christian Worship*, 77–78.

10. Casel, *Mystery of Christian Worship*, 93.

11. Jean-Luc Marion, *God without Being: Hors-Texte* (Chicago, Ill.: University of Chicago Press, 1995).

12. Mark Allen McIntosh, *Mystical Theology: The Integrity of Spirituality and Theology* (Malden, Mass.: Blackwell, 1998), 94.

13. Karl Rahner, *The Practice of Faith: A Handbook of Contemporary Spirituality* (New York: Crossroad Publications, 1983), xv, 63–64.

14. Jerome Bump, *Gerard Manley Hopkins* (Boston, Mass.: Twayne Publishers, 1982), 23–24.

15. D'Arcy also saw this. D'Arcy Wentworth Thompson, *On Growth and Form* (Cambridge: Cambridge University Press, 1968), 2 vols.

16. There is a parallel here with Maximus the Confessor who saw Christ as the inner principle of all things and is von Balthasar's model for the Form. In other words, Hopkins' "archetype" has analogy in von Balthasar's "Form."

17. Bump, *Gerard Manley Hopkins*, 37.

18. The interested reader might want to consult my treatment of Hopkins' poem "Pied Beauty" as found in Alejandro Garcia-Rivera, *The Community of the Beautiful* (Collegeville, Minn.: Liturgical Press, 1999), ch. 1.

19. McIntosh, *Mystical Theology*, 97.

20. Marion, *God without Being: Hors-Texte*, 26.

21. Marion, *God without Being: Hors-Texte*, 27.

22. This is a summary of Albert Borgmann's excellent exposition of technology in the postmodern world. I see in his work a more concrete illustration of Marion's abstract "idol." Borgmann is one of the few postmodern philosophers that actually see the connection between technology and the roots of postmodern thought. Postmodern thought's use of the many-reflecting image has roots, I think, in the technological culture that has brought us TV, computers, and the Internet. I also find myself in agreement with Borgmann's proposal. Only a revitalized liturgy can be a corrective to the corrosive mechanisms inherent in this technological way of life. See Albert Borgmann, *Power Failure: Christianity in the Culture of Technology* (Grand Rapids, Mich.: Brazos Press, 2003).

23. Marion, *God without Being: Hors-Texte*, 19.

24. Marion, *God without Being: Hors-Texte*, 171.

25. Marion, *God without Being: Hors-Texte*, 173–174.

26. Marion, *God without Being: Hors-Texte*, 167.

27. Marion, *God without Being: Hors-Texte*, 176.

28. Lewis Hyde, *The Gift: Imagination and the Erotic Life of Property* (New York: Vintage Books, 1983), 48.

29. Hyde, *The Gift*, 50.

30. Marion, *God without Being: Hors-Texte*, 181.

31. Marion, *God without Being: Hors-Texte*, 74.

32. Stephen Fields, S J, "Balthasar and Rahner on the Spiritual Senses," *Theological Studies* 57, no. 2 (June 1996): 227.

33. Hans Urs von Balthasar, *The Glory of the Lord: A Theological Aesthetics*, ed. John Kenneth Riches, vol. 4, *The Realm of Metaphysics in Antiquity*, translated by Brian McNeil et al. (San Francisco, Calif.: Ignatius Press, 1989), 7 vols., p. 322.

CHAPTER 2

✝

What Is Beautiful for God? (What Does God Like?)

Thomas Scirghi

Here we begin with the question: What makes Christian worship a work of beauty? We will answer that liturgy becomes a work of beauty when it has been inspired by God and then offered by the beloved community. This answer stands in contrast to a legalistic concern with the mere fulfillment of the rubrics. As mentioned earlier, while liturgical rubrics are essential for worship, they will not suffice to produce a work of praise and beauty. This answer also contrasts with an avant-garde ethos that encourages the production of art for its own sake.

To develop an answer to the question, What makes Christian worship a work of beauty? it may help to review the Scripture stories in which we hear how God accepts a person's offering with gladness. For example, recall how Jesus is moved by the prayers of the publican while he dismisses the pompous Pharisee. Referring to the publican (a tax collector) Jesus says, "I tell you, this man went home justified rather than the other; for those who exalt themselves will be humbled, but those who humble themselves will be exalted."[1] Of course not all offerings are so readily accepted. For example, the prophet Amos scolds the Israelites for their long-winded prayers and smelly sacrifices, demanding justice instead. Speaking for the Lord Amos says, "I hate, I despise your feasts, and I take no delight in your solemn assemblies. Your cereal offerings I will not accept, nor consider your stall-fed peace offerings. Away with your noisy songs! I will not listen to the melodies of your harps."[2] To listen to the ranting of the Lord we learn that not all acts of prayer and praise are pleasing to God. However, two biblical narratives in particular illustrate the proper way to render an offering to the Lord. The first is the New Testament account of the woman who washes Jesus' feet. Here we read of the Lord accepting an offering given in humility and Jesus uses the occasion to explain what makes an offering holy. The second is the Old Testament description of the construction of the tabernacle by the Israelites.

Here we find a description of the working relationship between God and the artist, to construct a work worthy of the Lord.

THE PARDON OF THE SINFUL WOMAN

One striking item about the story of the pardon of the sinful woman is that it is one of the few episodes found in all four gospels, giving it a certain significance in the canon of the Scripture.[3] The four accounts are told in a similar way. Each one focuses upon a dinner in someone's home to which Jesus has been invited. While Jesus and the guests recline at the table a woman approaches Jesus carrying a jar of ointment. She generously pours the ointment onto his feet as if to anoint them. A complaint is then voiced by someone in the room. In reading Mark, Matthew, and John, the complaint concerns the waste of precious oil. Each of these evangelists describes the oil as "costly." John calls it a genuine aromatic nard; and Mark adds that it was genuine spikenard. He then dramatizes the waste by noting that the woman "broke the jar," indicating that she kept nothing but used it all for Jesus. For some of those gathered in the room this display is wasteful. In both Mark and John someone protests that the oil could have been sold for more than three hundred days' wages and that this money could have been given to the poor. In each of these three accounts Jesus defends the woman. He mentions that the poor will always be with them, however, his presence is passing. Also, he interprets the woman's action to be a ritual preparing him for burial.

Luke's account differs slightly by focusing more upon the actions of the woman. Note that while the other three accounts are referred to as "The anointing at Bethany," and focus upon the anointing, this one uses the title of "the pardon of the sinful woman," and focuses upon the pardon. The other three give a detailed description of the precious oil. Luke simply mentions the oil, without indicating its value, but draws the reader's attention to the woman. She is, he says, a sinful woman, and we are left to imagine her sin. He positions the woman, standing behind Jesus at his feet. She weeps, falls to her knees, and with her tears washes his feet, then wipes them dry with her hair. She then kisses his feet and pours out the oil to anoint them.

The use of her hair suggests a scandalous action. She would have had to unloosen her headdress. The sight of her long hair flowing onto her shoulders and along her back would have been considered inappropriate in a public setting. And it would have reinforced the judgment of those who know her to be a sinful woman.[4] This scandalous sight infuriates the host, Simon the Pharisee. Thinking to himself he questions Jesus' authority, "If this man were a prophet he would know . . . that she is a sinner." Jesus can sense his anger and so responds with a parable. He tells a story of two debtors, one of whom owes a great sum of money, the other, a lesser amount. Both are forgiven their debts by the creditor. Jesus asks Simon which of the debtors will love the creditor more. Simon responds, quite reasonably, "The one whose larger debt was forgiven."

Agreeing with him, Jesus compares the two debtors to Simon and the sinful woman. He contrasts their actions: Simon did not wash his feet, which was an act of common hospitality; the woman washed them with her tears. Simon did not offer his guest a kiss, nor oil to anoint his head; she kissed his feet and anointed them. Then he states the lesson: because her many sins have been forgiven she has shown great love, but for those who have been forgiven little, they will love less. Jesus then assures the woman, "Your faith has saved you; go in peace." For Jesus, the woman washing his feet is a sign of gratitude for having been forgiven already, rather than a plea for forgiveness.

It is this blessing and sending forth—"Your faith has saved you; go in peace"—that marks the beginning of the liturgical *habitus*. Fitzmyer comments that the conjunction of salvation and peace encapsulates the Lukan view of the Christ event. "Salvation" (Greek: *sozein*) denotes one's deliverance from evil and from a state of negation, to a restored state of wholeness, that is, to a sound relationship with God. Likewise, Luke's use of the word "peace" (Greek: *eirene*) carries connotations of the Hebrew word *shalom*, which expresses the state of well-being that comes from God. This state of well-being goes beyond the absence of war and hostility, and includes the experience of harmony, security, order, and prosperity.[5]

We contend that this greeting marks the beginning of the liturgical *habitus* as the biblical reader is reminded here that genuine liturgical praise is initiated by God. As was mentioned in the previous chapter, the purpose for our liturgy is to give thanks and praise to God. We approach the liturgy with the recognition of what God has provided for us, namely through creation and redemption. It is these two themes that structure the Eucharistic Prayer, particularly the preface. For example, the preface of the second Eucharistic Prayer mentions these themes quite clearly.

> Father, it is our duty and our salvation,
> always and everywhere to give you thanks
> through your beloved Son, Jesus Christ.
> He is the Word through whom you made the universe,
> the savior you sent to redeem us.

In recognition of the divine gifts of creation and redemption, the faithful gather to express their thanks and praise. Here in this ritual they offer themselves to the service of the Lord. This priestly service is expressed precisely in the Prayer of the Faithful. At this point, responding to the Scripture proclaimed and preached, the people express their priesthood of the laity by offering up the various needs of the community, locally and globally, spiritually and socially. Thus liturgical worship is a response to the recognition of what God has done for humanity and the realization of our responsibility to continue the work of the Lord. Jesus makes clear that the woman washing his feet does so, not to attain salvation from her sins, but as an expression of the peace she has already gained from being forgiven. Interestingly, we do not know how she was forgiven. No mention is made of the moment of forgiveness or how she realized she was forgiven. But we hear Jesus, acting as a confessor with a penitent, pronouncing an absolution, a sacramental verification of what already has been accomplished. First he explains "Her many sins have been forgiven," then he pronounces, "Your sins are forgiven."

Thus the offering of this woman is found valuable. What makes it valuable is that it is marked by redemption. Now freed from sin and restored to a right relationship with God, she has become a new creation and kneels before the Lord. Her humble service is offered through Jesus, and he declares her offering worthy. In this way the woman's actions resemble the "presentation of the gifts," formerly referred to as the Offertory of the Mass. For the priest and assembly do not offer these gifts on their own. First of all, they are grateful for having received these gifts from the earth. Second, they invoke the Holy Spirit "to make them holy so that they may become for us the body and blood of our Lord, Jesus Christ." Notice that the presentation of the gifts is followed by a petition, that is, a plea for acceptance. At the altar the priest's prayer is followed by the bidding of the whole assembly addressed to the priest: "May the Lord accept the sacrifice at your hands for the praise and glory of His name, for our good and the good of all the Church."

THE WORTHINESS OF THE GIFT IS
RECOGNIZED BY ITS MARK OF REDEMPTION

Having attained redemption the woman's response is to offer praise to God. In this way she emulates the many figures in the gospels who benefit from a miraculous act of Jesus, or simply from an encounter with him. Consider the blind man Bartimaeus.[6] When Jesus heals him and restores his sight he doffs his cloak and runs through the streets praising the name of the Lord. Or when Jesus encounters the Samaritan woman at the well she returns to town to proclaim the good news which she has realized.[7]

Nathan Mitchell sees in the encounter of the woman with Jesus at Bethany a remarkable icon of Christian worship as she takes her costly jar of perfume, breaks it open, and gives it as a balm and a blessing. "As she takes, breaks, gives and blesses, this nameless woman names Jesus as God's *Christos*, the anointed one. Her body, broken open in love and tears, meets his body, broken open to receive her hospitality. Together, Jesus and this woman, form an embodied, Eucharistic icon of savior and saved. Christ is anointed for his mission (culminating in the cross), and the woman is released into freedom and forgiveness."[8]

THE ARTIST AT WORK: BUILDING
SOMETHING BEAUTIFUL FOR GOD

We can find a parallel narrative in Scripture with the account of the Israelites' building of the tabernacle, as described in the Book of Exodus. According to Pope Benedict XVI, in a discussion of aesthetics in the life of the church, the "Book of Exodus develops a theory of art in conjunction with the construction of the sacred tabernacle."[9] The pontiff argues that our own work may correspond to the greatness of God only if we respond to the fullest extent of our ability. For Benedict true art manifests the complete dignity of the beautiful. In order to attain this we must appreciate that artistic creativity begins with receptivity before engaging in productivity. This is to say that the artists do not plan for themselves what might be worthy of God and what is beautiful. Alone we are incapable of such a realization. Rather artistic creation reproduces what God has revealed to be the model, thus converting vision into form. Benedict argues that the understanding of artistic creativeness of the Old Testament differs significantly from its understanding in the modern age. Today "creativity" connotes the making of something original that no one has made, or thought of, before, and it is the invention of something that is completely one's own and completely new. However, in analyzing the account of the building of the tabernacle, creativity is more of a seeing together with God, participating in God's creation, and exposing the beauty that is concealed in creation. For Benedict this does not diminish the worth of the artists, but in fact justifies their work. So, he finds in the call of Bezalel, that artists are those to whom God has given understanding and skill so that they can carry out what God has instructed them to do.[10]

Benedict finds the roots of the modern concept of creativity in an anthropology, which holds that the human spirit is no longer primarily receptive but only productive. According to this view, "nothing meaningful precedes human existence (and) the human being comes from a meaningless factuality and one is thrown into a meaningless freedom. The person thus becomes a pure creator, but his creativity is pure whim and empty."[11] In contrast, Christian anthropology argues that human beings who are made in the image and likeness of God are a product of God's art. Consequently they can view God's creative ideas with the divine artist, and translate them into the visible and the audible. Thus service to God is not foreign to art for it is only by serving the divine that art exists at all. Following the lesson of Exodus, Benedict concludes that there are three conditions for true art: artists must be moved by their hearts; they must be skillful people; and they must have perceived what the Lord himself has shown.[12]

THE BUILDING OF THE TABERNACLE

The building of the tabernacle consumes a sizable section of the Book of Exodus, chapters 25–40. For the Hebrews, the tabernacle was a place where Yahweh could dwell with the people whom he had called into covenant. The Hebrew word for tabernacle used here is *mishkan*, literally meaning "dwelling." This section of the Book of Exodus describes in painstaking detail how the tabernacle is to be built. Reading somewhat like a builder's blueprint, we hear specific instructions for the materials—their size, color, quantity, and quality—to be used in the construction and how these instructions are to be followed.

The story begins on Mount Sinai where Moses receives the tablets of the commandments from the Lord. We then encounter one interruption: the creation and destruction of the golden calf. Chapters 32–34 describe how the covenant was broken and how it was restored. It is interesting to note that the Lord seems to pass over this offense with little anger or admonishment. Despite the outright defiance by the Israelites and the violence of Moses smashing the tablets on the ground and then grounding the gold of the calf into powder, pouring it into the water, and forcing the Israelites to drink it, we move through this section quickly and then resume the building of the tabernacle. It is as if there were but one concern for the Lord: to dwell with his people.[13] The Israelites are a new creation of God. The divine presence, which was lost through the sin of Adam and Eve, would be restored through the indwelling of the Lord. Hence there is an emphasis on obedience to the Word of God. Obedience, that is, receiving the Word of God, was essential to realizing the divine presence in their midst.[14]

Clearly the incident with the golden calf had its purpose in the developing relationship of Israel with the Lord. Later, in chapter four, we will discuss the episode of the golden calf in more detail. For now, we focus on how the Israelites were confronted with their sinfulness. Consequently they were forced to face the divine holiness, not only as a transcendent reality, but through an earthly presence as well. Neither is this incident overlooked. In what could be a sign of reconciliation, the Israelites contribute all they have to the construction of the Lord's dwelling.

The plunder they received from the Egyptians when they were liberated, was now used for the tabernacle.[15] They had been instructed to devote the best of their material goods to the enterprise, an obligation that entailed some sacrifice. They were called to hold nothing back in order to secure the presence of the Lord in their midst.[16] The Israelites responded generously and enthusiastically. In fact, they contributed so much material—much more than needed—that Moses had to ask them to halt their offerings.[17] Some centuries later a woman would re-enact this scene. Moved by her heart's desire to greet the Lord in her midst, she broke open her jar of expensive oil, and anointed the feet of Jesus.

For our purposes of answering the question—What makes Christian worship a work of beauty?—we could concentrate on the concluding chapter of Exodus. In chapter forty we reach the climax of Exodus. Here we learn that the preceding chapters provide more than just Bezalel's blueprint, but "a theological statement of the presence of Yahweh coming to dwell with his people."[18] A refrain runs through this chapter: Moses did "as the Lord commanded him."[19] Brevard Childs comments that the repetition of this phrase highlights the dominant intention of the author throughout chapters 35–40.[20] The tabernacle is the work of the Lord first received by the Israelite artisans, then produced by their hands, giving form to the divine vision.

Israel obeyed the Lord's commands by providing a free will offering to the Lord.[21] No longer acting as the slaves of Pharaoh, they willingly give their wealth and skill to the work of the Lord. Note that at the completion of the tabernacle, there is no mention of "it was good" as we read in the creation story. That is to say that we find no statement announcing the completion of the project or describing its magnificence. There's no description of its beauty. Instead we read: "Then the cloud covered their meeting tent, and the glory of the Lord filled the dwelling."[22]

On this consoling note of the Lord's presence among his people, we close the Book of Exodus.[23] Nevertheless the building of the tabernacle indeed became something beautiful for God. The Old Testament scholar Claus Westermann explains that, for the Hebrew people, the "beautiful" pertains to an event rather than to a being.[24] The western notion of beautiful, influenced by the Greeks, refers to a beholding of something, for example, an image, a statue, or a person, as we say, "beauty is in the eye of the beholder." For the Hebrews the beautiful is experienced within an encounter. Further, Westermann reminds us that the Israelites did not create pictorial art but that all art was realized in the act of speech and hearing. Thus the reaction to meeting something beautiful was neither in contemplating nor beholding it, nor passing judgment upon it, but a joy expressed in speech, which is praise, as the psalmist exults: "Bless the Lord, my soul! Lord, my God, you are great indeed."[25] Such joy in what is created expresses the belief that the world has its origins in the will and work of the creator and that the existence of humanity is founded in the same. Because everything that God created was good, the work of the artist is rendered beautiful in that it is something good in the eyes of God.[26]

The tabernacle provided the Jewish people with an opportunity to encounter the presence of the Lord. The beauty of the temple was found, not so much with the blueprints or with the precious metals adorning its surface, but in the activity of relating with God through prayer and sacrifice. Indeed the structure is necessary as it provides the setting for this encounter. Here we can find a parallel with the Christian liturgy. The rubrics, like the Church building, provide the structure and the setting for the community through which it may encounter the Lord. The liturgy leads the community into the source of belief, thereby exposing beauty. The role of the artist, then, is not only to expose beauty, but to help us believe in it as well. The liturgy helps to develop the proper disposition by which we recognize the presence of the divine.

NOTES

1. Luke 18:14.

2. Amos 5:21–23.

3. Matthew 26:6–13; Mark 14:3–9; Luke 7:36–50; John 12:1–8.

4. Raymond Edward Brown, *Anchor Bible*, vol. 29, *The Gospel According to John (I-XII)* (New York: Doubleday & Company, 1981), 450; Joseph A. Fitzmyer, *Anchor Bible*, vol. 28, *The Gospel According to Luke (I-IX)* (New York: Doubleday & Company, 1981), 689.

5. Brown, *Gospel Acc. John*, 450; Fitzmyer, *Gospel Acc. Luke*, 689.

6. Mark 11:46–52.

7. John 4:4–42.

8. Nathan D. Mitchell, "Other Voices, Other Rooms: The Future of Liturgical Language in Postmodern Cultures," *New Theology Review* 18, no. 4 (November 2005): 66.

9. Joseph Ratzinger, *A New Song for the Lord: Faith in Christ and Liturgy Today* (New York: Crossroad Publications, 1996), 129.

10. Exodus 35:30–36:1. Ratzinger, *New Song*, 130.

11. Ratzinger, *New Song*, 133.

12. Ratzinger, *New Song*, 134.

13. J. A. Moyter comments that, while the sin of the golden calf played an important part in the spiritual development of Israel, it "was not even a hiccough in the Lord's purposes. He picked up again at the point reached before the incident . . . as if to say 'As I was saying when I was so rudely interrupted!'" J. A. Moyter, *The Message of the Exodus* (Downers Grove, Ill.: Intervarsity Press, 2005), 318.

14. Moyter, *Message*, 323.

15. Exodus 12:33–36.

16. Moyter, *Message*, 321.

17. Exodus 36:2–7.

18. Moyter, *Message*, 897.

19. This refrain is repeated eight times in this chapter: verses 16, 19, 21, 23, 25, 27, 29, 32.

20. Brevard S. Childs, *The Book of Exodus; a Critical, Theological Commentary*, in *Old Testament Library* (Philadelphia: Westminster Press, 1974), 638. See also John E. Huesman, SJ, "Exodus," in *The Jerome Biblical Commentary*, ed. Raymond Edward Brown, Joseph A. Fitzmyer, and Roland Edmund Murphy (Englewood Cliffs, N.J.: Prentice-Hall, 1968), 47–66.

21. Moyter, *Message*, 318.

22. Exodus 40:34.

23. Huesman, "Exodus," 66.

24. Claus Westermann, *Creation* (Philadelphia: Fortress Press, 1976), 60–64.

25. Psalm 104:1.

26. Westermann, *Creation*, 60–64.

✝

In Whom We Live and Move and Have Our Being

Alejandro Garcia-Rivera

Irenaeus tells us: "the glory of God is man fully alive; moreover man's life is the vision of God."[1] In this concise statement, he summarizes a theology of the human person and, more remarkable, a breathtaking theology of worship, a liturgical aesthetics. In his powerfully put phrase, Irenaeus weaves the Glory of the Lord, human sensibility, and the nature and meaning of life. We live for a marvelous sensibility: to touch, taste, smell, hear, and see God. In turn, this marvelous life of sensibility is God's glory itself. These twin theological insights weave two aspects of theology that are not usually put together in such a direct way. Irenaeus seems to say that the glory of God is human life sanctified through a gracious and saint-C sensibility. Another way to put it is to say that God's glory becomes embodied in the human fully alive in the exercise of a wondrous sensibility. This is nothing less than a liturgical theology of the human person. It is a founding insight for a liturgical aesthetics.

A liturgical aesthetics gives reason for what may be *Sacrosanctum Concilium*'s most profound observation:

> From the liturgy therefore, and especially from the Eucharist, grace is poured forth upon us as from a fountain, and the sanctification of men in Christ and the glorification of God to which all other activities of the Church are directed, as toward their end, are achieved with maximum effectiveness. (SC, 9)

The liturgy, in other words, exists to glorify God and to sanctify us. These twin goods are not the sole raison d'être of the liturgy. All Christian life seeks to be sanctified as it follows Christ. All Christian activity in the

73

Church also means to glorify God. It is, in the liturgy, however, where both find their origin and end, where sanctification of the human person in Christ and the glory of the Lord are revealed as twin realities that cannot be separated. At least, this is an interpretation of the above through the eyes of a liturgical aesthetics. As such, it takes Irenaeus' insight seriously. Our sanctification and the glory of the Lord are inextricably connected through the spiritual elevation of human sensibility, an elevation that finds its highest effectiveness in the liturgical practice of the worshipping community of faith.

A graced and renewed human sensibility is, in this view, the means by which divine Glory becomes embodied in the world. As a theologian, I would say that this is the human dimension of a sensible Mystery. It is this human dimension that Fr. Scirghi and I wish to tackle in this chapter. Fr. Scirghi has spoken of the nature of embodiment in the liturgy. I would like to pursue his insights by asking whether there is an aesthetic dimension to such embodiment. This aesthetic dimension will be sought in the human embodiment of God's glory in a life that becomes one with Christ's. What is the aesthetic nature of this life? This living aesthetics, this living Beauty, is to be found in the life of praise and thanksgiving.

We have proposed that the Mystery of Christian worship is a sensible Mystery. A sensible Mystery, however, reveals another: human praise.[2] Indeed, why do humans praise? Praise often has been characterized as a response to divine Mystery. There is something problematic about this view. Does praise as response to divine Mystery really explain what praise is all about or does it merely describe a fait accompli? Let me suggest that praise is best understood as a mystery in itself, a mystery about the very nature of our humanity. As mystery, praise and thanksgiving need to be seen as more than acts of the will; they need to be seen as the very stuff of human life, or rather, as the very stuff that makes humans fully alive. The mysterious nature of praise becomes self evident with a little reflection. Whence praise? Where does praise originate? Do we praise to engage divine Mystery or does divine Mystery engage us in order for us to praise?[3] Is praise a response to an experience of divine Mystery, or is praise part of the experience itself? Is praise a reaction to a sensation, an act of the will, or an awareness of the mind?

Praise, it appears, is something of a mystery itself. Speaking of praise as response to divine Mystery does not do justice to the mystery that is praise itself. Praise seems to originate outside of us but also inside of us. Praise seems to be a response to an experience but also an experience itself. Praise seems to be more than an act or even a sensing; it is also a kind of knowing. Praise has, rather, the nature of a sensibility. Sensibility, however, is a word that requires some care in its use.[4] It does not mean sensation per se. Sensibility is more than pure sensation. It does not exactly mean to be sensitive either. It does mean, however, the capacity to sense as well as the capacity to respond. Sensibility captures a mysterious human ability, the capacity to perceive in such a way that such perception is also a response. In other words, sensibility concerns the capacity of the human person to rise above perceiving mere sensations to perceiving intelligently the emotion of such sensations.[5]

Such perception, a kind of emotional knowing, guides and encourages us to shape our lives in the light of such intelligent emotional sensing. Please make this note, however. Response and perception in intelligent, emotional sensing have a chicken-and-egg relationship in human sensibility. The shape of our life directly affects our sensibility. Human sensibility shapes a human life. Sensibility, in other words, speaks of the human ability to make visible the invisible. Sensibility, then, has a spiritual component. It concerns the ability of the human creature to rise above the merely sensate, the visible, into enjoying the sensuality of the spiritual, the invisible by making it visible in the course of a human life. Thus sensibility gives us access to understanding the process of sanctification. In other words, it is the process of the human becoming fully alive as he and she embodies the glory of the Lord through a sensibility that finds its fullest manifestation in praise and thanksgiving.

Whence praise? Human sensibility is our answer. To understand praise is to understand the glory of the Lord. To understand the glory of the Lord is to understand the human fully alive. To understand the human as fully alive is to understand sanctification as the ultimate manifestation of a full, human life. To understand the full manifestation of sanctity is to understand human sensibility. This, at least, is the chain of our reasoning. We propose it as the reasoning of a liturgical aesthetics for such reasoning has the merit if not of giving complete understanding, at least of giving a way of entering intelligently into the sensible Mystery of Christian worship and its corresponding mystery of human praise.

BIRDSONG

Why do birds sing? The reader may be justified in being puzzled by this question in a work dedicated to liturgy. What do birds singing have to do with liturgical aesthetics? It is actually a crucial question that must be answered if the theological assertions on human sensibility made above are to have any credibility. If human sensibility is the capacity to feel and respond to the emotion of sensation, then one must ask where the emotion in sensation comes from. Here we enter deep waters for the claim of emotion in sensation is a claim of considerable consequences not only for theology but also for philosophy and science. It is a claim that reveals how impoverished our theology has become since its split from its philosophical and scientific roots.[6] It is a claim, however, unavoidable for a liturgical aesthetics. The basis for the claim is the startling proposal that feeling is part of the cosmic reality and not solely of the human reality. Feeling, some philosophers proposed in the beginning of the twentieth century, is a variable in natural phenomena. The universe is awash in feeling. Its order and ways are guided and shaped in no small way through feeling. Such would be a nice, romantic claim except that one philosopher decided to apply it to a concrete, scientific phenomenon, birdsong. His method and his answers were truly remarkable.

Charles Hartshorne took seriously the idea that feeling is part of natural reality.[7] Hartshorne was an accomplished philosopher of the North American tradition. He was best known for his interest in the process philosophy of Whitehead. He became interested in the intersection of philosophy and natural science in a process aesthetics. He tested the scientific validity of his philosophical aesthetics with a unique study of birdsong that is still quoted by scientists today.

Hartshorne's aesthetics centers on an ancient philosophical principle. The Greek principle that the most truthful answer can be found as the means between two extremes, the principle of moderation, becomes the cornerstone of Hartshorne's aesthetics.[8] Hartshorne saw two pairs of extremes as the most compelling for such an aesthetics. One pair of extremes dealt with sameness and diversity. Hartshorne proposed that something is beautiful if it mediates between a boring monotony and a chaotic diversity. Applying the Greek principle of moderation to this axis defined by the two poles of monotonous homogeneity and chaotic diversity defines the aesthetic ideal. This ideal is nothing less than what is known as the "Great Theory of Beauty," namely unity-in-diversity.[9] This is the most long-lived consensus on the nature of the beautiful in Western thought. What is striking about Hartshorne's formulation is to reveal that the beautiful under this principle of the one in the many is not hierarchical but mediatory in nature. In other words, the beautiful is not valuing something over another. It is not judging a higher over a lower. It is, rather, the delight of mediation, a mutual consent of things agreeing with one another in such a way that both their unity and their individuality are preserved at the same time. If nothing else, this insight of Hartshorne clears much mischief done by a hierarchical view of the beautiful.

Hartshorne also proposed another pair of extremes or axis of aesthetic dimension. Intensity of feeling must be accounted for in aesthetics. Intensity of feeling, however, can vary between the drab and the unbearable. A reality that elicits mild or drab feelings can hardly be said to be worthy of the title beautiful. On the other hand, a reality that elicits such strength of feeling that is overpowering, even unbearable can hardly be enjoyed. The aesthetic ideal of true enjoyment is to be found in the mediation between these two extremes. True joy is found in that which unites both serenity and excitement without dissolving either one. Enjoyment is both a rest and an enchantment, repast and delight. Hartshorne, in a sense, reinterprets Aquinas' definition of the beautiful, *pulchra dicuntur quae visa placent*, beauty is that which pleases.[10] In recasting pleasure as enjoyment and as the mediation between two extremes of intensity of feeling, Hartshorne also avoids a hierarchy of aesthetic value. Enjoyment is not based on what pleases more but on mediating the intensity of feelings.

Hartshorne used the principle of moderation applied to these pairs of aesthetic extremes to explain the scientific observation of birdsong. Many birds have a singing repertoire that is quite often improvised. Against the "wired" hypothesis that birdsong is fixed by a bird's genetic material, Hartshorne documented some bird species as actually improvising and creating new songs. This penchant for variety and improvisation cannot be explained by genetic determinism. Indeed, it is hard to explain by any other hypothesis except the one suggested by the aesthetic mean. Birds improvise song because it is more enjoyable and beautiful to do so. Birdsong is neither drab nor unbearable. The capacity of birds to improvise song speaks of their capacity to vary the intensity of their feelings in song. It is an example of the intensity-of-feeling axis of Hartshorne's aesthetic theory. In this manner, Hartshorne convinced many scientists that birdsong has an aesthetic origin. Birds sing because they and other birds enjoy it!

When Hartshorne demonstrated the power of his aesthetics of the mean to explain birdsong, he also introduced a variable in scientific research that is close to heresy in conventional science: feeling. Feeling as part of the natural reality raises all sorts of alarms and questions to a scientist.[11] How can one measure feeling? Do animals actually feel and have emotion? Indeed, is feeling a component of the universe?

These are important questions for the theologian no less than the scientist for if feeling is part of the fabric of the universe, then a sensibility to divine Mystery may be found there too. In other words, the ability to experience divine Mystery may not be the sole province of the human creature. Perhaps birds sing because they experience Mystery and give praise through their song. And if experience of divine Mystery belongs to the spiritual, then birds must also be, in part, spiritual creatures. Acknowledging feeling in the non-human makes problematic the old dualism between matter and spirit. On the other hand, it opens up the true meaning of the spiritual and, with that, a renewed understanding of the Christian doctrine of the Incarnation. For whatever is spiritual about birds is also embodied in their singing. In singing, birds embody their experience of *that which can only be known by being enjoyed*: Beauty.[12] In the music of their

joy, birds embody their sense of life, become spiritual in their sensibility.
A bird's form of life, then, can be seen as a petit liturgy, the giving thanks
and praise by one of God's smaller creatures for the experience of a life-
giving Beauty.

CHURCH SONG

Why does the Church sing? Can we ask the same question of the Church
that we did of birds? If liturgical aesthetics is indeed a *Living* Beauty, then
yes, I believe we can! If birds sing because they enjoy their life and wish
others to enjoy it as well, then why not the Church? In the case of the
Church, however, Church song encompasses more than praise but also
thanksgiving. The Church sings not only in delight but also in gratitude
and while birds may sing gratefully, the Church's gratitude emerges out
of not only a present moment but also a sacred memory and a life-giving
anticipation. In understanding this, Acts 17, which has Paul speaking to
the Athenians on Mars Hill, may have much to tell us.

> Then Paul stood in front of the Areopagus and said, "Athenians, I see how
> extremely religious you are in every way. For as I went through the city and
> looked carefully at the objects of your worship, I found among them an altar
> with the inscription, 'To an unknown god.' What therefore you worship as
> unknown, this I proclaim to you. The God who made the world and every-
> thing in it, he who is Lord of heaven and earth, does not live in shrines made
> by human hands, nor is he served by human hands, as though he needed
> anything, since he himself gives to all mortals life and breath and all things.
> From one ancestor, he made all nations to inhabit the whole earth, and he al-
> lotted the times of their existence and the boundaries of the places where
> they would live, so that they would search for God and perhaps grope for
> him and find him-though indeed he is not far from each one of us. For 'In
> him we live and move and have our being'; as even some of your own poets
> have said, 'For we too are his offspring.'" (NRSV, Acts 17:22–28)

In this speech, Paul gives us what is perhaps the first liturgical theology.
Why do humans worship? Paul gives the Athenians two major reasons:
"we too are his offspring" and that "in Him we live and move and have
our being." To a naturalist, to say that you are of the same offspring is to
say different individual creatures are of the same species. More important
it is to say that different individual creatures possess similar forms of behavior shaped by the unique environment in which they exist, namely,
their *habitus*. To say that humans are one species, however, raises serious
issues. Humans, after all, live in all sorts of environments and exhibit a
great variety of behaviors. There is no one environment or behavior that

defines the human creature. As Paul himself admits there are many nations and races all living in different parts of the world. Animal species, on the other hand, are known by their singular behavior in a unique environment, their habitat. What kind of a species, then, is the human creature, a creature that has no apparent unique habitat?

Paul offers an answer that is more a statement of faith than a scientific observation. The habitat unique to the human species is the one God in Whom we live and move and have our being. This is the basis of our common humanity, why we can say we are one species. If this is so, then what is the role of human cultures and societies? If human culture and society is more than, as some theories of culture propose, a communication system or class struggle, then what role do they play in our humanity? Paul of Areopagus seems to tell us that culture and society exist as a gift of God to each nation and race by which they could "grope for him and perhaps find him." What is interesting about this is that this groping and searching is done while God is "not far from each one of us." In other words, Paul suggests that human culture exists as a means to be sensible to divine Mystery. Human culture provides the means by which the human creature engages the source of human life and being. What are these means? They are the means of culture in the wider, more traditional sense of the term.[13] Culture, of course, includes systems of communication, language, and kinship. Culture, in its wider sense, also includes the arts: music, painting, architecture, poetry, drama.

A theology of culture based on Acts 17 would see culture as a gift of sensibility from God so that we may "taste and see" God. It is not properly a habitat but a sensibility. In this sense, Paul critiques the Athenians' worship. They mistake the true nature of worship. True worship is a form of life; not the worship of a form of life.[14] And culture is a sensibility to that form of life. It allows us to experience it and celebrate it. Thus culture, especially culture in the service of worship, functions as a sense organ does. It senses the proper human environment, divine Mystery, and helps shape and express a form of life that is based on that Mystery.

Humans worship, then, because they sense and "grope" that it is in God in which they live and move and have their being. This is possible, however, because it is an embodied search, a search that takes place in time and space, in history and location, in social and cultural forms. In worship we "grope" for God and in that groping a form of life emerges. This is true worship and it is kin to those elements of culture that refine and define sensibility: music, visual arts, drama, poetry, and architecture. Worship, in other words, is kin to human song. It defines, in a sense, what might be called the human *habitus*.[15] The human *habitus* is the sensible Mystery in which "we live and move and have our being." The human *habitus* reveals the theological dimension of the question of why humans sing. The question now becomes: Why does the Church sing? The answer comes in the form of a wondrous sensibility, a specifically human embodiment of divine Beauty made possible through human culture but not identical with it. As sensibility to and embodiment of a great Beauty, human song becomes Church song and can be seen as a manifestation of a new form of life, a Living Beauty.

HUMAN SONG

Hartshorne's pioneering aesthetics provide the theologian with philosophical insights into the nature of the liturgy. Perhaps praise and thanksgiving are, like birdsong, how human creatures live and move and have their being. In other words, perhaps human worship is like a *habitus*. If birds sing because that is the way they live, and move, and have their being, then do humans live, and move, and have their being in such a way that praise and thanksgiving are a mark of this kind of life? Another way to put it is to ask if birds sing because it is their *habitus*, then do humans sing and give praise because there exists a human *habitus*? The term *"habitus"* suggests the idea of habitat or environment. Few theologians in the modern and postmodern era would be happy with the idea that human nature can be described in terms of a habitat or environment. The idea of a human *habitus* seems more appropriate to the natural sciences than to a theology of the human person. A person, they would say, cannot be defined by some naturalist category. A person possesses will and freedom. A human person is spiritual. A human person possesses a mind, indeed can build cities and control his and her environment. Music, in fact, makes the idea of human song as *habitus* nonsensical. Music belongs to the highest category of the human spirit, creativity, and art, not to the natural process of survival and evolution.

Such arguments, however, only make sense if one accepts an awesome discontinuity between human life and all other kind of life. And if such discontinuity is accepted or presumed, it would make any theology of embodiment problematic. Indeed, it would make a sensible Mystery absurd. For if what makes the human person unique as a creature is that it is discontinuous in every way from all other creatures, living and nonliving, then to be human is to be not of this world. In other words, the assumption that human nature is essentially different from the natural matrix in which it lives leads to a view of the human that is essentially Gnostic. On the other hand, one cannot accept the naturalistic extreme, namely that human life is essentially continuous with natural process. This assumption would also fail to do justice to human song. We do not sing like birds sing. Our form of life has a special quality that the form of life of birds is not.

What is this quality? Don Saliers, I believe, puts his finger on the answer to this question. There is something about human song that is inherently liturgical. As this respected liturgical scholar puts it:

> There is something about human beings that needs to make music, something that insists on song. Every culture sings about the world it experiences, in its own distinctive sound. In fact we come to know about a people by listening to what they sing and bring to expression in their music. *What* we sing and *how* we sing reveals much of who we are, and entering into another's song and music making provides a gateway into their world, which might be much different from our own. Sharing our song with others who do not know us is sharing a gift, akin to the sharing of food at a common table.[16]

Human song not only reveals what is most intimate to a particular people; it also helps us become intimate with other groups of people. In other words, when human creatures sing they not only reveal something intimate about who they are as a people but also open themselves to an empathetic dimension that helps them enter into an intimate knowledge of others. Human song is more than an expression of our humanity. It is a marvelous sensibility to a life-giving communion, a communion best understood in terms of sharing food at a common table. In other words, human song in its salvific sense is Church song.

The communion made effective in Church song was known by the Church Fathers as a mark of authentic Christian liturgy. It is this *symphonia* that inspired Clement of Alexandria to formulate a liturgical principle that guides the Church to this day:

> We want to strive so that we, the many, may be brought together into one love, according to the union of the essential unity. As we do good may we similarly pursue unity. . . . The union of many, which the divine harmony has called forth out of a medley of sounds and division, becomes one symphony, following the one leader of the choir and teacher, the Word, resting in that same truth and crying out: "Abba, Father."[17]

Clement of Alexandria expresses beautifully the element common to all theological aesthetics: a theology of revelation. The Scriptures reveal their revelatory (and saving) power as divine Word. But how is this Word made manifest? This has been a disputed question and has taken various forms in the history of theology. One thing is clear. The saving Word as found in the Scriptures is more than text or language. The early Church soon came to recognize that the words of Scripture found fuller meaning when sung. Indeed, the theological consensus of the Fathers finds that the text or words of the Scripture find their fullest expression when they are received as *una voce dicentes.*

The *Una Voce Dicentes* refers to the symphony above. It is a striving or groping for God, as Acts 17 suggests, so that many can be brought together as one. As such, the *Una Voce Dicentes* can be understood as a major principle of liturgical aesthetics. It describes the saving *koinonia* that is not only a gift of God's Word but also its response. In other words, God's Word not only comes to us creating a life-giving communion but also comes back to God in the form of a praise-giving communion. God's life-giving grace returns as praise-giving Church song. God comes to us as divine Word and returns to God as Church song. Church song, however, is more than text sung but a form of life, a saving *koinonia*.

The *Una Voce Dicentes* principle also reveals another element at work in the liturgical practice of our day that brings us back to our previous discussion on birdsong. We can assess dimension by asking a simple question. How common is the common table of the liturgy? Part of the answer lies within the liturgy itself. The preface of the Mass envisions the assembly singing *una voce dicentes* with the angels and archangels. The Table of the liturgy extends to the very heavens itself! Yet this is not vision enough. The early Church fathers also saw the *una voce dicentes* as including the entire natural world.

If this vision is more than mere metaphor, then how impoverished has our image of the common table become for it often signifies nothing more than an ordinary dining table addressed only to the human assembly gathered for worship. If the Word begins its divine trajectory with the Creation, and finds its full response at the Table of the One through Whom all things were made, then our celebration at the Table ought to reflect this awesome trajectory. But it does not, at least, very often.

What, then, is needed to make the necessary connections that would re-energize our liturgical practice into the ideal of the *Una Voce Dicentes*? In my long-about way, I have tried to clarify the elements needed to answer this question. Word and Table need find their intrinsic continuity in this cosmic trajectory. Word and Table, in other words, have a cosmic dimension that has been lost. The loss of this cosmic dimension, let me suggest, is responsible for the present theological insensitivity to the role of sensibility in the Mystery of Christian worship. Its recovery, however, needs a necessary step that takes us into a field that many today find distasteful and, even, irrelevant. I am speaking of metaphysics.

By metaphysics, I mean a reasonable account of the nature of reality. Metaphysics has been the way theology develops its cosmology. Theology gained in the last century by making a "turn to the subject" but it did so at the expense of ignoring the subject's embodiment in a cosmic matrix, that is, a metaphysics. Perhaps a more important concern, however, is the sense that the liturgical and theologcial insights that came out of Vatican II are being undermined due to a lack of a metaphysics to support them. Vatican II, some have said, proposed a profound theology in search of a metaphysics. Whatever the truth of this observation, it is certainly clear that to claim the Mystery of Christian worship is a sensible Mystery will need a metaphysics of sensibility as support. Another point is clear, however. Theologians cannot return again to the metaphysics of essences and hierarchies. Scientific honesty and social experience have discredited that approach. Metaphysics, however, need not be about essences. There is a relatively long tradition (300 years) in North America that has developed a distinctive metaphysics based on relationality. This philosophical tradition claims Ralph Waldo Emerson, Jonathan Edwards, Charles Peirce, Josiah Royce, William James, and Charles Hartshorne among others. One strand of this tradition developed an aesthetics based on such a metaphysics. It is here, I believe, that we can find the expansive commonality of the Table, its continuity with the Word through Whom all things were made, and the Church's song. It is furthermore, an aesthetic tradition that saw the connection between Beauty and holiness. The key to this relationship is the *habitus*. What follows is a (very) short introduction to a difficult philosophical term. I beg the reader's patience. It will be rewarded.

THE *HABITUS* OF HOLINESS

The word *"habitus"* can easily be translated as "habit." To do so, however, might result in reducing the tremendously rich meaning that word has in the history of theology. The term originates with Aristotle who uses the Greek word *hexis* as a way to understand the marvelous forms of marine and bird life of his native Greece.[18] The word *hexis* comes from the verb "to have." Aristotle used it in various ways as an attempt to understand what he saw in the thriving life of the Greek coast. One way in which he uses it is not to denote mere custom or "habit" but, rather, as a propensity toward a kind of behavior. Aristotle observed that animals tended to behave in their own characteristic way. Sandpipers behaved in a way unique to them and different from seagulls. Likewise, squids behaved differently than octopuses. This characteristic way to behave in a certain way, he called *hexis*. Aristotle did not stop there. He saw that *hexis* had other meanings.[19]

Aristotle observed that the characteristic behavior that marked every animal was passed on from parent to offspring. In other words, this behavior survived death. It was an abiding reality. It was abiding in a way that the theory of eternal forms of Plato, his mentor, did not adequately describe. In other words, Aristotle saw in the characteristic behavior of animals that continued through generations a different kind of abiding form, not the changeless forms of Plato but the dynamic forms of Nature. What is abiding, Aristotle saw, need not be changeless; it could also be the living. Finally, another way Aristotle used the word *hexis* referred to the human animal. The behavior of the human animal, Aristotle observed, was continuous but different with animal behavior. The human animal can transcend his characteristic behavior. In other words, the human animal can choose to live a virtuous life . . . or not. Here, Aristotle uses the word *hexis* as that which allows the enhancement of human life. The human *hexis* can enhance the human life both intellectually and morally.

Thus, in its origins, *habitus* has a richer meaning than what is meant today by "habit." It developed further meanings in its long history within theology. Aquinas, for example, gives habits the ability to enhance a human being's natural capacities. Habits give original powers a perfection. They are for Aquinas, "propensities to act well and with a greater strength." So *habitus* is a "mean between full actuality and pure potentiality." Aquinas saw the connection of the *habitus* to grace and designated sanctifying grace as an entitative habit, a habit that functions on the level of being. This is a considerable amplification of Aristotle's *hexis*. It allows for enhancement of one's being through the infusion of supernatural habits of being.[20] The eighteenth century brings additional elements to the understanding of *habitus*.

The empirical philosopher Locke believed that we know the world about us not by an intellectual act that abstracts form from a complex reality as the Scholastic theologians believed. We come to know the world through the senses. Locke saw the sensual as individual bits of sensation unrelated to one another but put together into meaningful associations by a process of the imagination. The imagination Locke refers to, however, is not the willy-nilly absolutely fanciful imagination of later philosophy but the imagination that brings order to the arbitrary. Another way to put it is to say that there exists a *habitus* to the imagination and allows the imagination to bring order to what is arbitrary in sensuality. The data of sensuality are habitually ordered by the human imagination. This added another dimension to our understanding of the habitus. It was not only a property of life but also a property of the mind. The *habitus* is not only a way to behave in the world but also a way to look at the world. More important for our purposes, the added element given to the *habitus* by philosophers of the eighteenth century is the role it gives the sensual in the role of knowledge.

The heightened role of the sensual in knowing terrified some philosophers like Kant who tells us that he was "awakened from his slumber" by the terror of the implications of the ideas that the likes of Hume, an empiricist like Locke, had wrought. What was terror for philosophers was grace for the Puritan theologian Jonathan Edwards. Edwards saw in the expanded role given the senses by the empiricists, an insight into process of human sanctification. Sanctification, Edwards believed, was a kind of *habitus* of the imagination shaped by human affections. He came to this conclusion in the following way.

If Locke is right and the senses are the key to the formation of knowledge, then ideas are known not by the mere operation of placing an idea under a more general idea, the logical equivalent of identifying a particular genus under a more universal species. Rather, ideas are known by the experience of the affections given motion by the idea itself. A powerful idea "excites" other similar ideas revealing their connectedness and relations. In other words, ideas are relational and the nature of those relations is affectual. But which affection pertains to the role of sanctification? Which affections are "religious" in the sense of taking us closer to God? Which are not? Edwards tried to answer this question in his influential work *The Religious Affections*.

In *Religious Affections*, Edwards distinguishes between notional knowledge and sensible knowledge. Sensible knowledge is

> of this sort, as it is of things that concern the heart, or the will and affections, so it all relates to the good or evil that the sensible knowledge of things of this nature involves; and nothing is called a sensible knowledge upon any other account but the sense, or kind of inward tasting or feeling, of sweetness or pleasure, bitterness or pain, that is implied in it, or arises from it.[21]

Notional knowledge, on the order hand, is knowledge attained in speculation or beholding by the mind. In short, sensible knowledge is knowledge "tasted" while notional knowledge is knowledge "beheld." But what is tasted? Or, rather, how does the mind "taste"?

The answer to that question takes us into the heart of Edwards' theological aesthetics. The mind "tastes" through a sixth sense, the spiritual sense Edwards called the "sense of the heart" and it tastes beauty itself. The "sense of the heart" is not a physical sense organ but involves the direction of the whole self, the habitus of the human creature. This sixth sense, this *habitus* found in human inclinations, inclines the whole self to move in one direction or another according to its taste of beauty. In this sense, Edwards' sense of the heart functions in much the same way as Augustine's psychology of love functions.[22] It speaks, however, in a way Augustine's psychology of love cannot. It speaks to a world and a theology riddled by dualisms of matter and spirit, nature and culture, holy and profane. Edwards' sense of the heart describes the nature of the spiritual senses in language that is quite modern but also challenges the assumptions of our modernity (and postmodernity). The sense of beauty is found in the marvelous sensibility that is the human *habitus*, the disposition of the human to form a way of life. In this sense, the *habitus*, the sense of the heart, becomes as well the means of sanctification. Through the religious affections that come from our sense of beauty, the believer inclines to shape his and her life toward the source of that beauty, the glory of God. By discerning correctly those affections that correspond to true beauty, a human life itself becomes part of that beauty. To be a saint, in other words, is to give human life to beauty by becoming sensible to beauty by means of that very life. Although Jonathan Edwards was a theologian in the Calvinist tradition and is separated from contemporary theology by more than two hundred years, his proposal on the relationship between *habitus* and holiness has taken new form in Roman Catholic liturgical theology.

Louis-Marie Chauvet with his work *Symbol and Sacrament* has discovered anew the relationship between a form of life and the life of the liturgy. In doing so, however, Chauvet introduces a profound iconoclasm in his liturgical theology. It is the nature of this iconoclasm that we shall investigate next not only to highlight the merits of a liturgical aesthetics but also to appreciate the brilliance of Chauvet's proposal. Let us now turn and take a closer look at the work of this brilliant thinker.

LOUIS-MARIE CHAUVET

Chauvet provided some of the most innovative thought in sacramental theology since the thirteenth century with the publication of *Symbol and Sacrament*. Building on the ground-breaking philosophy of Jean-Luc Marion's *God without Being*, Chauvet attempted to go beyond the influential sacramental theology of the Aristotelian-Thomistic scholastic tradition. Chauvet, like Marion, is concerned with the undue influence of the postmodern, economic marketplace on religious values. Or, rather, on the way the marketplace shapes our understanding of value. He is particularly concerned how marketplace forces shape, perhaps unconsciously, our philosophical understandings of sacramental grace, or, rather how sacraments "work" in the economy of grace. He is concerned, in other words, about "icons" and "idols."

Chauvet finds fault with the scholastic interpretation of the consensus achieved by the Church Fathers that sacraments not only signify but also cause grace. He examines with excruciating detail Aquinas' notion of sacramental causality. To a theologian, sacramental causality is an interesting problem. It involves trying to understand how free human acts can be within God's absolutely free actions. Putting it another way, if sacraments are absolutely free actions of God, are their effects, that is, the sanctification of the human, realized by human acts or is it God who realizes the effects? It is like asking which came first, the chicken or the egg. Only the condition of God's absolute freedom prevents it from becoming a chicken-and-egg type of question. On the other hand, human sanctification if it is to have any meaning whatsoever must be a free human act.

Chauvet argues that Aquinas' solution to this theological problem is to use the categories of sign and cause to explain how sacraments sanctify.

Aquinas uses the analogy of the instrument to give what Chauvet calls a productionist model of sacramental causality.[23] Such an analogy has led to understanding sacramental grace as an object or thing. The productionist scheme of sacramental grace tends to objectivize the nature of grace and loses its very essence, its roots in the individual subject. Chauvet goes back to Plato's dialogue in the Philebus on the difference between the process of shipbuilding and the finished product, the boat, to make an important point about the nature of sacramental causality. Plato's dialogue distinguishes between genesis, the process of building, and ousia, the thing built, and connects it to the observation that in every process of building an object there is a lover and a beloved. Plato then asks: where is the lover to be found? In the process or the finished product? Likewise, where is the beloved to be found? Plato's incisive question is taken up by Chauvet to illustrate what is at stake in sacramental causality. As Chauvet puts it:

> The lover is similarly oriented to the beloved, but he does not produce the beloved. He only causes the other to exist as a beloved, and thus as capable of making a response in return; he causes the other to exist—and this is a risk-as capable of not making a response in return. The boat is a finished product; but the beloved is precisely a product that is not finished—and is thus "infinite" in the sense of "indefinite," always in process; which is as much to say that the "beloved" is not a product at all. Because the beloved is a "subject," this person can never be simply reduced to an "achievement," but is always process, development-even a development without end.[24]

Chauvet makes a crucial point. Notions of causality are problematic when God's freedom and human freedom are intricately involved. Chauvet concludes that sacramental causality is hopelessly flawed by a philosophy of being that allows sacramental causality to be seen as "producing" grace. This makes grace an object or object-like. The danger in objectivizing grace is that, as object, it becomes subject to judgment of value and being given value, in turn, makes grace susceptible to being seen as a commodity in the reductive and dehumanizing forces of the capitalist marketplace.

Indeed, Chauvet argues that the entire logic of scholastic metaphysics is based on the creation of the "value-sign." Such signs are the same as "that of the marketplace."[25] Chauvet suggests another logic exists: the logic of "non-value," the logic of symbolic exchange. These two logics coexist in every society in different proportions but are better understood as two poles in tension with each other.

> But these two poles in dialectic tension belong to two different levels of exchange. The logic of the marketplace (under the form of barter or money) is

that of value; it belongs to the regime of need objects. The logic of symbolic exchange is of another order. For what is being exchanged through yams, shells, or spears, as through a rose or a book offered as gifts in our own culture, is more and other than what they are worth on the open market or objects are in themselves. One is here outside or beyond the regime of usefulness and immediacy. Rather, the principle which rules here is one of super-abundance. The true objects being exchanged are the subjects themselves. By the intermediary of these objects, the subjects weave or reweave alliances, they recognize themselves as full members of the tribe, where they find their identity in showing themselves in their proper place, and in putting others in their "proper place." As a consequence, what is transpiring in symbolic exchange is of the same order as what is transpiring in language.[26]

Chauvet has identified an important tension that is crucial to address in our postmodern, globalized world. Powerful economic forces are reaching into the intimate, inner sections of the human heart with breathtaking speed and horrifying efficacy. These forces work by transforming all human relationships into commodities. Chauvet fears above all that even our understanding of sacraments and the grace they confer in order to sanctify us is subject to being commodified.

What is the antidote? Chauvet suggests that what transpires in sacramental sanctification is "of the same order as what is transpiring in language." Chauvet here borrows heavily from French semiotics and the thought of Martin Heidegger. Heidegger, in a powerful reflection on the nature of Being, proposed that metaphysics had "forgotten" the revelatory nature of Being itself. He felt that metaphysics had confused this revelatory property with the ability to represent the entities of Being. In other words, Heidegger believed that philosophy had mistaken its ability to speak about things as they are and the very nature of Being itself. In other words, philosophy mistakenly understood language simply as a "speaking-about." Language, Heidegger thought, was more than speaking about things; it was also a place where the human makes him and herself. Although this is highly abstract, his proposal has profound implications in a technological world where things are commodified by slick media presentations. As such, Heidegger reveals why commodification has so powerful a grip on us today. Language, as Chauvet interprets Heidegger, is not the mere intermediary between being and humans but "the meeting place where being and humankind mutually [step] forward toward one another."[27] Thus, an innocent view of language makes us vulnerable to its formative ability. The antidote, then, is to recognize how language shapes a human life.

As Chauvet puts it:

It is thus impossible for us to get by without language; however, we only consent to this condition reluctantly because language poses an obstacle to this ideal transparency of the self to itself, to others, and to God which seems to constitute one of the fundamental presuppositions of the metaphysical tradition. Beyond this resentment of the necessity of a mediation through language, we discern a further suspicion of the very corporality and historicity of humankind: such is the unconscious paradigm that seems to control the metaphysical way of thinking. For the decision to describe either the body or language as an instrument presupposes an anterior existence, at least of the logical order, of humanity in relation to its "tools"; it presupposes an ideal human essence that, since its fall and exile, has been thus imprisoned "body-sign" (soma-sema) in the empire of the sensible. In spite of all its variations, metaphysics has never departed from this original Platonism; but it is impossible, when working under such presuppositions, to develop a positive evaluation for either the body or language as the environment in which both the subject may come to life and truth to happen.[28]

Chauvet applies Heidegger's proposal to a Christian anthropology. Language is more than a property of the human creature; it is where the human creature discovers and becomes itself! Language's main role is not to explain objects but to help the human creature become a subject. Thus, the language of the Scriptures aims not so much about explaining God but to "to insert human beings, insofar as they are summoned, into the being about which they are speaking."[29] The symbolic activity of the language of the liturgy or the sacraments has more to do about shaping a form of life than explaining the ways of God.

Since language shapes the human life, provides the "environment" or habitat of that life, then "the critical thrust for Christian theology does not consist in the apophatic purification of our concepts in order to express God but rather in the *use* that *we* make of these concepts, that is, in the *attitude*, idolatrous or not, they elicit from us."[30] Remarkably, Chauvet reaches a similar position to our own with respect to the apophatic nature of mystery. Purification of concepts is not the raison d'être of mystery. It is, rather, the inclination it gives our concepts. Is Chauvet proposing, as we have, that the Mystery of Christian worship is a sensible Mystery? I do not think so. Chauvet is not so much interested in divine Mystery as he is in the mystery of our humanity. He tells us that "what fostered this current criticism of classical sacramental theology was a request as profound as it was legitimate: *to reintroduce the concretely human* into liturgical celebrations and sacramental discourse."[31]

In these powerful reflections, Chauvet reaches a similar position to that of Edwards. One cannot separate the shape of a human life from that which gives it shape. The mystery of sanctifying grace made effective in the sacraments does not so much purify us as shapes us. As such, Chauvet comes close to identifying ritual language with *habitus*. As Chauvet nears the end of his reflection in *Symbol and Sacrament*, he touches on the nature of liturgical language itself. The ritual element of the liturgical text is more than a "festive garment" clothing theological propositions but is the "text of the text" itself. As he puts it:

> The aim, urgic by nature, of ritual texts (which also includes gestures, postures, movement, places, objects, music, decorative elements) . . . as well as spoken statements is pragmatic: the ritual text seeks neither to present an academic explanation or theological hypotheses nor to codify ethical norms nor to transmit information. The efficacious nature which characterizes them is such that their verbal formulations do not act as simple commentaries on an action that would be exterior to them but as actions symbolic in themselves. Whether it expresses praise, belief, petition, desire, or confession . . ., the liturgy is always within a particular kind of language whose unity seems assured, among other things, by its illocutionary modality. It is always the establishment of a new relation of place between the community and God which it seeks to accomplish and purports to achieve. And it is always, at the same time, the instauration or restoration of a cohesion among the members of the group, of their mutual reconciliation, of their communion in the same identity which is at work in the act of ritual language: it aims not at discursively thematizing the criteria of the community, but at constituting it by enunciating them. The "we" used in the present tense . . . truly functions as the illocutionary agent of the community.[32]

Language, in its specifically ritual form, is less about speech than about shaping. This is the "illocutionary dimension." What does it shape? Chauvet is clear. It shapes a "we," a community. As such, ritual language, because it shapes, is meant to be performed rather than spoken; it is an act rather than a speech. In its performance, ritual language is an "act which is its own result"; it is "the flesh of an intention born while taking significant form." Chauvet in this marvelous interpretation of sacramental efficacy as the illocutionary dimension of language gives us a new way of looking at the sacraments. He also gives a philosophical account of the nature of how the sacraments sanctify. Sanctification is less a dying to the world as it is a being shaped into a world. Sanctification is less a being purified as it is being shaped. It is no wonder that Chauvet's *Symbol and Sacrament* has been so well received among liturgical scholars. He puts his finger on the common experience of the liturgy. Liturgy shapes our humanity through human acts that somehow orient us toward a transcendent source. He also introduces a badly needed philosophical discussion to a field that has eschewed philosophy and concentrated mostly on biblical and historical scholarship. True, he critiques philosophy but his undeniable achievement is a philosophy of liturgy, a philosophy of language of the liturgy. Chauvet borrows heavily from the philosophy of Martin Heidegger and attempts a fundamental analysis of the liturgy. In his use of philosophy, Chauvet resembles Jonathan Edwards. Chauvet never mentions Jonathan Edwards but it is not hard to see how similar the illocutionary dimension of language is to Edwards' notion of the habitus. Both Chauvet's illocutionary dimension and Edwards' *habitus* describe the constitution of the saint as acts that shape a human life in conformance to God as absolutely transcendent (in Chauvet) or as supreme sovereign (in Edwards). They differ, however, as to the nature of these shaping acts. Chauvet focuses on language, albeit, the illocutionary dimension of language; Edwards on the affections.

Why does Chauvet eschew the affectivity of the senses? Chauvet fears the subject-object dichotomy. The senses function (in classical philosophy) to report an objective world to the mind. Chauvet apparently fears that exploring the role of the senses in worship would introduce the very dualisms he is trying to overcome. This means that he has no effective means to understand the affective nature of the liturgy. It also means that Chauvet apparently seals the human creature in the mode of language. Ironically, the Roman Catholic Chauvet appears to have become more puritanical than the Puritan Jonathan Edwards. Chauvet does have a theory of perception, however. He appropriates a phenomenology of perception that has its roots in the work of Merleau-Ponty.[33] A phenomenology of perception tries to catch sensation "on the wing." In this way, it avoids making what is sensed an object. Unfortunately, it also avoids giving an account of enjoyment. A sensation "on the wing" cannot be enjoyed only perceived. Chauvet's theory of perception may be able to catch a glimpse of God but it can never take delight in the Lord. And if Church song like birdsong has its origins in enjoyment, then this means that Chauvet's illocutionary dimension of language can never burst forth as Church song.

This suggests a profound iconoclasm. By iconoclasm I mean the denial that the immediacy of an original presence can be mediated by elements separate from that presence. In other words, iconoclasm denies that immediacy can be mediated. In Chauvet's system iconoclasm takes a new turn. Mediation, in the classical sense, presupposes an object to be represented to some subject. This scheme is unacceptable for Chauvet. To avoid such a view of mediation, he takes up Heidegger's analysis of Van Gogh's 1887 *A Pair of Shoes*. He quotes Heidegger that in *A Pair of Shoes* is found:

The essence of art: "the truth of the entity putting itself into effect." This has nothing to do with any "imitation" or "copy" of the real, with truth as the "conformity" (adaequatio) of traditional metaphysics. In opposition to this truth-as-exactitude, which bends everything to its "indiscrete calculation," the work of art, like all symbolic work, shows what the truth is: not something already given beforehand to which one only has to adjust oneself with exactitude, but rather a "making-come-into-being," an "advent" which, like a "fugitive glimpse," gives itself only in simultaneously "holding itself back" in a sort of "suspense" to the person who, against every utilitarian tendency, knows how to respect the "vacant place" where it discloses itself. No real peasant's shoe is more true than the one in Van Gogh's painting. The symbol touches what is most real in our world and allows it to come to its truth.[34]

Art, as Heidegger and Chauvet see it, does not imitate an original; it expresses the truth of a reality by letting it put "itself into effect." Thus mediation is not representation nor is it imitation of some original, but letting the original speak for itself beyond itself. Such is the role of symbol for Chauvet. It mediates in the manner that Van Gogh's *A Pair of Shoes* mediates by making truth come into being.

As such, Chauvet appears to have what may be characterized as a symbolic or semiotic aesthetics. But it is an aesthetics more concerned about the truth it presents than the delight it offers. Let me suggest this is a new kind of iconoclasm. It rejects the role of mediation in art by concentrating on its phenomenology. *A Pair of Shoes* is not the imitation of a pair of peasant shoes but an existential truth expressing itself. As such, I would argue it is a half-truth. All art is part imitation, part expression. The expressive dimension of all great art, however, would not be possible without its imitative dimension. Heidegger takes the expressive dimension of art to the extreme in his existential philosophy. He fails to appreciate that if *A Pair of Shoes* did not look like a pair of peasant shoes, its existential expressive dimension would not be possible. *A Pair of Shoes* expresses a powerful immediacy by its ability to render well an original pair of peasant shoes. By ignoring the mediating role of works of art, Heidegger introduces a powerful iconoclasm into the philosophy of art. Chauvet, I fear, carries this iconoclasm into his symbolic aesthetics of becoming. Such iconoclasm is dangerous for theology but is even more so for a liturgical theology.

In the past decade, theologians have tackled anew the role of aesthetics in theology. Part of that task was to distinguish what von Balthasar called a theological aesthetics from an aesthetic theology. By aesthetic theology, von Balthasar meant theology that uses aesthetics that solely concerns the work of art and ignores its religious dimension. Theological aesthetics, on the other hand, addresses the inextricable religious dimension of beauty. The crucial distinction lies in that an aesthetic theology only offers a theory of perception, while a theological aesthetics also offers a theory of rapture. Chauvet's theology of symbol gives us a theory of perception that has its base in Merleau-Ponty's phenomenology and Heidegger's existential philosophy. It is perception "on the wing," perceiving as becoming. As such, it is an aesthetics of symbol but it is also an aesthetics that has no room for the senses. This means it has no room for affectivity and, without affectivity, there can be no theory of rapture. As such, it appears to lie in von Balthasar's category of aesthetic theology. It knows little of beauty, or rather; it mistakes truth for beauty. Beauty in Chauvet's symbolic aesthetics is bypassed for the pure truth of presence becoming.

As such, Chauvet's ritual language may be the basis of a strange kind of aesthetics of presence as truth-coming-into-being but it can never find rapture as Church song. Nonetheless, Chauvet brings a crucial critique to theological aesthetics. A theological aesthetics must answer this basic question. How does perception become rapture? The corresponding question in liturgical aesthetics would be: How does God's Word become Church song as we gather around the Table of the Lord? These questions revolve around a category in theological aesthetics that Chauvet no doubt would reject: depth of form. Depth of form is crucial in theological aesthetics for it is the category that deals with the theological dimension of aesthetics: God's glory. As such, it is replete with it notions congenial to Platonism. Depth of form refers to what von Balthasar referred to as the subjective evidence of divine Beauty.[35] This evidence is the evidence of Christian experience as one with the light of faith. It is God's glory shining forth from within the beautiful form. The language of light shining from within a depth is far from the language Chauvet advocates in *Symbol and Sacrament*.

A NEW AESTHETIC AXIS

Chauvet, I believe, brings a needed corrective to this crucial category. Can we really speak of depth of form in a world that knows little of depth? Can we really speak of beauty in terms of depth when human suffering has reached such proportions that beauty itself is believed to be responsible for such suffering? I agree with Chauvet on this point. The older metaphysics that encourages Plato's metaphor of the cave cannot let us travel far into the twenty-first century. Chauvet's symbolic aesthetics of truth-coming-into-expression, however, suggests a way to re-think theological aesthetics' depth of form.

What Chauvet's symbolic aesthetics' lacks is Hopkins' notion of "instress." Hopkins' instress suggests a quality peculiar to a particular art form: drama. Heidegger fails to notice the truly aesthetic element of Van Gogh's *A Pair of Shoes*: dramatic beauty. The difference between dramatic form and aesthetic form is that the beholder sees himself as part of the form. This involvement is not like a contemplative "I-It" but like a dramatic "we." We do not simply see truth come into being in *A Pair of Shoes*, we are drawn into the life of the peasant who wore those shoes seeing in that imagined life some insight into our own life, a life of struggle seen "through a mirror darkly." No, it is not truth that comes into being but drama, the dramatic reality of our life revealed to us in the dramatic beauty of those peasant shoes. The glory of the Lord, in this case, comes to us not as a "depth" of form but as the instress of the very real struggle of lived experience.

Such reflection gives us a more profound way to look at Jesus' command: "Do this in memory of me." Memory, here, means more than remembering a rite or an event. Memory, here, carries a sense of that struggle and appears to call for a kind of communion that has a temporal dimension. In other words, memory, in Jesus' command, has dramatic form. Indeed, it could be seen as calling his followers to put on a play. In any case, dramatic form can also be seen in Chauvet's terms, as truth-coming-into-being, but it also encompasses more than a truth becoming; it is also like memory, a truth given. Dramatic form emerges from a script given but is given living form in its execution. This suggests an image for dramatic form, fire. If dramatic form is living form, form in execution, then fire is its very image. Perhaps the aesthetic power of Van Gogh's *A Pair of Shoes*, then, comes not simply as a truth that comes into being but a memory of struggling life come alive in the rapture of our appreciation of the painting.

Rapture comes not only as a light that illumines our darkness but as a fire that reveals the vitality of God's word in a world of death. That fire, that vitality revealed, is made visible in the vitality of Church song, indeed of all the arts that make the liturgy. For the arts themselves are vitalities expressed and not concepts represented. In this Chauvet is right. The glory of the Lord is life revealed, not an object represented. But Chauvet does not appreciate that while life revealed is more than a light that shines it is also a fire that burns and a fire that burns is also a candle that gives light. One need not negate the other. The images of fire and light correspond as well to the biblical image of holiness (the fire that did not consume the bush in front of Moses) and the Humanist image of human creativity. Fire and light, in other words, correspond to two poles of freedom: God's freedom and our own. It is here, I believe, that Chauvet's aesthetics flounder and, to some extent, all aesthetics.

Sacramental efficacy brings these two poles to the front. Ritual language does not make necessary God's action. On the other hand, without human performance such ritual is meaningless. Chauvet reconciles these two poles through the illocutionary dimension of ritual language, a dimension describing a kind of human *habitus* in which God's freedom becomes manifest along with human freedom in a phenomenology of becoming. This introduces a profound iconoclasm in the sense of a divine immediacy that can never be enjoyed because it must always be in the act of becoming. This has both a positive and a negative side. In introducing the crucial role that becoming plays in divine immediacy, Chauvet powerfully critiques aesthetic theories that ignore this dimension. Aesthetic religious "depth," in other words, must account not only the depth of being but also the depth of becoming. In developing a ritual theology solely based on a philosophy of becoming, Chauvet unfortunately jettisons the positive element of a ritual theory based on a philosophy of being. If something is to be enjoyed, it cannot always be in the act of becoming, it must also simply be. To resolve the poles of divine and human freedom, Chauvet chooses to reconcile the two through a philosophy of becoming. In doing so, he strips away the aesthetic potential of ritual language. It is hard to see how ritual language can become Church song in Chauvet's *Symbol and Sacrament.*

On the other hand, theological aesthetics has not appreciated Chauvet's insight about the role of becoming. Theological aesthetics has focused on the revelatory dimension of the beautiful rather than on the artistic underpinnings of beauty. What is needed, I believe, is Hartshorne's aesthetics of moderation. Hartshorne's principle of moderation cannot only be applied to understand birdsong, I believe it can be applied to understand Church song. Indeed, let us apply the aesthetics of moderation to the two freedoms that sacramental efficacy addresses, God's freedom and human freedom. These two freedoms are not extremes in the sense that they mutually exclude the other. Indeed, these two freedoms find their beauty precisely in their unity. But if these two elements do not apply as contrasting categories, then what does? What categories describe, in their contrast, the unitive revelatory experience of these two freedoms?

Let me suggest that an answer be sought in the experience that is artistic creativity. Artistic experience encompasses the possibilities of creative freedom. Creative freedom, in turn, is the key to the beautiful unitive revelatory experience of divine and human freedom working together. Let artistic creativity then become one of Hartshorne's aesthetic axes of moderation. Such an axis may be described by two elements that mark artistic creation, namely the constraints of the given material and subject and the freeing openness that is characteristic of artistic creativity itself. This brief analysis suggests the two poles of an aesthetic axis of creativity. One pole describes the opposite of creativity, the *datum*, or given. It is the pole of the materialist or of a theological aesthetics that limits its activity to mere beholding. The other pole describes the breakdown of creativity, the *donum*, or pure gift. Pure gift, pure creative freedom, would spiritualize creativity. The creative act would be reduced to a pure giving, a giving with nothing to give. It is the pole of an aesthetics that sees beauty only in its expression and not in its form or its content. Both these poles describe a new aesthetic axis.[36]

As such, this new aesthetic axis, artistic creativity, serves to describe the depth dimension of a liturgical aesthetics. It describes in a more profound way the aesthetic meaning of Jesus' command: "Do this in memory of me." For Jesus' command cannot be simply categorized as either *datum* or *donum*. It is a gift given, a *datum*, but it is also a gift given in the giving, a *donum*. It is the deeper meaning of Eucharist, giving thanks. In giving thanks, we acknowledge a gift given but we do so by giving, in *donum*, an offering of heart, mind, and soul to the One who gave us, once again, our hearts, our minds, and our souls. The intertwining of giving and gift, of *donum* and *datum*, is the intertwining of God's freedom and our freedom through the self-offering of God's Son. This is the aesthetic dimension of the liturgy's Christology.

The Mystery of Christian worship then turns on this command of the Christ, Jesus of Nazareth, who invites us at the table of the Eucharist to enter into a new kind of freedom, not the freedom of rebellion or self-assertion, not the freedom of autonomy or self-expression, but the freedom of true creativity, the artisanship of a way of life, a *habitus* of beauty that is both a gift for others and a gift received. As such, the Christ of Christian worship, where human and divine freedom became one, becomes more than a model of such unity of freedoms but its very means. Christ gives Himself to us in the mystery of the Eucharist so that we, in turn, may join our freedom to His and through Him to the Father's on the wings of that marvelous creative freedom that is the Holy Spirit.

This new aesthetic axis reveals the depth of remembrance, the aesthetics of anamnesis. It is more than a memory received, a datum, and more than a memory given, a donum, but a memory that can only be received by being given in the freshness and presence as it was given the first time. It is a memory come alive, with all the reverence and awe that is due God's freedom, and all the freshness and presence that is possible through human freedom. Thus artistic expression addresses the depth dimension of the liturgy not as a celebration of human self-expression but in its engagement of God's expression through his Son, which bonds Himself to us through the Spirit. A liturgical aesthetics, then, adds an aesthetic axis of artistic creativity defined by the poles of the *donum* and the *datum*. An aesthetics of moderation applied to this axis describes an artistic sensibility lying between pure giving and pure given, a sensibility where awe and reverence mix in fertile union with freshness and presence, where memory comes alive, becomes a life-giving presence, which, in turn, gives us a vision of the future.

A liturgical aesthetics of memory reveals the aesthetics of anamnesis as the temporal dimension of divine memory in its full potential under God's freedom. Liturgy's beauty emerges from the depths of a memory released from the chains of the temporally given into the beauty of a living anticipation. The aesthetic dimension of anamnesis may be found in the transformation of a memory into a life of anticipation whose very shape defines what Christians mean by the beautiful. The beauty of anamnesis awakes human freedom in its temporal dimensions. Human freedom understood from the perspective of Jesus' command to release the living potential of His memory uncovers what could be called the theodramatics of artistic creativity.

Theodramatics helps us understand the dimension of time that anamnesis engages. Time in a theodramatics differs from time in a theology of becoming (such as Chauvet's) in that theodramatics deals with "felt" time while the other absorbs time into a present. In other words, a temporal awareness purely concentrated on the present cannot be an awareness that is "felt." It is only because it is felt, however, that time in theodramatics makes possible remembrance and anticipation. As felt time, theodramatics is more than a datum of existence, static being, and less than pure donum of being, or perpetual becoming. But theodramatics is more than felt time; it is also felt space. Drama takes place on a stage. Drama aims to make such space felt by the ones who watch the drama. It aims to make the ones on the other side of the stage to find themselves within the stage itself. In other words, drama reveals a felt space, a space of separation and distance that nonetheless becomes the means through which a marvelous communion of freedoms and destinies is given form and shape. Drama's felt "time" is also a felt "space" where an almost magical empathy takes place. Such empathy not only makes what is given in time come alive and become present but also makes possible to anticipate, to hope for things not yet seen.

Theodramatics, then, is the temporal dimension of the aesthetic axis of human creativity. It adds another subtlety to a liturgical aesthetics. Aesthetic depth in the liturgy calls for dramatic sensibility. The distance between God's stage where all theodrama takes place and the human place of striving must be felt in order to be joined. The distance between the stage of divine action and the place of human striving must be felt so that the temporal dimension of Christ's memory can also be felt in all its aesthetic fullness. This fullness is found not in the impassable distance between the "Thou" and the "I," the sacred and the profane, but in the empathetic distance of the dramatic "We." This dramatic "We," in turn, gives the communal dimension of what we have called the *habitus* of holiness.

If artistic creativity may be represented as fire, then dramatic beauty may be imagined as the enfleshment of fire in time and space. Such enfleshment is the stuff of the saints. It is the aesthetics of holiness. As such, it gives a further dimension to what has been said about the human *habitus*. The human *habitus* finds sanctification in its sensibility to this embodying "fire." Thus, the depth of a liturgical aesthetics may be imagined through two principal images: Light and Fire. Light refers to the revelatory dimension of all theological aesthetics. It reveals that which can only be known by being enjoyed. Fire, on the other hand, refers to the element of rapture conceived as the uniting of human freedom with God's freedom. It is "ek-stasis" conceived as the embodying of "fire" rather than the leaving the sensual, the bodily behind. Revelatory beauty and ecstatic creativity give us the liturgical aesthetics of the unitive revelatory experience.

Embodying "fire" as the ecstatic element in the Church's liturgy helps us understand the relationship of the arts in the liturgy. Church song gathers up birdsong and all other human song into its own melody. It does not worry about its purity for in dramatic form, beauty is found not in the I nor in the Thou but in the We, the loving We that reveals our true cosmos, where you and I and It are given warmth by a fire born out a love of the Thou for all creation. A liturgical aesthetics, then, utilizes a sixth sense, the sensibility that is the *habitus* shaped by the instress that is the dramatic beauty of God's love calling out to our freedom in his Word to become an embodying fire of holy beauty so as to sing gathered around the Table with cherubim and seraphim and all the birds of the world, the Church song of Him in Whom we move and live and have our Being.

NOTES

1. Irenaeus, "Adversus Haereses," 4, 20, 7.

2. I use human rather than Christian praise because I believe praise is a mystery proper to our humanity not limited to our Christianity. I intend to give reasons for this belief in the section below on birdsong.

3. This is a version of Augustine's famous aesthetic musings: does beauty delight because it is beautiful, or is it beautiful because it delights?

4. The following understanding of sensibility has its roots in a long philosophical tradition developed in North America. This tradition engaged Locke's understanding of the senses in various and fruitful ways. A good discussion of this tradition can be found in Morton Gabriel White, *Science and Sentiment in America: Philosophical Thought from Jonathan Edwards to John Dewey* (London: Oxford University Press, 1973).

5. I understand sensibility to be one with the spiritual. The spiritual is the capacity to perceive intelligently the emotion of our sensations and the corresponding capacity to shape our lives according to such perception. That sensations bear emotion is a philosophical principle developed by Charles Hartshorne. He postulated that sensations are, in a sense, immanent emotions. The color red is more than a wavelength, it is also an emotion. As it turns out, this is more than a philosophical principle, it is a verifiable hypothesis. There exists an ever-growing body of scientific evidence that emotion pervades the universe, not only in animals, but also, perhaps, in the biology of nerve cells. See, for example, Charles Hartshorne, *The Philosophy and Psychology of Sensation* (Port Washington, N.Y.: Kennikat Press, 1968), xiv; Arthur Zajonc, *Catching the Light: The Entwined History of Light and Mind* (Oxford: Oxford University Press, 1993).

6. A word of explanation may be appropriate here. The basis of this judgment comes from a deep conviction I have argued elsewhere. I believe that theology has allowed its cosmological views to be relegated to the status of metaphor and myth because of its unfortunate troubles with Galileo and Darwin. Moreover, theology started a course in the late twentieth century that took it away from its organic

connections to philosophical thought, namely metaphysics. I do not argue for a return to a substance metaphysics but for a metaphysics of relations such as Charles Peirce and others in the North American philosophical tradition have given us. I believe only a metaphysics can mediate between science's cosmological views and theology's need of a cosmology. My arguments can be found in Alex Garcia-Rivera, "The Cosmic Frontier: Towards a Natural Anthropology," *CTNS Bulletin: The Center for the Theology and the Natural Sciences* 15, no. 4 (1995): 1–6; Alejandro Garcia-Rivera, "The Whole and the Love of Difference," in *From the Heart of Our People: Latino/a Explorations in Catholic Systematic Theology*, ed. Orlando Espín and Miguel H. Díaz (Maryknoll, N.Y.: Orbis Books, 1999).

   7. Cf. Charles Hartshorne, *Born to Sing: An Interpretation and World Survey of Bird Song* (Bloomington: Indiana University Press, 1973).

   8. It is striking to base an aesthetics on a principle of moderation rather than on a principle of hierarchy. Aesthetic value for Hartshorne is not based on a higher or a lower but on its ability to mediate between two oppositions. A more detailed argument for the principle of moderation in aesthetics can be found in Charles Hartshorne, *Wisdom as Moderation: A Philosophy of the Middle Way* (Albany, N.Y.: State University of New York Press, 1987), xi. For an excellent in-depth discussion of Hartshorne's aesthetics see Daniel A. Dombrowski, *Divine Beauty: The Aesthetics of Charles Hartshorne*, in *The Vanderbilt Library of American Philosophy* (Nashville, Tenn.: Vanderbilt University Press, 2004).

   9. As mentioned before, it was the great historian of aesthetics Wladyslaw Tatarkiewicz who coined the phrase in his exhaustive survey of theories of beauty. Cf. Wladyslaw Tatarkiewicz, "The Great Theory of Beauty & Its Decline," *Journal of Aesthetics and Art Criticism* 31, no. 2 (1972): 165–179.

   10. Aquinas' definition: *pulchra sunt quae visa placent* (ST, I q.9 a5 ad1) gives a new interpretation of the beautiful giving it a metaphysical character but in the epistemological order. By disclosing a metaphysical dimension in sensible but intelligible beauty, Aquinas gives an objectivity to the beautiful that frees it from pseudo-psychologizing. This insight of Aquinas was followed by Charles Peirce and also Hartshorne who interpreted Peirce.

   11. What is heretical to the conventional scientist is that if feeling is a variable in the observation of Nature, it is a variable that has metaphysical dimensions. Worse, it is but a short skip from metaphysics to religion. If feeling is indeed part of the fabric of the universe it opens up all sort of philosophical and theological avenues in the observation of Nature. This is not only a problem for conventional scientists. It is also a problem for many theologians. Theology made its peace with science a long time ago by creating strict boundaries between Nature and Revelation. There was a good reason for this. Science and its success embarrassed theologians still using metaphysics to develop a natural theology. This state of affairs was good for science. It kept dogmatic, narrow minded theologians from obstructing the free-wheeling nature of scientific research. Science paid a price, however. It simply is not able to account for emotion or feeling in the natural world. More tragic, science cannot enjoy its very success! The reader might be interested in my article; see Alejandro Garcia-Rivera, "Light from Light: An Aesthetic Approach to the Science-and-Religion Dialogue," *Currents in Theology and Mission* 28, nos. 3–4 (June/August 2001): 273–278.

12. This is a definition I offer based almost literally on the one Sang Hyun Lee mentions in his marvelous book: *The Philosophical Theology of Jonathan Edwards*. I find it attractive because it is another way of stating another of Aquinas' definitions of the beautiful, *Pulchrum dicatur id cujus apprehensio ipsa placet* or *Let us call that beautiful of which the apprehension in itself pleases*. If apprehension is allowed to encompass enjoyment (as distinct from pleasure) then apprehension here has the dimensions of a sensibility. This is another example of the connections that exist between scholastic and North American philosophy. For the Roman Catholic theologian, it is significant. North American thought allows a fresh philosophical approach that is not totally divorced from Roman Catholic philosophical tradition. Cf. Sang Hyun Lee, *The Philosophical Theology of Jonathan Edwards*. Expanded ed. (Princeton, N.J.: Princeton University Press, 2000).

13. By this I mean culture as measured by its institutions and, above all, its arts. It is an older understanding of culture that encompasses the dimension of civilization. It is the sense that Paul Tillich used in his theology of culture. Today we use culture more as a type of communication or information system. Although this is certainly a part of what culture is it is a rather impoverished view in my opinion. Tillich's understanding of culture can be explored in Tillich, *Theology of Culture*.

14. This distinction, I believe, has advantages to Marion's distinction between icon and idol. By concentrating on a form of life rather than a way of life, it avoids the moralism inherent in Marion's distinction. A form of life has wider connotations than a way of life. A form of life speaks of the creativity that is part of the living process itself. As such, it has moral dimensions and can be judged as right or wrong but, more important, it also has aesthetic dimensions in which the glory of the Lord can shine.

15. The notion of the *habitus* will be developed in greater detail below. *Habitus* is a general term describing the pre-disposition to behave or act in a certain way. Thus, it means more than habit or habitat.

16. Quoted in Wilma A. Bailey, *Music in Christian Worship: At the Service of the Liturgy* (Collegeville, Minn.: Liturgical Press, 2005), xvi, 29.

17. Clement of Alexandria, *Propepticos* 9, as quoted in Johannes Quasten, *Music & Worship in Pagan & Christian Antiquity* (Washington, D.C.: National Association of Pastoral Musicians, 1983), 67.

18. It is perhaps not stated enough that philosophy has deep roots in the observation of Nature. Contemporary philosophy, I believe, has suffered by abandoning these roots in the wake of the initial success of the natural sciences. This is a tragedy not only for philosophy but, especially, for theology. Theology, now more than ever, needs a cosmology, that is, an account of the natural world. A theological cosmology, however, would include the spiritual as part of that natural world. This would mean, in my opinion, that theology would see the natural phenomenon that is life as the tangible manifestation of the spiritual. This would, I believe, do much to overcome the dualism that has plagued both philosophy and theology since Descartes.

19. A nice summary of the philosophical development of the term *habitus* can be found in Lee, *Philosophical Theology*, 20ff.

20. Lee, *Philosophical Theology*, 24–25.

21. Jonathan Edwards, *The Religious Affections* (Edinburgh: Banner of Truth Trust, 1986), 272.

22. Lee, *Philosophical Theology*, 155.

23. Louis-Marie Chauvet, *Symbol and Sacrament: A Sacramental Reinterpretation of Christian Existence* (Collegeville, Minn.: Liturgical Press, 1993), 21ff.

24. Chauvet, *Symbol and Sacrament*, 24.

25. Chauvet, *Symbol and Sacrament*, 106.

26. Chauvet, *Symbol and Sacrament*, 106.

27. Chauvet, *Symbol and Sacrament*, 33.

28. Chauvet, *Symbol and Sacrament*, 34.

29. Chauvet is here quoting Jüngel. Chauvet, *Symbol and Sacrament*, 42.

30. Chauvet, *Symbol and Sacrament*, 42–43.

31. Chauvet, *Symbol and Sacrament*, 413.

32. Chauvet, *Symbol and Sacrament*, 429.

33. Chauvet, *Symbol and Sacrament*, 146ff.

34. Chauvet, *Symbol and Sacrament*, 117.

35. See von Balthasar's discussion in Joseph Fession and John Riches, ed., *The Glory of the Lord: A Theological Aesthetics*, vol. 1, *Seeing the Form*, by Hans Urs von Balthasar, translated by Erasmo Leiva-Merikakis (New York: Crossroad Publications, 1983), 7 vols., 442ff.

36. This axis also describes a medieval and modern theological *topos*, the relation of nature and grace. I have learned a great deal from Henri de Lubac's discussion of it in his historical treatment of the theological discussions on this relationship. Much of this debate occurred by an Aristotelian notion of nature. The discussion on birdsong has suggested the need to reconsider medieval notions of nature, indeed, even reconsider modern notions of nature. Doing so would bring us into a revitalized discussion on the relation between nature and grace. This new axis, I believe, puts modern insights about the intrinsic dimension of grace in all nature while at the same time providing a transcendent dimension into a new form, an axis where the *datum* takes the place of nature and *donum*, the place of grace.

CHAPTER 3

✝

It Is Right to Give God Thanks and Praise

Thomas Scirghi

The liturgy of the Eucharist begins with a three-part dialogue.

Priest: "The Lord be with you."
Assembly: "And also with you."
Priest: "Lift up your hearts."
Assembly: "We lift them up to the Lord."
Priest: "Let us give thanks to the Lord our God."
Assembly: "It is right to give God thanks and praise."

The last response from the assembly summarizes the purpose for the liturgy: "It is right to give God thanks and praise." The word "liturgy" derives from two Greek words, *leiton* (meaning "people," from which we get the word "laity") and *ergon* (meaning "work," from which we get ergonomics). Literally "liturgy" refers to the work of the people for God. It is the service that the faithful give to the Lord in response to the gift of creation and redemption they have received. And this work is a public, corporate act. Originally *leitourgia* referred to the public works of Roman society. So *leitourgia* was expressed through the requisite paying of one's taxes. The money collected from the taxes was spent on public works, such as the building of an aqueduct or a new road.[1] With the rise of Christianity throughout the Roman Empire this term was applied to the worship of Christians. They saw their thanks and praise as a form of service to God, a means of maintaining their fidelity to the teaching and work of Jesus Christ, the incarnate Word of God. Acting on this fidelity they gathered regularly, on "the first day of the week," following the command of

Jesus, which he spoke during His last supper: "Do this in memory of me." Their weekly gathering then, in which they discussed the teachings of Jesus and read letters from the itinerant apostles, and shared the meal of bread and wine, was an obedient response to the Lord's command.

This response to the Lord's command followed a three-fold scheme. The worship of God begins with Scripture: the recognition of Jesus as the Christ, the Son of God and the fulfillment of the prophets, the long-awaited messiah. Jesus called these disciples into a community—a church—to send them out again as "apostles," spreading His teaching and gathering others into this church. The worship of God continues explicitly in the liturgy. The praise of God in prayer and song, scripture and meal, recalls the story of the salvation of the world and directs the mission of the faithful today. Specifically, worship according to the Roman Rite is a setting for the Scripture, as the "prayers, collects and liturgical songs are scriptural in their inspiration."[2] As Christians praise God, remembering the divine gifts they have received, they also take note of the needs around them and pray to respond in a Christ-like manner. Thus the worship of God extends beyond the service of the liturgy to the community outside, to the needs on the street, to the poor and the oppressed, as well as to the leaders of government and business. So the worship of God begins with the Scripture's story of a community called into being by Christ, continues with a clear expression of faith and hope through the liturgy, and extends through the expression of moral behavior to the wider community. Scripture, worship and ethics are the necessary components for the genuine praise of God.[3]

When we discuss the aesthetics of liturgy, it will be important to maintain this three-fold scheme. To be clear, for our position, liturgical aesthetics means more than merely following the rubrics, as discussed previously. Further, it means more than creating a service that is pleasing to the senses. Indeed, many contemporary discussions of aesthetics seem to relegate the term to the sensuous, suggesting more of an "aesthete," that is, one who makes a cult of art and beauty. However, the word "aesthetic," derived from the Greek *aisthetes*, means "one who perceives." For the purposes of liturgical aesthetics this perception involves the purpose of the worship event, to which the sensuous elements contribute. We do not intend aesthetics to refer simply to the delightful qualities of art work, although they play an important role. Rather, beauty includes the purpose of the work, along with its appearance and performance. Thus a "beautiful liturgy" not only should be evaluated by its performance and the participation of the members of the congregation, but should take into account the transformative effect upon the worshipers. This is to say that the liturgy should lead toward a renewed and deepened sense of Christ's presence in their midst, coupled with a call to action in support of Christ's poor.

To state the matter simply, in evaluating a liturgical service we might ask two questions. First, where does this service come from? Does it express the tradition of the community in a genuine way? Second, where does it lead us? Does it send forth the congregation to incorporate the Word of God in daily life? This second question specifically addresses the transforming force of the liturgy by addressing the beauty around us. According to Richard Viladesau, "Christian solidarity with the poor and suffering . . . introduces a 'hermeneutic of suspicion' to our experience of the world and its beauties . . . for the Christian message is not merely that God is lovely, but that God is love; not merely that God is beautiful and is to be found in the pursuit of what is attractive and desirable in the world but that God is transcendentally and absolutely beautiful and is to be found even in what to the world's eye is ugly and deformed and unworthy."[4] Viladesau continues, saying that, given the context of this hermeneutic, religious experience does not entail simply one's personal spiritual elevation, or self-awareness, or inner peace. Rather it includes "an element of unrest and incompleteness, as well as a consequent imperative to action." It includes as well not simply the communion of an individual with God, "but a solidarity with others, including those whose lives are at present not beautiful."[5]

Accordingly this solidarity forms the basis for our communion. In sacramental terms we know the presence of Christ through the ministry to others. As Jesus explains upon healing the man born blind, "Neither he nor his parents sinned; it is so that the works of God might be made visible through him."[6] Likewise in the "final judgment" scene, according to Matthew, the king explains "whatever you did for the least of my brothers and sisters, you did for me."[7] In the first case Jesus models the behavior for his followers. In the second, he illustrates the lesson with a parable. Both passages point to the moment where God is found, namely, in caring for those who are neglected by the greater society. The recognition of the Lord in the ministering to those in desperate need is celebrated in the ritual of anointing of the sick. In the compassionate service of the other we meet the living God. This service in solidarity joins us in communion: servant, served, and savior. Further, as we know the presence of Christ in a unique way through the communal sharing of consecrated bread and wine, in a similar way we are drawn into communion by building solidarity with those who are neglected.

The transformation toward solidarity with others is expressed well by Archbishop Wilton Gregory: "Ours must be the question of how the Lord of the universe might in fact be using human hunger today to achieve his own purpose in our lives. How might human hunger today be a vehicle for God's transformation of our hearts?"[8] Thus, one transforming effect of the liturgy is to find beauty in what the world considers ugly. Viladesau warns that without this hermeneutic of suspicion applied to beauty, we run the risk of rendering the beautiful, as well as our worship, an idol. To be clear, he does not argue against the use of the arts in worship, but for the "creation of an explicitly and pastorally relevant theological aesthetic."[9]

THE FORMATION OF A LITURGICAL *HABITUS*

In order to develop a theological aesthetic for Christian worship we will need to focus on the notion of *habitus* for liturgy. By *habitus* we mean the development of the higher dispositions for worship. More than what is externally pleasing to the eye or ear, it is the proper disposition toward an embodied experience. This *habitus*, because it is an embodied experience, becomes virtually a "sixth sense" for appreciating liturgy.[10]

According to the tradition of the Eucharist developed in early Christianity, the celebration of liturgy necessitates a *habitus*. For the early Christians the way they worshiped meant more than procedural rubrics; it required a fundamental disposition toward the community. Consider Paul's chastisement of the community at Corinth: "When you meet in one place it is not to eat the Lord's Supper, for in eating each one goes ahead with his own supper, and one goes hungry while another gets drunk. . . . Therefore whoever eats the bread or drinks the cup of the Lord unworthily will have to answer for the body and blood of the Lord."[11] Without the *habitus*, that is, the developed disposition toward the embodied communion of the faithful, there can be no communion with Christ.

That final celebration—the Last Supper—has developed greatly through the centuries while the Church has adopted customs and practices of local cultures, and adapted them to a unified ritual of public prayer. Nevertheless the highly stylized liturgy of the twenty-first century serves to reveal the presence of God to the faithful, creating an experience somewhat similar to that of the first Christians gathered around the table with the Lord. The liturgy seeks to create such an experience of Christ's presence. Through this action of *anamnesis*, a remembering through action, the liturgy evokes an aesthetic ideal, heightening our perception, that is, our ability to perceive the presence of God in our midst. The interplay of Scripture, sacrament, song, and spoken prayer direct our attention to the presence of God. The *anamnesis* eventually gives way to a *prolepsis*, an anticipation of the coming reign of God.

Part of developing this disposition is to recognize the communal quality of worship. At first this may seem obvious, due to the fact that each Sunday Christians join together for an hour or so in a church. Yet in some cultures, especially western cultures, communal activity is countercultural. For Americans in particular, proud of their individualism, to become one with a community, to find one's identity through the community, rubs against the grain of popular culture. To be clear, Americans enjoy gathering for spectacles such as sporting events or rock music concerts. In the midst of these events the participants may enjoy a sense of bonding with the rest of the audience. Certain behavior for participation is expected from those attending. At a baseball game, for example, the masses huddle together in support of the home team. Cheers, applause, and song unite the group in a common cause. For a few hours there is a felt esprit de corps, but once the game ends, the individuals will return home, without knowing each other and with no responsibility to each other. The event promotes a feeling of camaraderie or common cause without any notion of commitment. Clearly no communion is formed. However, when the show ends, so does the bond. Sociologists refer to this phenomenon as part of a "loosely bonded culture."[12]

The Christian gathering calls for something quite different. In worship the present day disciples accept their mission as joining in the common cause of Jesus Christ. John Chrysostom expressed this sentiment well when he charged: "You cannot pray at home as at church, where there is a great multitude, where exclamations are cried out to God as from one great heart, and where there is something more: the union of minds, the accord of souls, the bond of charity, the prayer of the priests."[13] Chrysostom offers us a good description of ecclesial communion.

The obligation to attend weekly worship stems from this striving for unity of minds and souls, serving with charity for all, rather than from a legal requirement. The purpose of liturgy is to transform individuals into one body through the praise of God. The transformative action of the worship rite is linked to human emotion. Another dimension of aesthetics is to serve as a conduit for the emotions. The liturgy guides the emotions, orienting one's life toward the recovery of meaning. A liturgical rite is "a sequence of gestures regulated by rigorously codified norms."[14] Rite presents itself as a formal series of procedures of a symbolic nature that involve a code of social communication based on the belief that it possesses a specific efficacy by which, if performed and experienced in the provided conditions, it will have a transformative power on all who celebrate it.[15] In this way liturgical celebration has the potential to support both personal and group identity. For example, within the funeral liturgy mourners experience the disruption of affective bonds yet they are able to express emotion without the fear of losing themselves or their identity. The ecclesial community provides an echo and a container for the emotional expression of its members. In the first place, the community, in a manner of empathic understanding, responds with emotive resonance, that is to say that the community "re-sounds" or "echoes" the lamentation or exultation of its members. In the second place, the community acts as a container, checking that these emotions do not overflow into a debilitating despair or a disintegration of identity. Thus the liturgy of the Eucharist provides both a cathartic and reconstructive function as it regularly orients the emotions toward the Paschal Mystery of the death and resurrection of Jesus Christ.

More specifically, liturgy guides our emotions throughout the Church's year. We may ask, which emotions do we associate with the seasons of Advent or Lent? Embraced by the secular commercial society the liturgy seeks to re-orient us toward our collective source of meaning. Further we may ask, how should we "feel" collectively toward the Incarnation, the Crucifixion, or the Resurrection? As the liturgy guides the emotions of the worship body it leads to a unitive revelatory experience.

As we explore this notion of the unitive revelatory experience from a theological aesthetic, it will help to consider the significance of music in liturgy. Liturgical music serves both functions of this experience: it is unitive, as congregational singing helps to gather together the worshiping assembly; and it is revelatory, as the emotional force of music helps to evoke human feelings while its rhythm uncovers new meaning from the words.

THE MUSICALITY OF LITURGY

To understand the relationship of liturgy and music we need to ask: Is the liturgy inherently musical? It would be misleading to talk of the role or place of music in worship, as if music were something added to the spoken worship. As Don Saliers explains, liturgy is musical because it involves speaking, listening, movement, and rest. The congregation and its ministers need to be attuned to the rhythm and pace of the prayer and proclamation, as this is crucial for participation in the ritual dimensions of liturgy.[16] To speak of the inherent musicality of the liturgy means more than hymnody or the parts of the mass that may be sung. This musicality refers also to the way in which the liturgy is conducted with appropriate pacing and pausing, for instance. The contemplative quality we find in singing hymns or with chant may be applied to the spoken parts as well. For example, rather than rushing through the prayers, the congregation should speak them in a prayerful, deliberate manner, probably more slowly than usual. Moreover, as Frank Burch Brown notes, it is a cardinal principle of aesthetics that the message can never be separated entirely from the medium which conveys and shapes it.[17] Thus from the standpoint of liturgical aesthetics the manner in which we pray and proclaim will shape the meaning of the prayer and proclamation. Let us now look at how music contributes to the liturgy as a unitive revelatory experience.

THE UNITIVE FORCE OF MUSIC

An ancient Christian writer, Clement of Alexandria (d. 215), wrote: "We want to strive so that we, the many, may be brought together into one love, according to the union of the essential unity. As we do good may we similarly pursue unity . . . the union of many, which the divine harmony has called forth out of a medley of sounds and division, become one symphony, following the leader of the choir and the teacher, the world, resting in the same truth and crying out: 'Abba, Father.'"[18] Here Clement uses the metaphor of a symphony to describe the ideal of the church's union from a medley of sounds to a harmonious blend. What is it about music that produces this unifying effect? Note that this is an important question for liturgical aesthetics because, as was previously mentioned, if the liturgy is inherently musical, then our worship should display some sort of unifying effect.

To discuss the unifying effect of music we need to appreciate that sound itself is a fundamentally unitive act. According to Ed Foley, the production of a sound results in a web of relationships. The one who produces the sound is linked to the sound itself, as is the one who hears the sound, as well as with all others who receive the sound. Finally the producer of the sound is connected in a new way with himself. Foley compares this interconnectedness with the unitive character of God's interaction with humanity noting that "the experience of revelation not only unites an individual with God but forges a . . . network of relationships among a people who share the experience and commit themselves to it."[19]

One musician describes the unifying effect of music by simply contrasting song with speech. If two people were to speak at the same time their conversation would be inaudible. Yet several people may sing at the same time, and even though the words are different (as in for example, an opera) they are able to produce a beautiful song. In fact it is the union of the different sounds sung simultaneously that produces harmony.[20] Harmony stands between the cacophony of several voices speaking different words simultaneously, and the monotony of a group speaking or singing the same script in the same tone. The harmony of song maintains the difference while transforming the division into a union.

This notion of harmony may serve as a model for the Church. A vibrant church could be compared to a well-trained choir in that the members of a church should not follow along in some monolithic structure with monotonous repetition, but resonate as a choir with its distinct voices of soprano, alto, tenor, and bass, singing the same song with varying tones. It is the latter that produces the beautiful sound.

To sing with others contributes to the building of a community. Basil of Caesarea appears to echo Clement of Alexandria when he writes: "Who can consider as an enemy one with whom he has sung God's praises with one voice? Hence singing the psalms imparts the highest good, love, for it uses communal singing, so to speak, as a bond of unity, and it harmoniously draws people to the symphony of one choir."[21] For Basil, the transformative effect of singing may heal the division between enemies.

The purpose of the Church's singing, as is shown here, is to build the community into a communion with God. Don Saliers makes this clear as he argues that liturgical song is not meant merely for listening; nor is it designed for spiritual edification or the expression of personal piety. Rather our song is intended to be a corporate prayerful action as heard in the liturgy's acclamation and antiphons, responses and refrains, and through the traditional hymnody.[22]

As we are developing a theological aesthetic for liturgy we need to realize that the assembly of worshipers is essentially a "gathering." Recall the words of Jesus to Peter: "I say to you, you are Peter, and upon this rock I will build my church."[23] A footnote for this verse explains that "church," from the Greek *ekklesia*, refers to the community that Jesus will gather.[24] The Church is essentially a gathering, a group of disparate individuals called into union by Jesus Christ. The weekly worship in the presence of Christ reminds us of this vocation: as God's people we are being gathered. As mentioned in chapter one, the entrance procession, in some sense, begins at home rather than at the church door. This is to say that the actual preparation for Sunday worship starts at home, as we rise from sleep, wash, dress, and eat, then travel to the house of worship. The Lord continues to call His people together and through the Church's ritual He continues to fashion this collective into a body. The Church still strives to recognize its unity. Moreover, this unity includes those who gather throughout the world in praise of Christ, as well as those who have gone before us, and the kingdom of heaven.

This gathering entails a certain disposition because it is a counter-cultural activity. We leave the comfort of home, the material world and the individualistic mindset of the surrounding culture, to be united in one body entering into a Spirit-filled world. All the more reason that the Church's singing is necessary as it helps the transition from the street to the sanctuary. According to Saliers, sung prayer aids in the formation of affections and dispositions of the faithful who dwell in the Word of God.[25]

As we sing the praise of God our voices blend with all of God's kingdom. Indeed the early church spoke of a *"koinonia* of singing," by which the Church's singing was united with that of the angels in heaven.[26] This may be difficult to appreciate because much of the current western culture treats music as a passive form of entertainment. We no longer "make" music, that is, perform by singing or playing an instrument, as much as we listen to music, usually from recordings, and sometimes in the concert hall. Moreover, music is often played for mere background ambiance in which attentive listening is not even required.

MUSIC AS A REVELATORY EXPERIENCE

"In addition to expressing texts, music can also unveil a dimension of meaning and feeling, a communication of ideas and intuitions which words alone cannot yield. This dimension is integral to the human personality and to growth in faith. It cannot be ignored if the signs of worship are to speak to the whole person."[27] This quote is taken from the document "Music in Catholic Worship," published in 1982 by the U.S. Bishops' Committee on the Liturgy. Accordingly, the regular practice of worship should "unveil," or reveal, some aspects of meaning and feeling which speech or script fails to uncover. Also, they note that worship should "speak to the whole person." The liturgy should "move" the worshipers as well as teach the tradition.

It was mentioned earlier that worship is inherently musical. It reveals the nature of communion through the experience of praying in unison. Again, the purpose of music in liturgy holds more than an entertaining value. Music is not intended as an addition to the spoken service in order to enhance our worship. Rather music serves to reveal to a disparate group the real possibility of a saving communion through a loving community. Moreover, if liturgy is to provide a unitive revelatory experience, then this "experience" requires more than an intellectual comprehension, but more of a knowing of the mind as well as of the heart. In the words of Dom Gregory Dix, "We have forgotten that the study of liturgy is, above all, a study of life, that Christian worship has always been done by real men and women, whose contemporary circumstances have all the time a profound effect upon the ideas and aspirations with which they come to worship."[28]

Because the liturgy is, in the words of Dix, "a study of life," we need to consider human emotions as well as the ideas proffered in worship. However, the emotions we speak of here are not concerned with a person's mood or personal feelings at this point in time. Liturgy evokes those deeply rooted emotions "which become part of our way of being through time."[29] Liturgy develops a *habitus* for the community. For the first Christians, it was one thing to recognize Jesus as the Christ, the Messiah; it was another to leave everything behind and follow Him. True discipleship joins the intellect and the will, bringing a person to a point of conversion. The liturgy provides an encounter with Christ, to cite Schillebeeckx,[30] through which we experience our deep-seated desire for union with God.

Music touches the heart, revealing this desire, bringing it to expression in a way that normal discourse cannot. In the words of Arthur Schopenhauer, music provides us with "that profound pleasure with which we see the deepest recesses of our nature find expression . . . we must attribute to music a far more serious and profound significance that refers to the innermost being of the world and of our own self."[31] According to Schopenhauer, music stands out among the arts as it directly articulates the noumenal, that is, the inner essence of things, rather than the phenomenal. Moreover music allows a composer to express profound wisdom in a language that his or her reasoning faculty does not understand.[32]

THE INTERPRETIVE ROLE OF MUSIC

So far we have discussed the power of sung worship to unveil our deeply rooted beliefs. From another perspective we can appreciate its part in helping to understand the content of our belief. When the words of Christian faith are set to music, when they are heard in song rather than in speech, the congregation will hear then in a new way. According to Viladesau, singing is not our normal form of address, it takes the word out of the "I-Thou" context of speech and places it in the "we" context of shared musical experience. Singing replaces the irregular cadences of speech with artfully constructed cadences, following rhythm and melody. In this way music serves a hermeneutical function: it interprets the word by taking it out of the context of a dialogue, bestowing upon it an emotive value. Congregational singing allows us to contemplate and celebrate the word rather than simply to hear it or speak it.[33] The sung prayer allows for a new hearing of the words.

One caution should be noted here: emotional expression should not deteriorate into simple emotionalism. Worship is not about encouraging a feeling of excitement so much as enabling enthusiastic expression. To be "enthused" (*en theos*) literally means to be inspired by God. Sung prayer should awaken the congregation to the meaning of its praise of God through a language that unveils who God is. Likewise, liturgical music should not fall into sentimental self-expression but must be orthodox, that is, it must convey true thanksgiving and praise of God; it must be able to confront the reality of sin and suffering; and petition for the mercy of God.[34] Indeed throughout the history of the Church some have held music suspect, fearing that it could be a distraction from right worship. Several of the Church Fathers railed against the use of musical instruments for worship. They cited the prophet Amos: "Away from me with the noise of your songs; the playing of your harps I do not wish to hear."[35] Here Amos charges that such music resembles the lifestyle of the complacent wealthy who ignore the plight of God's people.[36] Citing this passage, Theodoret of Cyrus writes, "We know that God takes no pleasure in songs and music because of what he says to the Jews." And Isidore of Pelusium equated music in liturgy with offering sacrifice: "If God received sacrifices and blood by reason of the foolishness of the men of that time, why do you wonder that he should also have borne with the music of the cithara and the psaltery?"[37] Because of its great emotional force music can enchant the listeners, either by distracting them into a state of emotionalism, or by evoking the deep-seated desires and truths of the Christian tradition. We could distinguish this emotionalism from the deep-seated desires as external and internal participation. The participation of liturgical singing calls for more than a campfire songfest, simply uniting a group in a circle together. Worship music connects the community and fosters the disposition of openness to the divine. So it is this latter movement of internal participation which concerns the worshipers. The notion of "active participation" is discussed rather extensively in the document of the Second Vatican Council, "The Constitution on the Sacred Liturgy." There we read, "In the restoration and promotion of the sacred liturgy . . . full and active participation by all the people is the aim to be considered before all else; for it is the primary and indispensable source from which the faithful are to derive the true Christian spirit."[38] Furthermore, "Pastors . . . must promote the liturgical instruction of the faithful, and also their active participation in the liturgy both internally and externally."[39] Within the realm of liturgical music, the Church discusses this distinction in the document "Musicam Sacram."[40] Here it is explained that the participation of the faithful should be, above all, internal. This is to say that the faithful join their minds to what they speak and hear, creating a disposition of cooperation with the Lord's grace. This participation must be external also so much as the physical activity of singing responses and hymns, along with gesture and posture, promotes an internal awareness of, and readiness for, the public prayer. "The faithful should be taught to unite themselves interiorly to what the ministers or choir sing, so that by listening to them they may raise their minds to God."[41] By adhering to the guidelines presented by the Church, and by developing a liturgical aesthetic, the music of worship will contribute to a unitive revelatory experience.

NOTES

1. Cf. Aidan Kavanagh, *On Liturgical Theology*, The Hale Memorial Lectures of Seabury-Western Theological Seminary, 1981 (New York: Pueblo Publishing, 1984), 57.

2. "The Constitution on the Sacred Liturgy," in *The Documents of Vatican II*, ed. Walter M. Abbott (New York: Herder and Herder Association Press, 1966), no. 24.

3. Louis-Marie Chauvet, *The Sacraments: The Word of God at the Mercy of the Body* (Collegeville, Minn.: Liturgical Press, 2001), xxv, 29–31.

4. Richard Viladesau, *Theology and the Arts: Encountering God through Music, Art, and Rhetoric* (New York: Paulist Press, 2000), vi, 52–53.

5. Viladesau, *Theology and the Arts*, 53.

6. John 9:3.

7. Matthew 25:40.

8. "Where Hunger is Found," *Origins* 35, no. 8 (July 7, 2005): 129.

9. Viladesau, *Theology and the Arts*, 54.

10. In the following section, Prof. Garcia-Rivera will discuss this sixth sense in more detail.

11. 1 Corinthians 11:20, 27.

12. A "loosely bonded culture" is defined as a culture of exaggerated individualism with the need for political and social consensus. Here people will attempt to overcome their isolation and make common cause with each other. Richard M. Merelman, *Making Something of Ourselves: On Culture and Politics in the United States* (Berkeley: University of California Press, 1984), 120.

13. *De incomprehensibili*, 3, 6: PG 48, 725. In *Catechism of the Catholic Church*. (Ligouri: Ligouri Publication, 1994), no. 2226.

14. Lucio Maria Pinkus, OSH, "The Psychosociological Aspect of the Liturgy," in *Handbook for Liturgical Studies*, ed. Anscar J. Chupungco, OSB, vol. 2, *Fundamental Liturgy* (Collegeville, Minn.: Liturgical Press, 1997), 5 vols., 179.

15. Pinkus, "The Psychosociological Aspect of the Liturgy," 179.

16. Don Saliers, "Integrity of Sung Prayer," *Worship* 55, no. 4 (1981): 297.

17. Frank Burch Brown, "Christian Music: More Than Just Words," *Theology Today* 62 (2005): 228.

18. Johannes Quasten, *Music & Worship in Pagan & Christian Antiquity* (Washington, D.C.: National Association of Pastoral Musicians, 1983), 67.

19. Jan Michael Joncas, "Liturgy and Music," in *Handbook for Liturgical Studies*, ed. Anscar J. Chupungco (Collegeville, Minn.: Liturgical Press, 1997), 314.

20. Borja Iturbe, *Music and Theology of the Eucharist*, unpublished manuscript. I am grateful to Mr. Iturbe for directing me to several of the sources mentioned in this chapter.

21. Quasten, *Music & Worship in Pagan & Christian Antiquity*, 70.

22. Saliers, "Integrity of Sung Prayer," 300.

23. Matthew 16:18.

24. *The Catholic Study Bible: New American Bible*, ed. Donald Senior et al. (New York: Oxford University Press, 1990).

25. Saliers, "Integrity of Sung Prayer," 298–299.

26. Quasten, *Music & Worship in Pagan & Christian Antiquity*, 69.

27. "Music in Christian Worship," edition no. 3, in *The Liturgy Documents: A Parish Resource*, ed. Elizabeth Hoffman and Catholic Church. Archdiocese of Chicago (Ill.), Liturgy Training Program (Chicago, Ill.: Liturgy Training Publications, 1991), no. 24.

28. Gregory Dix, *The Shape of the Liturgy* (London: Adam & Charles Black, 1993), xix, 741. Cf. Saliers, "Integrity of Sung Prayer," 294–295.

29. Saliers, "Integrity of Sung Prayer," 296.

30. E. Schillebeeckx, OP, *Christ, the Sacrament of the Encounter with God* (Kansas City, Mo.: Sheed & Ward, 1963), 3–20.

31. Arthur Schopenhauer, *The World as Will and Representation* (New York: Dover Publications, 1966), 2 v, I:256–257. Cf. Lewis Lockwood, *Beethoven: The Music and the Life* (New York: W.W. Norton, 2003), 15–16.

32. Schopenhauer, *The World as Will and Representation*, I:256–257. Cf. Lockwood, *Beethoven: The Music and the Life*, 15–16.

33. Viladesau, *Theology and the Arts: Encountering God Through Music, Art, and Rhetoric*, 48.

34. Saliers, "Integrity of Sung Prayer," 297–298.

35. Amos 5:23.

36. Viladesau, *Theology and the Arts*, 52.

37. Quasten, *Music & Worship in Pagan & Christian Antiquity*, 63–65.

38. "The Constitution on the Sacred Liturgy," no. 14.

39. "The Constitution on the Sacred Liturgy," no. 19.

40. "Musicam Sacram: Instruction on the Sacred Liturgy." Sacred Congregation of Rites, March 5, 1967. "Adoremus: Society for the Renewal of Sacred Liturgy." www.adoremus.org/MusicamSacram.html (accessed October 1, 2005).

41. "Musicam Sacram," 15.

✛

The Glory of the Lord

Alejandro Garcia-Rivera

In the previous chapter, Fr. Scirghi and I tackled the mystery of human praise as it manifests itself in the liturgy. Human praise was connected to the first of the two principal dimensions of the Mystery of Christian Worship: the sanctifying of the human creature. Human praise (as Church song) is a sanctifying *habitus*, which disposes us and reveals to us the true nature of human sanctification: the One in Whom we live and move and have our being. In this chapter we turn our attention to the second dimension of this mystery: glorifying God. The dialogue leading to the Sanctus is our entrance into this dimension. The dialogue highlights the Church's effort to glorify God. The dialogue begins with human thanksgiving, the lifting up of human hearts, and takes what is human into the company of seraphim and cherubim giving glory to God.

As such, it reveals another element of Church song: thanksgiving. If praise led us to discover the nature of human sanctification, then thanksgiving will lead us to discover the nature of giving glory to God. Thanksgiving, then, is as much a mystery as human praise. As such, praise and thanksgiving are but two sides of this fundamental mystery. If praise opens up to us one side of this Mystery, the sanctification of the human, then thanksgiving takes us to the other side, giving glory to God. But why is this mystery? It is important that a liturgical aesthetics ask this question if for no other reason than giving glory to God in the context of the liturgy often involves the arts. Giving glory to God in the liturgy takes concrete form in the artistic expression of the liturgical texts, the fleshing of the liturgy's rubrics, and the aesthetic design of the liturgy's context as shaped by the worship space and scheduled celebrations. Such nitty-gritty details as music chosen, vestments worn, paths processed, texts chanted, incense burnt, and lessons read all revolve around a truly profound, ultimately aesthetic but highly problematic question: what pleases God?

If thanksgiving is to be truly a gift of our thanks then it is given in such a way so as to be enjoyed. Gifts are given with the aim to delight. When the recipient of our gift is God, however, then thanksgiving may appear blasphemous. How can the human creature possibly know what is pleasing to God? Even if we assumed we knew, would it not be a dangerous assumption? Could not what is assumed to be pleasing to God turn out to be the pleasing of potentialities and powers that are far away from God? One can hear God's distaste with human thanksgiving in Isaiah 1:11:

> What to me is the multitude of your sacrifices?
> says the Lord;
> I have had enough of burnt offerings of rams
> and the fat of fed beasts;
> I do not delight in the blood of bulls,
> or of lambs, or of goats. (NRSV, electronic ed.)

There are plenty of warnings in Scripture that it is foolish, even foolhardy, to assume what pleases God. Perhaps this explains the many careful prescriptions for ritual found in Leviticus. What is offered, even if it is thanks, must be offered with trepidation and great care.

Yet the question cannot be so easily dismissed. Scripture, after all, is replete with instances of God being pleased. God is pleased six times in the Creation story and this pleasure is marked by a day of rest that becomes Israel's day of praise and thanksgiving, the Sabbath. God is pleased with Abraham as well as with Job's stubborn calls to justice. And in the gospel of Matthew we hear God Godself tells us that "This is my Son, my Beloved, with whom I am well pleased" (Matthew 3:17, NRSV electronic ed.). This Son, the Son of God, then himself is pleased when a sinful woman kisses and anoints his feet. There are more instances that can be noted but the point, I trust, is made. It is not only possible to please the Lord. It is just and right to do so.

As such, God's pleasure is a complex mystery. An approach to this great mystery from an aesthetics perspective suggests looking at God's own artistic activity. God's delight, after all, is first revealed when God looks over the artistry of his own work. The singular, most revealing moment of this divine delight takes place at the end of this divine artistry, the Sabbath rest. Thus, an important connection becomes evident between divine delight and the Christian liturgy in the connection between divine artistry and the foundation of the Sabbath. The cosmic creation, however, is not the only instance of divine artistry. Christians also speak of the New Creation. This New Creation is not set over against the First Creation but is continuous with it and fulfills it. What is the nature of this New Creation? It is, of course, the Kingdom of God that Jesus proclaimed and revealed to human hearts through the Holy Spirit. Yet the shape and contours of this Kingdom, this New Creation, has been difficult to discern. It is given vision in that most beautiful of Scripture texts, Revelation. It is, I think, also significant that this text also provides us with a vision of the liturgy laced through with incredible artistic expression. As such, it suggests another important dimension of God's delight.

God delights at the sight of a new creation, the human heart created anew and turned toward God, a human work but a work made possible by God. In other words, the liturgy revealed in John's vision in the Apocalypse is, in essence, a new Sabbath. By this, I mean that the liturgy of John's vision is also, like the First Sabbath, a vision of God's delight at his own artistry except that in the New Sabbath it is the artistry of divine grace on human hearts. It is the nature of this artistry that this chapter wishes to address. It is, in its theological essence, the nature of the relationship between divine freedom and human freedom not in its ethical dimensions but in its aesthetic or, rather, artistic dimensions. The category of the arts where this relationship is best explored is not hard to find. It is drama. Dramatics, or rather, a theodramatics best illuminates how God's artistry that shapes human hearts becomes manifest in truly human works of art. Thus, this chapter seeks to expand upon the theodramatics dimension discovered in the reflection of the last chapter.[1]

A liturgical aesthetics recognizes that these two divine "works" define the complex mystery of God's delight. The Sabbath and the human heart are connected and intertwined in profound and beautiful ways. What is the structure around which they intertwine? It is what may be called the human side of divine Mystery. The Mystery that is God's delight is also the human mystery known as the *capax Dei*.[2] How can the finite be capable of the infinite? How can the human creature bear the knowledge, indeed, the love of his and her divine Creator? Yet this is what marks us as truly human. More than the doctrine of the *imago Dei*, it is the doctrine of the *capax Dei* that reveals the true nature of our humanity. It is the *capax Dei* that reveals our ultimate human goal, which, as the Catechism says, is "to know and love God." As such, the *capax Dei* is at the heart of a theological aesthetics that takes human experience seriously. It is the heart of a theological aesthetics that is concerned not only with divine Beauty but with its grasp, the human experience of divine Beauty, the beautiful.

Under the doctrine of the *capax Dei*, the beautiful becomes more than a mere reception of Beauty by human experience but a grasp, an insight, or, even better, an encounter with Beauty that stretches human experience to the point of self-transcendence in its grasp and encounter with Mystery's Beauty. The Mystery of God's delight reveals its gracious aim, the human capacity to know and love God. Theological reflection of the past two or three hundred years has given poor service to this fundamental mystery. This mystery may have been passed over too quickly in an overly rational understanding of faith.[3] In the rational account of understanding, knowing, too often, was separated from loving. Such separation took the "gift" out of theological reflection and replaced it with the "given-ness" of semi-magisterial statements. It is only in the rise of a liturgical theology that the profound question of God's delight can be raised in our day. It is a question, however, that can only be answered in a liturgical aesthetics.

In a liturgical aesthetics, a strictly rational separation between knowing and loving cannot be sustained. Under the synoptic view of a liturgical aesthetics, knowing and loving follow from the other and are ultimately inseparable.[4] Thus, if we are to love God, we must know God. If we are to know God, we must love God. Knowing leads to loving, loving leads to knowing, and the both are one. In any case, the implication is clear. In order to love God, we must also come to know God and vice-versa. But what sort of knowing is proper to loving? What sort of loving is proper to knowing? This, I believe, can only be answered from the perspective of a theodramatics. The reason lies in the way God revealed to us not only his love but also the way to know him. Christ's passion, death, and resurrection make clear that the category of delight addressed by a liturgical aesthetics is more than mere pleasure. It is also clear that the Resurrection cannot be the sole source of Christian delight. This means that if God's nature and love is revealed to us in Christ's passion, death, and resurrection, then it is revealed to us through a story we must experience from beginning to end and that is made our own in the end. In other words, we come to know and love God through the drama that is Christ's passion, death, and resurrection. Dramatics reveal a way of knowing that can only be known by loving and a loving that becomes a way of knowing.

The Paschal Mystery, then, is the key to a liturgical aesthetics that tries to answer the question of God's delight. The actual form of this Mystery in the liturgy, indeed, its very origins (Jesus' command "Do this in memory of me"), leads us to suspect that we are on the right track in emphasizing a theodramatics. For it is the very nature of this mystery to demand a dramatic approach. Such an approach revolves around an awakened or, rather, graced *capax Dei* that is not only able to receive God's mystery but also return it. This aesthetic-dramatic understanding of the *capax Dei* highlights the gift-like nature of human receptivity of divine Beauty. The aesthetic-dramatics of divine Beauty received means also human beauty returned.

This dynamic view of the *capax Dei* is revealed to us in the very human encounter with the risen Christ made possible through the Spirit come down through the liturgy. As mentioned above, the encounter with the risen Christ in the liturgy finds its origin in Jesus' command: "Do this in memory of me." It sets up the form of the encounter with the Mystery of Christian worship. The encounter with the sensible Mystery of the liturgy is an encounter made possible through dramatic form that weaves God's freedom and ours into truly beautiful works of thanksgiving. It is here where a liturgical aesthetics ultimately leads us. The Mystery of Christian worship is a sensible mystery that is received and returned. It is a mystery in which human praise and giving thanks emerge out of an awakened *capax Dei* awakened in the dramatic encounter with the living Christ through the Spirit. It is the work of carrying out Jesus' command: "Do this in memory of me." As such, it awakens the human *capax Dei* to the extent that encountering the Christ becomes the infusion of a new way of life, a new creation, a new Sabbath.[5] We meet Christ not as some stony presence or as a mental phantasm occasioned by a symbol or sign in a liturgical celebration. We meet God in Christ through the Spirit-inspired encounter with Mystery, an encounter involving a heightened sense of a living presence within us and outside of us, a new way of life, a breathing together, a true inspiration. It is indeed, a new Sabbath, a new creation seen now as communion and community radiating God's living presence through the charm and joy of the beautiful. In this encounter with the living Christ, we meet the Father and the Spirit as well.

This inspired encounter with Mystery has as a practical aim the human *capax Dei*. It acts to awaken our capacity for God with the practical aim to please the Lord. It calls for an inspired response in the form of a human sensibility to, and creative attitude toward, pleasing God. Such inspired response takes dramatic form and is the subject of this chapter. In this chapter, I develop further the aesthetics of moderation outlined previously and draw out its implications. In particular, I now explore the nature of theodramatic form, which I believe is what I have called the anagogical imagination. The anagogical imagination provides the means in which human hearts receive the given-ness of Christ's living presence and are able to move gratefully into the midst of that presence. Theodramatic form, then, in the sense of the anagogical imagination reveals a further shape to the *habitus* formed by and forming our praise and thanksgiving.

It is a *habitus* characterized by communion and community, or put in aesthetic terms, an invisible communion made visible through community. Indeed, the interlacing of communion and community interprets what we have called the unitive revelatory experience. It becomes the answer of a liturgical aesthetics to the question of what pleases the Lord. It is the shape of the New Creation, the new Sabbath, a community in communion with God and with each other. As new Creation it reveals the aesthetic shape of the human *capax Dei*. As new Sabbath, it reveals mutual delight and joy in God and in us taking place in the interlacing of communion and community. Moreover, it is a delight that goes beyond mere pleasure but is very life itself. It is an inspired communion creating a community of new life. It is one breath giving life to many. It is a community of the beautiful. It is the delight of a Living Beauty; it is, indeed, the Glory of the Lord.

THE ANAGOGICAL IMAGINATION

In the last chapter, we proposed a third axis for an aesthetics of moderation. It is an axis whose poles were marked by that which is received as given, the *datum*, and that which is sent as gift, the *donum*. It is the axis of creativity, the axis that concerns the depth dimension of the beautiful. The axis, however, proved to have some complexity. We noted that a temporal dimension must be acknowledged to the aesthetics of creativity. For the theologian, the beautiful cannot be truly understood solely by philosophical reflection. The beautiful has a dimension that philosophy can only point to but not address. It is this dimension, the depth dimension, that began to be explored at the end of the previous chapter.

Depth, in a theological aesthetics, refers to the theological dimension of the beautiful. Previous work on this depth dimension focused (almost exclusively) on the revelatory nature of the experience of divine Beauty.[6] This revelatory dimension is often characterized as light. In the previous chapter, however, we proposed another element in the depth dimension of divine Beauty. This dimension was characterized as fire. We characterized this element as a theodramatics and suggested it functions empathetically. Theodramatics reveals the empathetic dimensions of the artistic creation of beauty, the creation of the dramatic "We." This dramatic "We" gave us the embodiment of "fire," the element of passion that acts as a corrective to an otherwise unbalanced preoccupation with light as the depth dimension of the beautiful form.

The depth dimension of divine Beauty, we felt, needed to be characterized both as fire and light because divine revelation is not only a "lamp unto our feet." It is a passion that burns brightly across the night of the human heart. Such passion has the character of a divine drama in which the human is asked to enter. In doing so, divine Beauty takes aesthetic form as a dramatic "We." As such, this depth element of passion points to the unitive nature of Beauty's call. The beautiful is not only a call to appreciation but a call to union. Further reflection on the nature of revelation would have suggested this finding. Such reflection would have suggested the unitive roles that empathy and sympathy play in both art and revelation.

Divine revelation has two corresponding partners: empathy and sympathy. God reveals Himself at least in part out of sympathy for us and in order that we may empathize with God and with neighbor. This is even more the case with the revelatory nature of divine Beauty. Beauty reveals so that we may understand God not in mental abstractions or indifferent detachment but through a passionate union that delights. In other words, what is revelatory in divine beauty comes to us as a passion, a passion intrinsic in Beauty's call. It is a passion that unites. Such passion is best understood in terms of dramatic form. The dramatic "We" that takes place in good drama is also the "We" offered to us by God in the liturgy. But how is this "We" accomplished? What are the elements of this dramatic accomplishment?

Certainly the basic ingredient of such an accomplishment must be the human imagination. All artistic form but, especially, dramatic form engages the imagination. Dramatic form is particularly dependent on the imagination. It relies on its effectiveness on the principle known as aesthetic distance. Aesthetic distance in drama refers to the paradox that to become one with the action on stage, the audience understands such action is an imitation, a *mimesis* of actual action. A very young child, for example, cannot experience drama for she would not be able to distinguish the action on stage from actual action in life. It is precisely holding present this distance that makes overcoming the distance possible.[7] Such distance takes passion to overcome. Indeed, the dramatic "We" achieved through aesthetic distance relies ultimately in the unitive passion of the human imagination.

In drama, however, such unitive passion also becomes revelatory of the human condition. Dramatic form allows humanity to observe the human heart at work revealing to us the nature of our selves. In theodramatic form, unitive passion also reveals the nature of our selves but it does this through the nature of God's love for us in the living presence of the risen Christ encountered through the Holy Spirit. Theodramatic form awakens the human *capax Dei*, weaving human hearts into intimate communion with divine Beauty itself. In summary, the depth dimension of divine Beauty is not only revelatory light but also unitive fire or passion. Together they circumscribe the full aesthetic experience of divine Beauty, a unitive revelatory experience of living form and mutual delight.

It is the thesis of this chapter that such an experience comes about through the work of the human imagination, a work of theodramatic form. Furthermore, this imagination functions in an anagogical manner. By anagogical, I mean an experience of spiritual "uplifting." Anagogy was first proposed by Pseudo-Dionysius as an element of mystical knowing. Abbot Suger, however, demonstrated that Dionysius' anagogy could also be an aesthetic experience by commissioning the famous "Anagogical Window" at the Abbey of St. Denis.[8] That anagogy, or spiritual "uplifting," can be an aesthetic experience corrects some misunderstandings or reductions in the understanding of experience in the encounter with Mystery. Anagogy understood as spiritual "uplifting" without a sensible component tends to conflate the spiritual with the mental. Anagogy, under these terms, tends to be associated with revelatory theories emphasizing the ineffability of knowing God or the transcending of the conceptual. As such, anagogy devoid of aesthetic experience tends to support images of elevation. Indeed, anagogy has often been described in terms of a ladder. The ladder image, however, has come to ill repute. It has been used to justify all matters of oppression and has led to a discrediting of religious experience itself.

Our suggestion that anagogy be given a sensible component aims to correct such abuses of what is a profound religious insight. When anagogy is linked to aesthetic experience, the predominant metaphor for the experience is not mere elevation but the more encompassing metaphor of depth. Depth refers to the unitive, revelatory experience of divine Beauty. If such an experience is not only a knowing but a loving, then depth is the more appropriate metaphor. Unlike knowing, loving is best described as a going "deeper" rather than a going "higher." As such, the metaphor of depth allows transcendence to be seen not merely as that which transcends the limits of the conceptual but that which transforms our humanity itself. For it is human nature that carries the paradox of divine revelation not God's transcendence. It is human experience that carries the *capax Dei*, the capacity to know and love God, not divine revelation. Transcendence, then, must be seen as something more than a horizon to human concepts or an abyss against human experience. Transcendence involves the capacity to know a love greater than our loving, and to love a knowledge greater than our knowing. In other words, we ought to understand transcendence as a capacity not an ineffability.

This claim comes from an effort to understand the theological aesthetics of anagogy. Anagogy, or spiritual "uplifting," does not take place merely in the realm of the conceptual. It takes place in a broader dimension found in human experience. It is the dimension found when human experience transcends itself. It is the dimension found when human striving reaches its own limitations and takes a step into another dimension, or rather, an Other's dimension. It is the apophatic dimension of a Sensible Mystery. This dimension, this place where our knowledge and our loving are challenged, taken to a limit, indeed stretched to the breaking point is also the place known as the imagination. It is there a liturgical aesthetics must go if it is to understand the nature of the mystery that is the *capax Dei*. Let us suggest it is the anagogical dimension of the human imagination. It is what might be called the anagogical imagination.

THE "GOOD" IMAGINATION

The heart of the Hebrew Scriptures may be found in the great call to passionate love of Deuteronomy 6:5, the *Shema* of Israel: " You shall love the Lord your God with all your heart, and with all your soul, and with all your might." Such passion is unique to our understanding of passion itself. One view of passion is that which is a threat to reason. It is a "taking leave of your senses." Yet the *Shema* is a call to use all your reason, indeed all your senses in order to love God wholly and unconditionally. Another view sees passion as a risk to society. Passion leads people to abandon social conventions and laws. Yet the *Shema* calls us to forge a marvelous community with God. It is a call to build a new society not to destroy society.[9] What is truly unique about the passion described by the *Shema* concerns the human resource needed for such passion. I am speaking of the human imagination. The *Shema* reveals a unique dimension intrinsic to a passion connected to loving God. Such passion calls for imagination. But are we talking about any kind of imagination? Actually no, passionate love of God calls for a very special kind of imagination. It is what the rabbis called the *yetzer ha'tov*.

The earliest rabbinic interpretation on Deuteronomy 6:5, for example, is found in the Mishnah, *Berakhot* IX.5. In reference to the phrase "*with all your heart*," the comment reads: "with your two inclinations, with the good inclination [*yetzer*] and with the evil inclination [*yetzer*]." The rabbis saw the human heart as having two distinct inclinations: one toward evil (the *yetser ha'ra*) and one toward good (the *yetser ha'tov*).[10] These inclinations are not identical with the modern understanding of the imagination but they do have the same sense of a forming or shaping power. In rabbinic thought, this power is at the same time dangerous and ennobling to the human for it is related to the same power of God the Creator. As such, it forms the basis for a rabbinic theology of sin. The forming power of the human inclination is a primordial drive that can lead one to sin or, as Richard Kearney puts it,

> if sublimated and oriented towards the divine way (Talmud), can serve as an indispensable power for attaining the goal of creation: the universal embodiment of God's plan in the Messianic Kingdom of justice and peace. . . . In short if the evil imagination epitomizes the error of history as a monologue of man with himself, the good imagination (yetser ha'tov) opens up history to an I-Thou dialogue between man and his Creator.[11]

Kearney's comment on the rabbinic interpretation of what we might today call the imagination reveals the paradoxical nature of the human imagination. It is the means by which the human loses his humanity. It is also the way in which the human gains it. Perhaps the fruit of the tree of good and evil was the *Yetzer*. Martin Buber's illuminating commentary on Deuteronomy 6:5 makes another point:

> Evil is lack of direction and that which is done in it and out of it as the grasping, seizing, exploiting, humiliating, torturing, and destroying of what offers itself. Good is direction and what is done in it . . . with the whole soul, so that in fact all the vigour with which evil might have been done is included in it.[12]

It answers, I believe, the question with which we began this essay. What pleases God? That which is good. But what is good? If Buber is correct, it is the work of the *yetzer ha'tov*, the work of the good imagination.

This work, the work that is good, however, must not be understood in purely moral terms. It is, as Buber says, more than an act; it is, above all, a direction. What is this direction? One answer comes from the mystical tradition through Pseudo-Dionysius. It is *anagogē* or anagogy, "to uplift" or "raise higher." The mystical tradition, however, can be interpreted as being one that diminishes the relationship of anagogy and the imagination. We have argued in the first chapter that such an interpretation may not do justice to the full content of that tradition. Nonetheless, it is not the only place for the theologian to find a theology of direction. The liturgical tradition provides us with one. It is the *sursum corda*, the "lift up your hearts." It is the direction of all sacrifice, offering, and thanksgiving. It is as well a work. A liturgical aesthetics would be more precise. It is the work of the *yetzer ha'tov*, the good imagination that passionately involves the whole heart, soul, and mind into a love affair with God and neighbor.

It is indeed, here in the liturgy where the Christian theologian finds Israel's *yetzer ha'tov*. In the New Testament, the *yetzer ha'tov* takes a fresh interpretation. It becomes mixed up in the root meaning of the Greek term, the *nous*, which originally meant an inner sense directed toward an objective reality "out there."[13] One of these new terms that has its roots with the *yetzer* of Israel is the *dianoia kardias* found in the Magnificat of Luke. The heart (*kardias*) in the New Testament (as in the Hebrew Scriptures) has a rich association as the seat of feeling, thoughts and desires.[14] Moreover, in the New Testament, the imagination becomes the "eyes" of the heart. In other words, the *yetzer* of Israel takes on an even closer association with the rich theological category of the human heart as its *dianoia* or "eyes." As such, *dianoia* means more than a "beholding." It is, essentially, like the *yetzer*, a direction, a disposition of thoughts, feelings, and desires. In other words, it is a *habitus* of thought, feeling, and desire.

This is expressed clearly in the Magnificat. The *dianoia kardias* of the powerful corresponds to the *yetzer ha'ra*, the evil inclination, of rabbinic anthropology. It becomes a *habitus* of the evil imagination of the powerful that the Lord aims to reverse. In its place, a different *habitus* is to take its place. It is the *habitus* of *hupsosen tapeinos*, "lifting up the lowly," or "exalting those whose dispositions are humble." In other words, the promise of reversal of the imagination of the powerful is the good news that causes Mary's soul to be delighted. Such reversal addresses not simply the hearts of the rich and powerful but any imagination of the heart that enthrones its thoughts, desires, and feelings in a direction that points proudly and idolatrously to itself. The *yetzer ha'tov* of Israel reveals itself in the good news that delights Mary's soul to be what Jesus and the apostles called *metanoia*.

Metanoia, I believe, is the equivalent of Israel's good imagination. As such, it brings subtle complexity to Israel's *yetzer ha'tov*. It is not, for example, an imagination that beholds some utopia. Neither is it strictly a moral disposition, a disposition to do good. Nor is it merely a reversal of a previous disposition. It is more subtle than that. What makes difficult to grasp the nature of Christian *metanoia* lies in the nature of the Magnificat's sense of "lifting up the lowly." To lift up the lowly, for example, cannot mean to give a higher value to the humble than to the proud for it is the very problem of value that is addressed. In other words, the *dianoia kardias* of the powerful was evil in the values it holds up to its possessors. If *metanoia* means merely a reversal of values, then, it seems to me, there is no real *metanoia* just a change in regime.

Metanoia, I believe, refers more to a direction than a value.[15] It is, however, a "felt" direction. It is direction with a sensible component. It is, I think, anagogy understood as an experience, an aesthetic experience. As such, it is a disposition of the heart but a disposition that "feels" or senses a contrast, or rather a direction, a "higher" and a "lower." It is the disposition of the heart David so well described in Psalm 51:

> O Lord, open my lips,
> and my mouth will declare your praise.
> For you have no delight in sacrifice;
> if I were to give a burnt offering, you would not be pleased.
> The sacrifice acceptable to God is a broken spirit;
> a broken and contrite heart, O God, you will not despise.
> (Ps. 51:15–17, NRSV electronic ed.)

The sense of a "higher" and a "lower" refers to the *dianoia* of the contrite heart, or as the philosopher Josiah Royce would put it, the heart that knows a need of salvation. Let's be clear, however, about this need. It is not simply a need that finds awareness from a brokenness caused by dehumanizing humiliation. It is a need that finds itself not in chaos but within a felt direction. It is a need of salvation that senses the shape of that salvation. It is a heart taking shape in the spiritual gravitational pull of a "higher" and a "lower." It is, I think, the deeper meaning of the *Sursum Corda*. The lifting up of our hearts is the lifting up the lowly. It is the recognizing of our need of salvation in the context of a glimpse of the shape of that salvation. This is the work of the good imagination, the *yetzer ha'tov* of Israel, and the *metanoia* of Christianity.

ANAGOGICAL TRANSCENDENCE

A brief exploration of the nuances behind the tradition of the *yetzer ha'tov* and its continuation into the New Testament notion of *metanoia* took us into the deep waters of Psalm 51 and the Magnificat. These two texts circumscribe for us an answer to the question: what pleases God? The answer takes form as a heart become aware of its need of salvation, a heart whose very awareness affords a glimpse of the shape of that salvation. This form is experienced as a felt direction, a sensible experience of a higher and a lower. It is the experience of depth, a going deeper into a marvelous experience. As felt, depth is a direction that does not attribute the higher (or the lower) to any one thing or idea. It does not pit the higher against the lower. Depth, as metaphor, refers to the felt direction given human experience in the encounter with sensible Mystery. It is the felt direction of hearts, a direction shaped by theodramatic form, the experience of hearts created anew in the dramatic engagement with the risen Christ made possible through the Lord and Giver of life. It is a new creation, the thrust of a marvelous imagination that takes the human person to the threshold of creativity itself. It is the anagogical imagination.

Such a view has aesthetic implications. The sense of a higher and a lower then refers to more than a sense of value or judgment of taste. It refers specifically to a unitive process that is also revelatory. It refers to a new aesthetic form that is a new form of life, the sharing of one breath as the Body of Christ. Thus, "higher" and "lower" refer to a direction in life itself. It refers to a life lived in the depth of Mystery, a life of anagogical transcendence, a *habitus* that disposes us constantly to the *metanoia* of conversion to a new form of life. This new form of life is, by its very nature, unitive. Indeed, it is its very delight. A unitive life is a life of concrete community lived in spiritual communion. A unitive life is a life lived in anagogical transcendence, in the threshold of the human *capax Dei*, a capacity best represented by artistic creativity, a form given life in an encounter with the risen Christ inspired and guided by the Lord and Giver of life and lifted up in offering and sacrifice to the Father. Such unitive life is a communion with the risen Christ through the Holy Spirit, which together takes this living form, this new song, and lifts it up into the heart and joy of the Father.

Yet such unitive communion only has salvific sense in the form of a concrete community. But concrete community, as any who has tried to live it knows, is more ephemeral than communion. The Scriptures reveal to us the secret of real community: the contrite heart. Reaching the contrite heart, however, is no easy task. Those who have come to Christianity by such a heart know this. Yet no more powerful source of community exists than a heart that has come to know its need of salvation and found grace as the shape of that salvation. Here we come to the heart of a liturgical aesthetics, for I believe that this is one of the main goals of such an aesthetics: to reach the contrite heart so that it may be lifted up. This is, I believe, what ultimately delights the Lord: the prodigal heart that returns to the authentic source of its own loves and desires.

THE COMMUNITY OF THE BEAUTIFUL

We have opened up another element in the aesthetic axis of creativity. A theodramatics requires the element of an anagogical imagination. The anagogical imagination highlights a unitive dimension that is often ignored in a theological aesthetics. The theological dimension in a theological aesthetics is not only revelatory but also unitive. In the anagogical imagination this unitive dimension takes form as the experience of a higher and a lower. It is the experience of Mystery's depth taking shape as a new form of life, a form shaped through its awareness of a need of salvation giving a glimpse of the shape of that salvation. This unitive dimension can be characterized as anagogical transcendence into a new form of life occasioned by a living encounter with the risen Christ through the action of the Holy Spirit that together lift up our hearts into true delight of the Father.

This new form of life is a living communion in concrete community. As mentioned above, such concrete community is rare and difficult to achieve. So what can a liturgical aesthetics reveal about the secret of forming such a community? I believe it can say much. The key notion that opens up the insights of a liturgical aesthetics is the *habitus* discussed previously. The concrete community that is part of the living communion that is the Body of Christ is to be found in the *habitus* cultivated in our encounter with Christ. It is this *habitus* that becomes our ultimate aesthetic aim, the offering pleasing to God and what ultimately glorifies God. This *habitus* refers not simply to the individual but to a community. It is this community I now wish to address, the community of the beautiful.

In the previous section, we discussed the anagogical transcendence of our senses in the experience of Mystery's depth, the sense of a higher and a lower. It recast anagogy from an image of elevation to the image of depth. Anagogical transcendence, however, has a more concrete dimension: a community of praise and thanksgiving. Indeed, anagogical transcendence reveals another subtlety in the axis of creativity, a subtlety inherent in the creative, artistic act itself. Creativity can only flourish in a humble attitude toward our human creations. The practical details of making visible our praise and thanksgiving demand an attitude of what Charles Peirce called fallibility in our self-transcendent but very human attempts at pleasing God. In other words, a contrite heart not only applies to our daily lives but even in our praise and thanksgiving. The axis of creativity in a liturgical aesthetics calls for a critical and humble attitude in our efforts to please God, an attitude that is willing to modify and, even attempt new approaches in the practical implementation of Church song.

Such an attitude actually speaks to the heart of the creative process, at least the creative process understood spiritually. Creativity, too often, has been associated with artistic expression. It is the realm of artistic genius, a particularly gifted individual. While artistic creativity is indeed a gift and a highly spiritual work, a liturgical aesthetics would deny that it is absolute gift or, even, the work of a purely individual nature such as the category of genius might suggest. A liturgical aesthetics would point those who want to understand the creative process to the metaphor of depth and the category of the anagogical imagination as *metanoia*. Jacques Maritain has, I think, one of the best descriptions of this process. As he put it,

> In order that there should grow unceasingly, conforming to its law, the life of the creative spirit, it is necessary that the center of subjectivity where this creative spirit awakens to itself in suffering the things of the world and those of the soul should unceasingly be deepened. In following this line of reflection one would probably be led to ask oneself whether, beyond a certain degree of depth, this progress in spirituality can continue unless, under one form or another, a religious experience properly so called helps the soul of the poet to quit the surface levels.[16]

In any case, what I want to keep in mind here is that creation takes form at different levels within the spiritual fabric of the soul—everyone by this very fact confesses what he is. The more the poet grows, the deeper the level of creative intuition descends into the density of his soul. Where formerly he could be moved to song, he can do nothing now, he must dig down deeper. One would say that the shock of suffering and vision breaks down, one after another, the living sensitive partitions behind which his identity is hiding. He is harassed, he is tracked down, he is destroyed. Woe to him if in retiring into himself he finds a heaven devastated, inaccessible; he can do nothing then but sink into his hell. But if at the end of the ends the poet turns silent, it is not that the growth of which I speak may ever come to an end, it is not that of itself the song does not still ask to be more deeply born in him, less distant from the creative untreated spirituality, archetype of all creative life: it is that the partition of the heart has been attained, and the human substance consumed.[17]

Maritain, of course, does not speak of the anagogical imagination but I believe that his term the "creative intuition" comes close. When Maritain tells us, for example, that the creative spirit awakens "in suffering the things of the world," he is not far from describing what we call the contrite heart. What is striking in Maritain's description is the metaphor of descent rather than ascent. Maritain sees the creative process as a process of going "deeper" not "higher." Indeed, Maritain's description describes an intuition whose sensibilities are stretched to the limit but in being so stretched, it reaches the "archetype of all creative life." In other words, artistic creativity in its spiritual dimensions is more than an expression, it is also a reception. It is more than spiritual agency; it is also spiritual passion.

It is a passion, however, that humbles even as it gives life. It is an imagination of descent that, ultimately erupts in form that is full of life and, we would add, a life full of form. Indeed, Maritain describes the crucial element of artistic creativity, the humility to descend into the depths of a sensible mystery. Descent into sensible mystery means a willingness to experiment with new forms. It means a willingness to see the world anew. This element guarantees true creativity, the very stuff of living form. Living forms adapt and evolve precisely due to a creativity born out of a willingness to leave old patterns behind and discover new patterns of life. Anagogical transcendence develops the *habitus* of a critical and open attitude to the practical incorporation of our liturgy's praise and thanksgiving. Indeed, a pre-requisite toward a true sympathy for God's delight means a willingness to explore what truly pleases God.

This critical attitude of our artistic efforts to delight God gives rise to a socially binding force, a loyalty, toward a concrete community. Such loyalty is not the loyalty appropriate to a fortress in siege, the loyalty of an "us" versus "them." Rather, it is a loyalty defined by its willingness to be fallible. It is loyalty to a direction, the anagogical experience of a higher and a lower, a direction whose aim is God's delight. It is loyalty to offering a truly pleasing sacrifice. Such loyalty binds a community in the concreteness of a self-conscious fallibilism that is the mark of the truth, and goodness, and indeed the beauty of its artistry. In this sense, the concrete community itself becomes the ultimate offering, a contrite heart in social form. Indeed it becomes beautiful as God's delight. It becomes the community of the beautiful.

As such, the community of the beautiful is not merely a community that is beautiful. It is a community bound together through a loyalty to give anagogical direction to every concrete aspect of its life as community. In such endeavor, the community of the beautiful brings all of creation to participate in such a direction. It is a community whose common cause is to bring human experience to a point where human nature reveals itself by transcending its own resources in the inspired encounter with the Son of God who revealed the fullness of our humanity to ourselves. He also sought God's delight and brought creation to participate in such delight.

Indeed, He was the One whom seas and wind obey. He was the One who made water into wine, who sang psalms and danced in the Temple. He was the One who spoke of banquets and feasts, of raiments more beautiful than those of Solomon and found only in flowers. He was the One who let a broken woman anoint his feet with precious oil and mark the encounter with the sweet smell of orange scent. He was the one who brought to every encounter both pleasant and unpleasant a sense of the higher and the lower, the experience of Mystery's depth and the anagogical transcendence of human experience, the experience of the truly beautiful.

Thus the deeper meaning of the beautiful reveals itself in the very way our Lord created a concrete community. Clay pots revealed to be more precious than golden chalices. Stony hearts become living stones. Water turns to wine. Lilies-of-the-field become fashion shows and sparrows are found to be more precious than pearls. This is the work of the anagogical imagination, the artistic process of anagogical transcendence. Such transcendence works in all artistic creativity that has sympathy for and empathy of God's delight. Artistic creativity based on such an imagination provides a measure of distinction from other aspects of artistic production. It attempts the work of the good imagination, the *yetzer ha'tov* that formed Israel and the *metanoia* that John the Baptist so effectively lived. It is artistic creativity going to the very marrow of human experience in order to transcend it not by obliterating it but by revealing its very source, the human *capax Dei* that is the anagogical imagination.

Such artistic creativity shows all our creations to be fallible not in the sense of shoddy workmanship or artistic incompetence but by its very imagination, the anagogical sense of depth that makes all human creations of true beauty also a direction, a direction into the heart of Mystery. Entrance into this imagination, however, requires a contrite heart, the awareness of the need of salvation. Such a contrite heart also has a social form. It is the living form that gives the contrite heart a glimpse of the shape of that salvation, a saving communion made visible through the concrete living form that is the community of the beautiful. It is, indeed, not only the community of the beautiful but also the Glory of the Lord.

We give glory to God, then, by becoming the Glory of the Lord, a saving communion made visible through the living form of the community of the beautiful. We give glory to God by offering the contrite heart, the anagogical imagination willing to enter into the dramatic "We" of concrete community lived in the theodrama that sets the stage for the sorrows and joys of our pilgrimage to heaven. It is the gathering up of creation into the worship life itself, all creatures giving glory to God by being given anagogical direction in the self-transcendence that is human creativity, or in theological terms, the human *capax Dei*. In a liturgical aesthetics, the transcendental of the beautiful takes concrete shape. It is more than a mental abstraction. It is the community come alive in the unitive, revelatory experience of Church song. It is the community of the beautiful. It is, indeed, a Living Beauty.

NOTES

1. It was the great theologian Hans Urs von Balthasar who had the genius to recognize that the ancient theological reflection that tries to understand the relationship between divine and human freedom is best understood as a kind of drama. Our understanding of a liturgical theodrama although inspired by von Balthasar's brilliant insight also differs from it in significant ways. Von Balthasar locates the heart of this theodrama in the inner life of the Trinity. We would locate it in the Paschal Mystery. Von Balthasar locates the "action" of the drama in human acts and concerns. We would locate the "action" of the drama in all of creation. It is this difference that took us to the equally brilliant insights of the logician Charles Peirce and his interpreters, Josiah Royce and Charles Hartshorne. Through these insights, von Balthasar's theodrama gets relocated in a way that is amenable to liturgical interpretation the interlaced reality of God's creation and human hearts. Hans Urs von Balthasar, *Theo-Drama: Theological Dramatic Theory*, translated by Graham Harrison (San Francisco, Calif.: Ignatius Press, 1988–1998), 5 vols.

2. The *capax Dei* refers to our capacity as finite human beings to know and love the infinite God.

3. This claim raises issues that go back to the Church's struggle in trying to understand the relationship between faith and reason. That feeling, or more specifically loving, has been neglected in this struggle and has, in my opinion, led to that separation of theology from spirituality. I believe, like von Balthasar claims, that theologians ought to do their theology on their "knees." Cf. Hans Urs von Balthasar, "Theology and Sanctity," in *The Word Made Flesh*, vol. 1 (San Francisco, Calif.: Ignatius Press, 1989), 181–209.

4. By synoptic I mean a view of understanding that distinguishes itself from an analytic view, a view that seeks understanding by taking things apart, or a synthetic view, a view that seeks understanding by seeing things as a whole. A synoptic view, inspired by Charles Peirce's suggestion of the image of the multistranded cable in understanding, seeks understanding by seeing the parts as one, and the one in the parts. It corresponds to the most ancient view of beauty, unity-in-diversity.

5. In other words, the anagogical imagination is our attempt to understand the dramatic form in which an audience becomes one with the action on stage. The action of the liturgy then provides the basis of theodramatic form in which the assembly becomes one with the presence of the risen Christ in the Mystery of Christian worship. Such an at-one-ment serves to distinguish the dramatic nature of the

encounter. It is more than the stumbling onto a presence, symbolic, mystical, or otherwise. It is also more than an event or occasion.

6. An excellent review on this point can be found in Harold Osborne, "Revelatory Theories of Art," *The British Journal of Aesthetics* 4, no. 4 (October 1964): 332–347.

7. Note here how this has the potential to change our understanding of the way signs and symbols act in the liturgy. As most liturgists would be prepared to admit, they do more than represent. On the other hand, if signs and symbols have a dramatic dimension, they also do more than "present" or make present a spiritual reality. They also serve to unite, to make us "one" with the reality, and they do so precisely because they are not the same as the reality. In other words, a semiotic aesthetics includes the notion of aesthetic distance in signification. This allows for the unitive, revelatory experience of which the liturgy is exemplary in producing. A good discussion on the nature of aesthetic distance and its origin in Aristotle's understanding of tragedy can be found in Walter Arnold Kaufmann, *Tragedy and Philosophy* (Garden City, N.Y.: Doubleday, 1968).

8. For a fuller discussion of Abbot Suger's "Anagogical Window," in a sense the exemplar of all stained glass windows, see my discussion in the chapter "Heaven-With-us" in Alejandro Garcia-Rivera, *A Wounded Innocence: Sketches for a Theology of Art* (Collegeville, Minn.: Liturgical Press, 2003).

9. These two views of reason are taken from Roberto Unger's marvelous work on the nature of passion. See Roberto Mangabeira Unger, *Passion an Essay on Personality* (New York: Free Press Collier Macmillan, 1984), 101ff.

10. G. H. Cohen Stuart, *The Struggle in Man Between Good and Evil: An Inquiry Into the Origin of thé Rabbinic Concept of Yetzser Hara* (Kampen: J.H. Kok, 1984).

11. Richard. Kearney, *The Wake of Imagination: Ideas of Creativity in Western Culture* (London: Hutchinson, 1988), 46.

12. Martin Buber, *Good and Evil: Two Interpretations* (Upper Saddle River, N.J.: Prentice Hall, 1997), 130–131.

13. "Nous," in *Theological Dictionary of the New Testament.*, ed. Gerhard Kittel (Grand Rapids, Mich.: Eerdmans, 1964).

14. "Leb," in *Theological Dictionary of the New Testament.*, ed. Gerhard Kittel (Grand Rapids, Mich.: Eerdmans, 1964).

15. This is an insight I take from the aesthetics of Charles Peirce. Peirce noticed that aesthetic value could not be associated with an absolute value but could only be described as a "higher" or a "lower." The interested reader can consult Potter's excellent summary of Peirce's aesthetics in Vincent G. Potter, *Charles S. Peirce on Norms & Ideals* (Amherst: University of Massachusetts Press, 1967).

16. Jacques Maritain, *Creative Intuition in Art and Poetry* (New York: Pantheon Books, 1953), 105.

17. Maritain, *Creative Intuition*, 103–105.

CHAPTER 4

✛

Go in Peace . . . Then What?

Thomas Scirghi

Why do we call it the "Mass"? As mentioned previously, the liturgy does not begin with the presider's greeting, nor with the congregation's singing; rather the liturgy begins at home, with our preparation for the celebration. Likewise, it is commonly understood that the weekly practice of Christian worship does not end with the final blessing of the congregation. This is understood by most of the assembly, if only in theory rather than in practice, and despite the custom of some to dart out of the church right after receiving Communion. In one sense our worship prepares us to encounter the risen Lord in daily life, throughout the week. In this chapter we will discuss the relationship of the liturgy and justice.[1] For Christians, justice is the work performed in response to the Gospel message. This relationship is sometimes referred to as "the liturgy that does justice." In this chapter, we will look first at the meaning of the dismissal that we hear at the conclusion of each liturgy, then we will consider the relationship of liturgy and justice, a relationship that we hope to show is an intrinsic one. This relationship is witnessed on two levels: by the way in which the community members interact during worship, and through their responsibility to care for the greater society outside of the church community.

ITE MISSA EST: DISMISSAL OR MISSION?

The Mass concludes with a blessing and a dismissal. For the dismissal usually we hear a prayer such as: "May almighty God bless you, the

Father, and the Son, and the Holy Spirit. The Mass is ended, go in peace."[2] According to the *General Instruction of the Roman Missal* (GIRM), the purpose of the dismissal is "so that each may go out to do good works, praising and blessing God."[3] It is interesting to note that while the literal meaning of the dismissal is just that—a granting of permission to leave the assembly—throughout the Church's liturgical tradition meaning has unfolded creatively, suggesting more of a mission than a simple sending away.

For the dismissal, the early church used the phrase *Ite, missa est* ("Go, you are dismissed"). From the Latin word *missa* comes the English word "mass." Here, *missa* is derived from the Latin word *dimissio*, meaning "dismissal. " There is some discrepancy as to the meaning of this phrase in early Christian worship. On the one hand, some claim that it was merely an announcement of dismissal. Indeed, the meaning of *Ite, missa est* sounds somewhat similar to what we might hear today at the conclusion of a business meeting or a session of court, for example, "This meeting (or court) is adjourned," that is, the business of this gathering is suspended to a future time. During the Patristic era, this dismissal referred to the dissembling of a secular group after a public gathering. In Christian liturgy it announced the closing of the assembly. Several commentators from the Middle Ages argued that the phrase holds solely a practical meaning. For example, Amalarius, a liturgist and bishop of the early ninth century, explains: "What is *Ite, missa est* but if not 'Go home in peace'?" While some claimed that *missa* is derived from *missio*, meaning "mission," this claim appears to have no foundation.[4]

On the other hand, other early church sources indicate that the phrase may be more than a mere announcement. For example, according to Hippolytus, writing in the third century, the catechumens were sent away from the liturgy with a laying on of hands. Here, the dismissal itself becomes a religious act, a sign of the church drawing her children near with motherly affection before sending them away. Jungmann explains that it is in the very nature of the Church for its members to experience a refuge of grace and blessing. Such a refuge would have been especially significant for members of the church during this time. Christians faced persecution regularly so the way home was fraught with danger and temptation. This sign of sending forth—the laying on of hands—served to strengthen them for their journey. Eventually, by the fifth century, the word *missa* came to stand for the final blessing within the liturgy and from this developed the custom of calling every service of worship a *missa* because it included a blessing.[5] Furthermore, for Hippolytus the liturgy directs the worshiping assembly toward good works in the care of others, whether or not this direction is specifically expressed in the dismissal. In his words: "When these things have been done, then each person shall hasten to do good works and to please God and to conduct himself rightly, being zealous for the Church, doing what he has leanrt (sic) and advancing in piety."[6] Thus while the Church celebrates the liturgy, the Church is more than the liturgy as the Eucharist flows outward into the daily lives of the assembly.[7] It is a matter of finding God in all things, to use a popular notion. In this way the liturgy creates artists, artisans of a new life. Having practiced the discipline of worship, the congregation is free to discover the presence of God in daily living. Moreover, the sending forth commissions the Christians to transform the way they live so that Christ's presence may be revealed. In responding to the living Word of Jesus Christ, Christians conform their lives to the commandment that promotes harmony and equity for all people. Hence Christians are committed to a practice of justice, which is the lived expression of finding God in all things.

Recently, the meaning of the dismissal has been given a stronger connection with the Church's mission, as found in the Bishops' Synod on the Eucharist: "*Ite, missa est*. To make more explicit the relationship between Eucharist and mission . . . it is suggested that new dismissal formulas be prepared (solemn blessings, prayers over the people, or others), which underline the mission in the world of the faithful who have participated in the Eucharist."[8] Here the bishops appear to follow the lead of Pope John Paul II who recommended that "the final blessing and dismissal need to be better valued and appreciated, so that all who have shared in the Eucharist may come to a deeper sense of the responsibility entrusted to them."[9] In this brief look at the rite of dismissal, from both ancient as well as contemporary sources, we find an outward thrust to the liturgy, a clear indication that the Christian worship of God continues after the close of the service.

THREE-FOLD PURPOSE OF THE CHURCH

The relationship of liturgy and justice becomes clear when we consider the three-fold purpose of the church. In his recent encyclical, Pope Benedict XVI lists these purposes with their Greek titles: *kerygma, leitourgia,* and *diakonia*, translated as proclamation, worship, and service. It is the Church's responsibility to proclaim the good news of the risen Christ, to worship God in gratitude for creation and redemption, and to continue the salvific work of Jesus Christ in daily life. In the liturgy, the three are brought together as scripture, sacrament, and service.

We find a paradigm for this three-fold scheme in the Scripture story of the two disciples on the road to Emmaus, at the conclusion of the Gospel of Luke.[10] Recalling the story, we find the two disciples, Cleopas and an unnamed companion, walking along a road toward Jerusalem. It's later in the day of Sunday, the day Jesus rose from the tomb. As they walk, they discuss the news of the day: the rumors of Jesus' resurrection and his appearance to several women. They are confused, not knowing how to understand this fantastic report. Suddenly a stranger appears; it is Jesus but they do not recognize him. In a sorrowful tone, they recount these stories to him. When they finish speaking, Jesus interprets the scripture for them, from the prophets to the present, explaining how Christ is the fulfillment of the prophets. The two disciples then invite Jesus to join them for a meal and to spend the evening with them. At the table, Jesus is invited to pray the blessing over the meal. Following the Jewish custom, he takes a piece of bread, blesses it, breaks it, and gives it to the two men. Suddenly there is a flash of recognition by the men: in the breaking of the bread they recognize Jesus as the Christ. They then express to each other their amazement and run outside to tell the other disciples of their experience: "The Lord has truly been raised!"

The apparition on the way to Emmaus offers a paradigm for the three-part structure of the liturgy: the Word, the meal, and the dismissal.[11] At first the disciples stand sorrowfully before Jesus, in need of hearing God's word. Their expectations of Jesus as the messiah are confused. Jesus then opens the Scripture for them, as a preacher would, applying the lesson of the text to the current context. Then, at the table, Jesus breaks the bread, following the four-fold action of take, bless, break, and give. This is the same action we find first in the feeding of the five thousand and later at the Last Supper.[12] The Word of God disposes the hearers to a deeper awareness of the presence of God in their midst. As they move to the table Christ's presence is rendered clear to them through the meal, which he commanded his followers to celebrate. At this point they express an awareness that their "hearts were burning as he opened the scriptures for them." It is interesting to note the use of the word "open" (in Greek, *dianoigo*) as used here by Luke. Sometimes we find this word translated as "explain."[13] Used here, "open" means a deeper understanding of revelation.[14] Luke mentions it twice in this passage as both their eyes and hearts were opened. Early on in the Gospel, with the presentation of Jesus in the temple, we hear of such an opening, as Luke records: "Every first born male will be called holy to the Lord."[15] Again, we find in the Greek text the word *dianoigo*, as the phrase "every first born male" refers literally to "every male opening the womb."[16] The encounter at Emmaus is more than pedagogy; it is drama. As their eyes and hearts were opened the disciples are drawn into the scripture; they become part of the story. They now "see" in a new way. They have been transformed. Finally, this good news cried out to be shared. The two disciples ran from their home to tell the others. In their telling of the story and interpreting its meaning for themselves, the Christian community was born. Those who worship the risen Christ today, leave the liturgy intent upon telling the story through the spoken word and good works. The dramatic dialogue of proclamation and response continues to reveal the presence of Christ as the hearers participate in this story.

Through this activity of word and works—the *diakonia*—the Christian community continues to thrive. Before this term became associated with a specific office within the church—the "deacon"—it referred to service in a broad sense, that is, the ministry of the whole church. Traditionally this service took the form of social ministry with an emphasis for the care of the poor and of those in need. This service was seen as a continuation of the ministry of Jesus Christ. As Christ cared for the poor, and showed compassion toward those in need of healing and forgiveness, the church as the Body of Christ would manifest the presence of the Savior through its service.[17] In this way Christians strive toward building a community of justice.

THE LINK BETWEEN LITURGY AND JUSTICE

Throughout the Scriptures we find a connection between the activity of worship and the practice of justice. The Hebrew prophets as well as the apostles rail against those who practice an elaborate worship, adhering to the rules while ignoring the needs of their neighbors. Consider two of the scripture passages already discussed. We hear one such rant by the prophet Amos: "I hate, I despise your feasts, and I take no delight in your solemn assemblies. . . . But let justice roll down like waters, and righteousness like an ever-flowing stream. Alas for you who desire the day of the Lord. . . . It is darkness, not light."[18]

The biblical scholar John Donahue finds the imagery of the "flowing waters" striking. He explains that during their feasts the Israelites would pray for the flowing streams as a way to assure fertility and life to the land. By comparing justice with a flowing stream, the prophet, speaking in the name of Yahweh, warns that life will be barren without justice.[19] In this passage we also find the phrase "the day of the Lord." This is the earliest reference in the Old Testament to this phrase. "The day of the Lord" was a popular expression anticipating the victory of Yahweh over Israel's enemies; it was meant to be a day of exaltation. However, in the vision of Amos, it will be a day to be feared since it is the Day of Judgment: on that day God's own people will be destroyed. Amos condemns, not so much the ritual worship of the Israelites, but their religious formalism. Their external rites belie their interior morality and negate their worship of Yahweh.[20] In his plea for justice, Amos speaks for all the prophets. According to G. von Rad, "There is absolutely no concept in the Old Testament with

so central a significance for all relationships of human life as that of justice and righteousness."[21]

St. Paul resembles the prophet when he criticizes the Corinthians for
their manner of worship. He focuses his criticism on the divisiveness that
is clearly evident within their celebration of the Lord's Supper. So ram-
pant is their division that they really do not celebrate the Eucharist; in fact
they make a mockery of it. In Paul's words, "When you assemble as a
church, I hear that there are divisions among you. . . . When you meet together, it is not for the Lord's Supper that you eat. . . . Whoever eats the
bread or drinks the cup of the Lord in an unworthy manner will be guilty
of profaning the Lord."[22] Further, according to Paul, the rubrics were indeed followed through the use of the correct ritual words, but the division
among them and the lack of care for one another denied the reality of the
Eucharist.[23]

Jesus appears to sum up both the criticisms of Amos and Paul in his de-
nunciation of the scribes and Pharisees.[24] According to Jesus they have
taken the seat of authority and made a show of their religious practices.
Meanwhile they create burdens for the Jewish people. They do not practice what they preach. His criticism to them: "On the outside you appear
righteous, but inside you are filled with hypocrisy and evildoing." Hence
throughout the Scripture we find that the hallmark for genuine worship
is sincerity. Sincere worship consists of the praise of God and the practice
of justice for the people of God.

The lack of correspondence between what is prayed within a worship
service and what is practiced throughout the wider community calls into
question the sincerity and effectiveness of the worship. This disjunction
between what is prayed and what is practiced—between word and
deed—nullifies the *habitus*. The Pharisees had mastered a religious formalism but never developed a *habitus* for living the religious life. A sincere liturgy is marked by the genuine expression of devotion to God
through which a community is opened to God's power of transformation.
If the devotion is insincere, that is, if some attend worship merely to rat-
ify their personal beliefs, or simply to fulfill an obligation, then they will
not be transformed. We need to be clear here: while we profess that all
things are possible with almighty God, we must recognize as well our
ability, in freedom, to deny the divine gift of God's grace. While the gift is
offered, human beings may choose to either accept it or reject it.[25]

Christian worship will be judged effective by the fruit it bears amid the
greater community, and this fruit is borne through the work of justice. As
it is written, "By their fruits you will know them."[26] The notion of "producing fruit" is an important one for the dynamic of liturgy. Christian
worship may be judged effective by the fruit it bears amid the greater
community. While this is an ancient notion, something was lost during

the Middle Ages, yet revived later with the liturgical reform movement of the twentieth century, and elaborated upon at the Second Vatican Council.[27] However, it is interesting to note that in the Council's document "The Constitution on the Sacred Liturgy," there is no specific mention of "justice." Nevertheless there is a clear connection between the community's worship and the fruit to be borne from it, namely that what the congregation has received by faith and sacrament in the celebration of the Eucharist should effect their way of life. Strengthened by the "heavenly food," they should live joyfully and gratefully, eager to perform good works.[28]

This notion of "fruitfulness" shifted the Church's concern with liturgy from a legal mind set to a vocational view. With the development of a universal liturgy during the Middle Ages the emphasis fell upon the rubrics with a scrutiny that they should be carried out correctly. The principle of *ex opere operato* ("by the work worked") ensured that so long as the ritual was celebrated properly, that is, that the rubrics were followed carefully, and despite the disposition of the minister, the sacrament would prove effective; God's grace would be conveyed. Through the more recent emphasis on "fruitfulness" the Church does not deny the principle of *ex opere operato*, but sees it as a minimum condition, as one of validity rather than productivity.[29] Returning to our metaphor of the gift, we could think of *ex opere operato* as a principle that is concerned with the conveyance of the gift, that by following the prescribed procedure we know the gift was received properly. But fruitfulness is concerned with how the gift will be used. It is concerned with the transforming effect that the sacrament has on the recipient and the shape it takes within the community. It asks "what will the community make of this gift?" And this gift is Christ's memory as a way of life.

How the community will make use of the gift points us in two directions. Christians are directed outward as they are called to share the gift with those around them in need. They are also directed inward, so that they will be re-oriented along the path of faith. Moving outward, we find an intrinsic link between the community's worship and its good works. This intrinsic link could be called the *lex agendi*. Earlier we described the relationship of the activity of the Church's worship and the content of the Church's faith in terms of the ancient principle coined by Prosper of Aquitaine, *ut legem credendi lex statuat supplicandi*, or the shorthand version, *lex orandi, lex credendi*. For our discussion here we could add a third component—*lex agendi*: the rule of doing or acting—to indicate a necessary link of faith, prayer, and action.[30]

Writing in the second century, Justin Martyr declared that the meal and the offering associated with it were also for the orphans and the widows, that is, "Those who are needy because of sickness or other causes, and the captives, and the strangers, who sojourn among us."[31] Justin's description of the liturgy shows that the connecting link between worship and works is found in the liturgy itself. For this community the liturgy did not merely conjure up an ethereal unity beyond themselves, as if it were some spiritual entity to which they aspired. For them the weekly celebration of the Lord's Supper extended their family meal to include the entire church.[32] The first Christians brought with them to the table both food and the needs of the community. The bread and wine for the meal were prepared at home and carried to the place of worship. Some of it would have been used for their Eucharist and the rest was to be distributed throughout the community. They also carried with them the needs of the community and voiced them during the intercessory prayers: prayers for the sick and the dead, the physically weak, and the socially vulnerable. To be sure, their concern was not so much out of pity but more from an awareness of the dignity of each person. An authentic celebration of the Eucharist helped to deepen their awareness of the value of each person for the Creator.[33] Also, this act of compassion contributed to their conversion as they came to recognize Christ in those who were suffering. This practical concern was a response to Jesus' command "By this all will know that you are my disciples, if you have love for one another."[34] The celebration of the Eucharist, then, becomes a unitive revelatory experience.

This deeper awareness brings us to the second direction, the inward movement: the Eucharistic worship helped to re-orient the members of the community. This is to say that genuine worship of Jesus Christ served to re-direct them by which they recognized their existence before God; a wondrous creation yet tainted by sin, turned away from God in freedom. Although a Christian may boast with the psalmist, "I praise you, so wonderfully you made me!" (Psalm 139:14), there are days when he must lament along with the psalmist, "But I am a worm, hardly human, scorned by everyone, despised by the people" (Psalm 22:7). Through the worship of Jesus Christ, the Holy Spirit turns the faithful away from sin and despair, toward salvation and renewed hope. This re-orientation is demonstrated in the ritual of baptism as practiced by the Eastern Orthodox, in a movement referred to as the *apotaxis* and *syntaxis*. According to this rite, the candidate for baptism turns toward the west for the renunciation (*apotaxis*) of a worldly life. This renunciation is expressed in the form of questions and answers. Then the candidate turns toward the east (or "orient," hence the term "orientation") for the acceptance (*syntaxis*) of Jesus Christ. This acceptance is expressed through the recitation of the Creed of Nicea and Constantinople.[35] The Roman Catholic Rite of Baptism expresses this orientation through first the renunciation of sin, then the profession of faith, all in a question and answer format, immediately preceding the immersion of the candidate.[36]

In light of the relationship of liturgy and justice we realize that the orientation of the liturgy is toward building up the kingdom of God. It enables the worshiping body to perceive the world in a new way. As the bread and wine are transformed into the Body and Blood of Jesus Christ, we come to recognize the sacredness of all reality, that all creation is, according to the poet Gerard Manley Hopkins, "charged with the grandeur of God," that is, that all creation is a gift waiting to be used in the service of God. Walter Cardinal Kasper refers to this new perception as the "universal cosmic dimension of the Eucharist." In his words, "The bread and wine are the gift of creation and the fruit of human work; when they are brought into the Eucharistic event, the eschatological transformation of all reality is in a certain sense accomplished in them even now. . . . (T)he heavenly world penetrates our world and is present when the Eucharist is celebrated."[37]

LITURGY AND JUSTICE: AN AESTHETIC APPRECIATION

Within the context of aesthetics, *diakonia* can be thought of as a creative act, a work-in-progress, constructing the community. The service of God that comes as a response to the proclaimed Word and the sacramental meal is more than an obligation performed under fear of a penalty. Rather, *diakonia* becomes a form of expression through which the modern-day disciples realize the presence of Christ in their midst and understand the meaning of Christian discipleship.

Note that this creative act is not merely a form of self-expression, but an expression of the Body of Christ. This is to say that the just actions of the community members give expression to the faith of the community, as they are rooted in the teaching and work of Jesus Christ. He provides the model for *diakonia* and this service finds new expression throughout the multi-faceted context of Christianity.

When service deteriorates into self-expression, we no longer build a Christian community, but a golden calf. It is interesting to note that the molding of the golden calf of the Exodus story was done as an act of faith to bring the Israelites closer to God. We read this story in the thirty-second chapter of the Book of Exodus. At this particular point in their journey from slavery in Egypt to freedom in the Promised Land, the Israelites had reached Mt. Sinai where they would receive the Ten Commandments. Here the covenant between Israel and God would be ratified and the nation of Israel established. But before this would happen, Moses left his people to climb the mountain in order to stand in the presence of God. His long absence worried the Israelites. Out of fear they went to Aaron, Moses' brother, and he instructed them to give over their jewelry, which he melted and molded into the form of a golden calf. This statue was intended to be a symbol of Yahweh. Presenting it to the people, Aaron cried out, "This is your God, O Israel, who brought you out of the land of Egypt. Tomorrow is a feast of the Lord," and the Israelites enjoyed a day of revelry. The calf, which was actually a young bull, symbolized strength, leadership, and fertility. It served as a symbol for several deities and was found throughout the ancient Near East.[38] Here such cultic objects were used to bring people into the presence of a divine being so as to focus attention on their god. This in itself may be helpful, actually, for promoting one's relationship with God. A problem occurs for the Israelites when such objects were used to manipulate the will of Yahweh. The Commandments made clear that the Israelites were to shun idols and graven images. The Commandments also regulate their behavior to one another. The juxtaposition of these two regulations suggests that the Israelites' understanding of Yahweh was not to be found in a hand-made image but in the way they lived within their community. The prohibition of idolatry was joined with the command for living a life of justice.[39]

The molding of the calf was not intended to be a defiant act but an act of devotion. The problem came, not so much from infidelity, but misdirection. As we hear when God speaks to Moses: "They have turned aside from the way I pointed out to them, making for themselves a molten calf and worshiping it, sacrificing to it and crying out 'This is your God, O Israel, who brought you out of the land of Egypt.'"[40] The problem is that Aaron's act of worship was not inspired by God; rather it was of his own making. The genuine ways of worship are revealed to human beings rather than invented by them. The prophets make clear that they speak in the name of God and not in their own name; King David listened attentively to the Lord's instructions concerning the construction of the ark of the covenant. In the New Testament the evangelists were inspired in their writings of the Scriptures. Jesus Christ commanded that his disciples remember him through the breaking of the bread. Also he promised that he would be revealed to them through their care of one another.[41] For Christians sincere worship follows the commandments and the example of Jesus Christ. By following the example of Jesus Christ they imitate him and become one with him. The worship which responds to the Lord's command provides a unitive revelatory experience.

Sincere worship relies upon the intermingling of the three duties of the Church: proclamation, worship, and service. Taken individually these duties may be reduced to self-serving activities. For example, reading or hearing the Scripture alone, without the proper response in praise of God or in works of justice, may reduce a living faith to fundamentalism. When the worship celebration is separated from its scriptural roots it risks being tied to a medieval format or drifting into the avant-garde.

And when justice loses its moorings from the Church, it becomes social action rather than an act of discipleship. Mariane Sawicki illustrates clearly the relationships of these three duties. She refers to them as "three tables," that is, the table of the Gospel narratives, of worship, and of solidarity with the poor.

We have, then, three tables . . . and we must become adept at all three. The table of the Gospel narratives teaches us to retain and process factual information about who Jesus was. That skill was essential for recognizing him. But if we learn no other skill, then we imagine Jesus as someone from the past, dead and gone now although nostalgically remembered. We will miss seeing Jesus in the present because we will think of him as only a historical figure. The table of worship equips us to taste the volatility of the power of the spirit flowing through a community at prayer. That skill too is essential for recognizing Jesus, but it is not sufficient in itself. If all we can do is pray, we will start seeing Jesus everywhere, and we will hear him saying whatever we like. The table of solidarity with the poor trains us in the literacy of hunger. When that competence is added to charismatic sensitivity and factual recall, then we begin to approximate a receptivity to what the gospel traditions intend by the phrase "seeing Jesus."[42]

For Sawicki, the unity of the three tables provides us with the competence we need to recognize the Lord. In her words, "To meet the Lord at the table, you have to know how to behave."[43] The three duties taken together prescribe that behavior.

CONCLUSION

From this discussion we see that the rite of dismissal is more of a charge than merely a conclusion. It is the necessary response to the proclamation of the Scripture that enlivens the Word of God. It is the response, as well, to the recognition of Christ in the breaking of the bread and the sharing of the cup. The Judeo-Christian tradition proclaims the necessity of living justly, for this is how the faithful will know the presence of God. We come to worship in order to deepen our awareness of Christ in our midst. When Jesus proclaimed the Kingdom of God he displayed the effects of this Kingdom in the ordinary events of life, especially through his teaching, healing, and forgiving. He demonstrated the power of God acting in the world. He confronted the powers of the world by living for the poor and the oppressed. The Son of God is present in the least of humanity. To fulfill the law of Christ, then, Christians are called to live in justice, that is, to live faithfully to the demands of their relationship with all the people of God.

The liturgy cultivates our ability to recognize the living Lord, not only in the church's ritual and in the confines of this sacred space but also in the world, and to help others come to recognize him as well. We do not bow before a golden calf, a container for the divine. Instead we stand before God, in gratitude and service, opening ourselves to discovering the divine in those we are called to serve.

Once again, we must take care not to turn the gift into a commodity. The golden calf was an attempt to turn the gift of God's presence into a manageable form that could be manipulated by the Israelites. So too, Christians can fashion those they serve into a commodity, forsaking the gift of the divine presence and treating the needy as a problem. Citing Sawicki once more, she warns that we may turn the table of charity into a commodity when we regard the poor as a problem to be solved by applying our surplus goods or time as a remedy. In doing so we fail to see how "they are flesh of our flesh, transubstantiated now into the Body of Christ, indispensable to the possibility of our ever looking Jesus in the face."[44]

Hence the necessity of living justly poses an obligation to the faithful, but this obligation is imposed from within rather than from without. It is the obligation that comes from a vocation, something like the drive to achieve one's own desire. It is similar to a situation in which two people, who are very much in love and devoted to each other, realize the need to make sacrifices for each other for the sake of a harmonious life. Their obligation to one another emanates from their vocation to live as one. From this perspective we may appreciate that such an obligation is personal rather than institutional. By this we mean that the obligation is necessary to develop an inter-personal relationship rather than following the dictates of an authority for the sake of being a member-in-good-standing of an organization, the way one is obliged to pay dues or attend regular meetings to maintain one's membership. This obligation is personal because it follows from one's own vocation, in this case, to become a true disciple of Jesus Christ.

Through living out their lives in the practice of justice, following the example of the Lord, Christians continue to respond to Christ and recognize him in their daily existence. Given the tools of the trade by the Church, Christians set out to fashion a world in which Christ is recognized. The social setting of the community becomes a workshop for the disciples. In this way *diakonia* is a creative work, nourished and guided by the liturgy.

NOTES

1. For an explanation of what we mean by "justice" we can turn to the *Catechism of the Catholic Church*: Justice is the moral virtue by which we render what is due

to God and to our neighbor. Justice toward other people disposes a person to respect the rights of others and to establish in human relationships the harmony that promotes equity with regard to persons and to the common good (No. 1807).

2. Other formulas for the dismissal read: "Go in the peace of Christ," and "Go in peace to love and serve the Lord." In all cases the response of the assembly is "Thanks be to God." Cf. *Sacramentary*, p. 567. GIRM no. 168.

3. GIRM no. 90.

4. Marcel Metzger, "A Eucharistic Mission," in *Handbook for Liturgical Studies*, ed. Anscar J. Chupungco, O.SB, vol. III, *The Eucharist* (Collegeville, Minn.: Liturgical Press, 1997), 3. Metzger cites others on this issue; for example, Florus of Lyons, following Isidore of Seville, states: "The word *missa* has to be understood as nothing else than the dismissal, that is, the dissolution [of the assembly] which, at the completion of all parts of the celebration, the deacon pronounces as the people is dismissed from the solemn rites just observed." Also, Honorius of Autun, of the twelfth century, states: "*Ite, missa est* is the permission to leave" or "the meeting is adjourned."

5. Josef A. Jungmann, *The Mass of the Roman Rite: Its Origins and Development (Missarum Sollemnia)*, 2 vols. (Westminster, Md.: Christian Classics, 1986), vol. 1:173–174, vol. 2:433.

6. Christopher S. Weakly, "'Go to Love and Serve': The Concluding Rite (the Sending) of the Eucharist Ecumenically Observed" Thesis S.T.L., Jesuit School of Theology at Berkeley, 1999, 42.

7. John Francis Baldovin, S J, *Bread of Life, Cup of Salvation: Understanding the Mass* (Lanham, Md.: Rowman & Littlefield, 2003), 149.

8. Zenit News Agency, *Propositions of the Synod of the Eucharist*. October 31, 2005, http://www.zenit.org/english/visualizza.phtml?sid=79161.

9. John Paul II, *Dies Domini*, Apostolic Letter, Keeping the Lord's Day (1998), no. 45. Cf. Weakly, "Go to Love and Serve," 5.

10. Luke 24:13–35.

11. By way of clarification, the current liturgy includes a rite of entrance, a rite that was added during the fourth century. However, for the early church's worship, the entrance was rather simple. In some of the early descriptions of liturgical practices, the gathering is but briefly mentioned, moving immediately to the letters of the apostles and the writings of the prophets. Cf. Justin Martyr, "First Apology," 67.1, in Ronald Claud Dudley. Jasper and G. J. Cuming, *Prayers of the Eucharist Early and Reformed*, 3d ed. (Collegeville, Minn.: Liturgical Press, 1990), 29.

12. Luke Timothy Johnson and Daniel J. Harrington, *The Gospel of Luke*, Sacra Pagina, vol. 3 (Collegeville, Minn.: Liturgical Press, 1991), 396–399.

13. See, for example, the *Jerusalem Bible*: "Did not our hearts burn within us as he talked to us on the road and explained the scriptures to us?"

14. Carroll Stuhlmueller, CP, "The Gospel According to Luke," in *The Jerome Biblical Commentary*, ed. Raymond Edward Brown, Joseph A. Fitzmyer, and Roland Edmund Murphy (Englewood Cliffs, N.J.: Prentice-Hall, 1968), 177:29.

15. Luke 2:23.

16. Johnson and Harrington, *The Gospel of Luke*, 54.

17. Susan K. Wood, *Sacramental Orders*, Lex Orandi Series (Collegeville, Minn.: Liturgical Press, 2000), 144. See also, Donald K. McKim, *Westminster Dictionary of*

Theological Terms, 1st ed. (Louisville, Ky.: Westminster John Knox Press, 1996), 71, 76.

18. Amos 5:21–24. See also Hosea 6:6 and Isaiah 1:10–17.

19. John Donahue, SJ, "Biblical Perspectives on Justice," in *The Faith That Does Justice: Examining the Christian Sources for Social Change*, ed. John C. Haughey (New York: Paulist Press, 1977), 75.

20. P. J. King, "Amos," in *The Jerome Biblical Commentary*, ed. Raymond Edward Brown, Joseph A. Fitzmyer, and Roland Edmund Murphy (Englewood Cliffs, N.J.: Prentice-Hall, 1968), 250; John Barton, "Amos," in *The New Interpreter's Study Bible* (Nashville, Tenn.: Abingdon Press, 2003); Donahue, "Biblical Perspectives on Justice," 69.

21. G. von Rad as cited in Donahue, "Biblical Perspectives on Justice," 68.

22. 1 Corinthians 11:17–33.

23. Jerome Murphy-O'Connor, "The First Letter to the Corinthians," in *The New Jerome Biblical Commentary*, ed. Raymond Edward Brown, Joseph A. Fitzmyer, and Roland Edmund Murphy (Englewood Cliffs, N.J.: Prentice-Hall, 1990), 809.

24. Matthew 23:1–36. See also Mark 12:38–40 and Luke 11:37–52.

25. Geoffrey Wainwright, *Doxology the Praise of God in Worship, Doctrine, and Life: A Systematic Theology* (New York: Oxford University Press, 1980), 399–403.

26. Matthew 7:16.

27. L. Edward Phillips, "Ethics and Worship," in *The New Westminster Dictionary of Liturgy and Worship*, ed. Paul F. Bradshaw (Louisville, Ky.: Westminster John Knox Press, 2002), 167.

28. "Instruction on the Worship of the Eucharistic Mystery," in *Vatican Council II: More Postconciliar Documents*, ed. Austin Flannery, OP (Collegeville, Minn.: Liturgical Press, 1982), no. 13.

29. According to the "Constitution on the Sacred Liturgy" (no. 11), when the liturgy is celebrated more is required than the mere observance of the laws governing valid and licit celebration. The faithful should take part knowingly, actively, and fruitfully. Walter M. Abbott, SJ, *The Documents of Vatican II* (New York: Herder and Herder Association Press, 1966).

30. Teresa Berger, "Lex Orandi—Lex Credendi—Lex Agendi: Auf dem Weg zu einer Okumenisch Konsensfahigen Verhaltnisbestimmung von Liturgie, Theologie, Ethik," *Archiv Fur Liturgiewissenschaft* 27 (1985): 425–432. See also Kevin Irwin on *"lex vivendi*: The rule of living," in Kevin W. Irwin, *Models of the Eucharist* (New York: Paulist Press, 2005), 30.

31. Justin Martyr, *Apology*, chapter 65. Cf. Don Saliers, "Afterword: Liturgy and Ethics Revisited," in E. Byron Anderson and Bruce T. Morrill, *Liturgy and the Moral Self Humanity at Full Stretch Before God: Essays in Honor of Don E. Saliers* (Collegeville, Minn.: Liturgical Press, 1998), 221.

32. Rafael Avila P., *Worship and Politics* (Maryknoll, N.Y.: Orbis Books, 1981), 100. See also Phillips, "Ethics and Worship," 168; and Bernd Wannenwetsch, *Political Worship Ethics for Christian Citizens*, translated by Margaret Kohl, Oxford Studies in Theological Ethics (Oxford: Oxford University Press, 2004), 79.

33. Bishop Roger Mahony, "The Eucharist and Social Justice," *Worship* 57 (1983): 52–61.

34. John 13:35.

35. Stefano Parenti, "Christian Initiation in the East," in *Handbook for Liturgical Studies*, ed. Anscar J. Chupungco, OSB, vol. 4, *Sacraments and Sacramentals* (Collegeville, Minn.: Liturgical Press, 2000), 5 vols., 35. See also Joseph Ratzinger, *The Spirit of the Liturgy* (San Francisco, Calif.: Ignatius Press, 2000), 68.

36. Rite of Christian Initiation, nn. 217, 219. *The Rites*, op. cit., pp. 98–100.

37. Walter Cardinal Kasper, *Sacrament of Unity the Eucharist and the Church* (New York: Crossroad Publications, 2004), 127.

38. William H. Propp, "Golden Calf," in *The Oxford Companion to the Bible*, ed. Bruce Manning Metzger and Michael David Coogan (New York: Oxford University Press, 2003), 257. See also, *The New Interpreter's Study Bible New Revised Standard Version with the Apocrypha* (Nashville, Tenn.: Abingdon Press, 2003), 131.

39. Douglas A. Knight, "Idols, Idolatry," in *The Oxford Companion to the Bible*, ed. Bruce Manning Metzger and Michael David Coogan (New York: Oxford University Press, 2003), 298.

40. Exodus 32:8.

41. Matthew 25.

42. Marianne Sawicki, *Seeing the Lord: Resurrection and Early Christian Practices* (Minneapolis, Minn.: Fortress Press, 1994), 297. For a fine summary of Sawicki's discussion, see Nathan Mitchell, "Present in the Sacraments," *Worship* 80, no. 4 (July 2006): 351.

43. Sawicki, *Seeing the Lord*, 298.

44. Sawicki, *Seeing the Lord*, 297.

✝

Do This in Memory of Me

Alejandro Garcia-Rivera

A liturgical aesthetics, as we have seen, leads a community to a *habitus* of holiness. Such a *habitus* takes shape and form through the three aesthetic axes of order, intensity, and creativity. Inasmuch as these axes define the aesthetics of Church Song, it behooves us to note an important but often neglected dimension of such aesthetics. There is a dark side to Church Song. It is implicit in the question asked in the previous chapter: whence praise? This question can only arise in a context where the possibility of despair is real enough to make praise itself a question even as it is a wonder.

In our discussion of Church Song, we concentrated only on its wondrous dimension, the dimension of praise and thanksgiving. This wondrous dimension has its roots in the *Una Voce Dicentes* that reveals a marvelous life-giving communion. Not all who come to worship, however, experience such communion. Church Song, after all, is based on Human Song and the human person who comes to sing and take part in the liturgy is, at times, someone who has felt alone and isolated, even forsaken. In other words, a liturgical aesthetics must not only give an account of praise. It must also account for lament.

LAMENT

There are many instances of lament in the Bible. Perhaps the most significant of these for a liturgical aesthetics occurs in the book of Genesis. The well-known story of Cain and Abel is, in a sense, a story about the role of lament and the nature of worship. The story revolves around the difference in quality of worship between Cain and his brother. In the contrast between Cain and Abel, the Scriptures also contrast two different views on worship. Indeed, God favors the worship offered by Abel over the one offered by Cain. We are not told, however, why. We are not told what makes one's offering more pleasant to the Lord than another. We can note the contrast between shepherd Abel and farmer Cain and wonder if, in this contrast, lies the reason for God's favoring Abel's offering over Cain's. In the final analysis, the best explanation for God's favor has to do with the interior attitude or the spirit in which the offerings were given. What is this interior attitude? The story, as it develops, gives us an idea.

> Cain said to his brother Abel, "Let us go out to the field." And when they were in the field, Cain rose up against his brother Abel, and killed him. Then the Lord said to Cain, "Where is your brother Abel?" He said, "I do not know; am I my brother's keeper?" And the Lord said, "What have you done? Listen; your brother's blood is crying out to me from the ground!" (NRSV, Gen. 4:8–10)

Cain, jealous of Abel, murders him. God seeks out Cain and confronts him: "Where is your brother Abel?" Cain's response to the Lord suggests something profound about a proper attitude in worship: "Am I my brother's keeper?" Was God's distaste of Cain's offering due to its irrelevance to Abel's life and well-being? Did Cain offer God the first-fruits of his hard-won toil with no thought of sharing it with his brother Abel? While somewhat speculative, these questions appear to hit the mark in God's subsequent accusation: "Listen; your brother's blood is crying out to me from the ground!"

God not only hears our praise; God also hears the cries of injustice. God not only hears praise and thanksgiving; God also hears the cries of protest and supplication. The story of Cain and Abel, as I see it, has powerful implications for liturgy. Worship ought to encompass what happens outside of worship because God, in the language of Isaiah, hears the cries of the poor. Worship entails not only that offered in life-giving community but also those cries uttered in life-taking isolation. God, in the language of Isaiah, hears the cries of the poor. More important, God, in hearing the cry of the blood of Abel, reveals a further depth in this sad and tragic story. Blood, the biblical equivalent of the human soul, that which represents the essence of human life and identity, is that which cries out to God in supplication and outrage. Such cry defines an aesthetic, perhaps deeper understanding of justice.

For what is protested is the loss of life or, rather, the joy of such life. Indeed, injustice has a profound connection to sorrow. Like sorrow, injustice involves a loss of joy in living life itself. Injustice's sorrow, the loss of joy in life, circumscribes what may be a deeper understanding of injustice. The category of joy founds an understanding of justice. An aesthetic understanding suggests justice is not to be seen solely in terms of social categories or noble principles or, even, noble causes. Justice has aesthetic roots. It cannot be understood solely in terms of what is right or wrong or even, what is deserved, but in the joy and delight of a life lived in justice with other lives. Moreover, justice, seen from an aesthetics perspective, is sacred. It is a gift given by God that no one has the right to diminish or take away. Justice, in other words, reveals its depths in a sacred joie de vivre. It is the proper condition for the human *habitus*. It is the sine qua non of Human Song.

Many, however, fail to notice the aesthetic underpinnings and its liturgical significance that justice demands. In the case of Cain and Abel, for example, it is reasonable to see in Cain's jealousy and wickedness something powerful at work in our humanity. Nonetheless, to see in Abel's murder only Cain's wickedness is to miss what is perhaps the most essential revelation about what is truly human: our ability to know what is just. What ought to make us wonder is our response to Cain's wickedness not the wickedness itself. For in our response, our recognition of the injustice done to Abel, lies a marvelous ability to know justice as God knows it and to respond as God responds. We too are shocked by the brutality and injustice of Cain's murderous acts. This is the perspective of justice. The ability to know justice is the ability to see human acts from the perspective of heaven. It is the ability to have a bird's-eye view of our humanity. It is a wondrous and, essentially, aesthetic divine gift to the human creature.

There is a corresponding ability to the bird's-eye view that justice demands. It is the ability to be moved by what one sees and hears. Our hearts are also moved by the cry (and sight) of Abel's blood. What is seen from heaven moves us on earth. Our bird's-eye view from heaven is one with our ground-based experience on earth. It is this double ability, to see as God sees and to experience what another feels, that allows us to address God out of the experience of suffering and injustice.[1] Indeed, it is the ability to lament suffering and injustice that is most human, not our ability to inflict it.[2]

The implications for a liturgical aesthetics are significant. There is a deep connection between lament and praise. Lament protests the loss of joy and delight of life that makes possible praise and thanksgiving. Indeed, there must be room for lament in the liturgy in order that there may be praise. This means that liturgy must somehow encompass not only what happens within the sanctuary but also the life and diminishment of that life that occur outside the church's walls. It is for this reason, that the *ordo* of the liturgical rites cannot be seen as an end in themselves but must be oriented to the wider action that takes place in the world. The liturgy's action, if it is to include lament in its work of praise, must somehow encompass the world's action. This introduces a tragic element into the liturgy, the tragic story of Cain and Abel as played throughout the world every day and every hour.

But the liturgy is not a tragedy and here is where lament reveals a deeper dimension of a liturgical aesthetics. A liturgical aesthetics sees lament as intrinsic to the labor of gratitude that is the work of the liturgical action. Such lament enters the liturgy by encompassing the world's action within the liturgical action itself. But how can the tragic dimension in the world's existence that enters into the liturgy through lament not destroy the labor of praise and thanksgiving that is the liturgy? Here lies the heart of the Mystery of Christian Worship. For liturgy's structure, as revealed by its aesthetics, appears to be torn asunder by two opposing forces.

On the one hand, the liturgy must embrace the world's suffering, its lament, the tragic dimension of lives diminished by injustice and suffering. The liturgy must give voice to such cries as come out of the loss of joy and delight in the living of life itself. On the other hand, the liturgy must finish its sacred work, the fashioning of a new human *habitus*, a holy work of praise and thanksgiving. These two appear to be at odds with one another. Can the cries of injustice avoid becoming cries of revenge? Can the sorrows of tragic sufferings avoid despair? More important, can the work of praise and thanksgiving be based on lament? Can praise emerge from lament without destroying the integrity of such lament? Can the tragedy of lament become a comedy of praise? Only one artistic form can rise up to the challenge such difficult questions raise: drama.

THE TRAGIC SENSE OF LIFE

There is a tragic sense to life. At least, many have observed and commented on this sense for centuries. The Spanish philosopher Miguel de Unamuno has reflected deeply on it. In his classic book *The Tragic Sense of Life*, Unamuno insightfully describes this sense:

> Yes, perhaps, as the Sage says, "nothing worth proving can be proven, nor yet disproven"; but can we restrain that instinct which urges man to wish to know, and above all to wish to know the things which may conduce to life, to eternal life? Eternal life, not eternal knowledge, as the Alexandrian gnostic [St. Clement] said. For living is one thing and knowing is another; and, as we shall see, perhaps there is such an opposition between the two that we may say that everything vital is anti-rational, and that everything rational is anti-vital. And this is the basis of the tragic sense of life.[3]

Unamuno, I believe, puts his finger on what may be called an aesthetic insight into the nature of human suffering. This insight may be found in attempting to answer the following question: "How do I know that I suffer?" The question may seem trivial at first glance. "It is self-evident," might be our first response. Yet with further reflection, one becomes aware how profound a question it really is. For, one thing is sure, we all are aware that we suffer. And, another thing is sure. None of us can really explain how we became aware of it. In between these two certainties lies the profundity that points to the nature of knowing our own suffering. If suffering is common to all, then what serves as the contrast that alerts us that suffering is more than a status quo, a condition taken for granted? Indeed, what gives us the sense that suffering is not the way life was meant to be? How do we know that suffering is alien to our humanity, that it diminishes it?

The story of Cain and Abel only points to an answer, it does not explain why we are aware of our own suffering. The answer, let me suggest, can best be answered from an aesthetics perspective. There is no life so free of suffering that we can use as a contrast to our own life and thus make the logical comparison that reveals our suffering to ourselves. Something else informs this strange knowing. Such knowing cannot be understood in a purely epistemological sense. Such knowing is more than a logical comparison between an ideal life and a broken one.[4] An alternate to such idealized contrast, there is aesthetic grasp of the whole in the many that moves the human heart to deep empathy for the human condition. We sense in the fragmented, broken experiences of our life, a possible unity, a marvelous continuity of life which, as such, is profoundly beautiful. It is not the unity of a completed syllogism but the potential unity of a life now broken yet continuing into a work of beauty. As such, this sense, the sense of a brokenness yet to be unified, is not yet tragic, at least, in the sense that Unamuno means. What makes it tragic begins with the realization that a life meant to be a work of beauty depends on the actions taken in gathering the broken shards of our life and shaping it into a beautiful unity. The tragic becomes clear with the realization that such shaping depends on a kind of knowing that must come from a depth that is beyond the individual self. We were made for eternal life but such life depends in our being able to know what makes for a beautiful whole of a life not only as individuals but as a community.

The story of Cain and Abel can be thought as a story that reveals this tragic sense. What was it that Abel knew that made his offering pleasing to the Lord? Conversely, what did Cain fail to understand? Was the secret of God's pleasure with Abel's offering that his offering included thanksgiving for Cain's life as well? In contrast, was Cain's offering disjointed from Abel's life? Was God's displeasure with Cain's offering that it did

not offer a share of its blessings to Abel? The story, of course, does not answer these questions but it does suggest Unamuno's tragic sense of life. If
eternal life is a life shared with others in union with God's own life, then
Abel's death reveals the fissure that separates what was meant to be from
what is. It is a fissure arising from the difference between the kind of
knowing that takes us communally into a true sharing in the life of God,
and one that does not. It is a fissure born in the disjointing our knowing
from our living. It is the difference between a selfish knowing and a living shared. In this fissure lies the tragic sense of life and, if I may boldly
suggest, the heart of a liturgical aesthetics.

What is this heart? It is, I believe, what Rosemary Haughton called the
"drama of salvation," what Hans Urs von Balthasar called the "Theo-
Drama," and what we call a "theodramatics."

DRAMA, THEO-DRAMA, AND THEODRAMATICS

The tragic sense of life does not necessarily suggest that life is a tragedy.
Nonetheless, it calls attention to the dramatic character contained in the
experience of suffering itself. If I may fault many recent theologies, it is
the lack of taking into account the dramatic dimension inherent in all human suffering. Such theologies emphasize the victimization due to injustice and ignore the tragic loss of innocence that is also one more bitter fruit
of injustice. In emphasizing victimization without a corresponding treatment of the tragic, such theologies can easily cross into a shallow moralism that is an inadequate understanding of justice. For such moralism effectively disengages a concern for justice from the dynamics of salvation.
Only by taking account of the dramatic, can a theology of justice truly account for the dynamics of salvation. Rosemary Haughton, in her book *The
Drama of Salvation*, puts it eloquently:

> [The dramatic ways salvation is depicted in the Scriptures] is not accidental,
> this is how it has to be, for neither abstract doctrine nor historical figures nor
> allegorical personifications are sufficient to explain the nature of the trans-
> formation that is offered. Only the combination of history and symbol and
> myth and personal experience, presented in a form that the mind can take
> hold of but never exhaust or fully comprehend, will do the job. And that is
> drama. The talk of the drama of salvation, or salvation history as a play, is
> not a mere metaphor; it is about as accurate a description as it is possible to
> give of the way in which the real availability of salvation is made known, and
> its character explained to human minds.[5]

What Haughton so succinctly points out to the theologian is that addressing the world's suffering must make possible not only the need of

salvation but also a real sense of its availability and character. This was liberation theology's marvelous and enduring insight, *orthodoxy*, right knowing, is one with *orthopraxis*, right action.[6] So what happened to it? What happened to the passion for justice that marked the emergence of liberation theology in the sixties and continued through the eighties?

Many would say that the world has shifted to a more conservative perspective. I would disagree. The world may have, indeed, shifted to a more conservative stance but I believe there are deeper reasons for the demise of the passion for justice in theology. The Latin American theological insight on justice became quickly diminished when its fundamental aesthetic character turned moralistic. Liberation theology rightly saw that *theoria* and *praxis* could not be seen as independent of one another. *Theoria* followed upon *praxis*. This suggested an ecclesial dimension of justice: *orthopraxis*. The Church is concerned not only with *orthodoxy*, right knowing, but also with *orthopraxis*, right action. Indeed our understanding of salvation encompasses these two dimensions.[7]

For some of us, this exciting and powerful vision has become distorted.[8] What was meant as a project of working to make a broken community into a just whole through the union of right knowing and acting became a moral code for proper behavior. The great humanistic vision of a community in *shalom* became a community haunted by moral imperatives. In other words, a compassion and a call for solidarity for the poor got distorted into a world of good guys and bad guys. The pristination of salvation was, in my opinion, the demise of a vibrant and important theological contribution. There is, let me suggest, one area of theology that may bring back its passion: the liturgy. But only if liturgy itself finds once again its proper vision. This means two things for liturgical theology. It must somehow find its essential reference to salvation and resist becoming obsessed with rubrical propriety. The right knowing, the *orthodoxy*, of liturgy is not to be found in the rubrics but in its insight into salvation. Liturgical theology must also find a way to see the action of the liturgy as *orthopraxis* but in its profound meaning as right action and not as right behavior. These two crucial elements of right knowing and right action are best integrated in the liturgy's most powerful form: *orthopoesis* or drama.

Drama, for example, is an exceptionally appropriate analogy to salvation. Knowledge of salvation requires what may be called a bird's-eye view. It is the view from heaven. Suffering, on the other hand, is ground-based. Suffering inflicted by human beings on other human beings is ground-based. It is the view from earth. No wonder, then, it is so tricky to speak of salvation to a suffering world. To do so risks our talk of salvation sounding irrelevant or, worse, condescending. Indeed, a suffering heart may ask: What has heaven to do with earth? Nonetheless, there is a form that is open to the meeting between heaven and earth, the offer of salvation and the experience of suffering. The bird's-eye view of salvation and the ground-based view of suffering come together in dramatic form. Drama involves the unity of a bird's-eye view and ground-based experience. Dramatic form takes shape when the bird's-eye view of an audience becomes one with the ground-based action on the stage. When these two meet and become one, something truly magical occurs, the distance between stage and audience disappears, heaven and earth join together and form a horizon, a measure of vision that also measures the human condition. This dramatic horizon judges and reveals human motivations, failures, and, even, tragic innocences. It provides insight into our humanity even though as a horizon it is not an infinite gaze into the depths of the human spirit. Nonetheless, the horizon that takes place in the dramatic form of the stage is an apt analogy that helps us understand the strange knowing that is our own experience of suffering. Horizons, indeed, are the stuff of drama that refers to salvation and suffering. It is a term that is used very effectively in the Theo-Drama of Hans Urs von Balthasar.

Dr. Haughton and Miguel de Unamuno are not the only ones who have noticed this dramatic element in the Scriptural witness and in the universal experience of human suffering. Hans Urs von Balthasar, the great Swiss theologian, wrote (in translation) five volumes on what he called the Theo-Drama. Von Balthasar took the Baroque metaphor first proposed by the Spanish playwright Luis Calderón, of the "world is a stage," and developed it into a profound Trinitarian theology.[9] Von Balthasar has the unique honor of being recognized by both Eastern and Western theologians as one of their own. This is due to von Balthasar's prolific studies of the great Church fathers such as Origen, Gregory of Nyssa, and Gregory of Nazanzien.[10] His most profound work, in our opinion, must be his Theo-Drama. In this work, von Balthasar imagines the inner life of the Trinity in a most creative way.[11] The internal processions of the Father, the Son and the Holy Spirit are inherently dramatic. The Trinity's *perichoresis* can be understood dramatically! Moreover, this dramatic inner life is offered to the world though the work of the outer life of the Trinity that men and women may truly participate in God's very life. Such offer of divine life makes the world a stage in which the Father is the Author, the Son is the Actor, and the Holy Spirit is the Director of a divine Drama that corresponds to the very life of the Trinity.[12] Rosemary Haughton's notion of the drama of salvation takes breath-taking theological substance in von Balthasar's Theo-Drama. Salvation history now becomes a Theo-Drama, the real availability in participating in the inner life of the Trinity by participating in the alternative script God offers to the tragic scripts written for the world by human machinations and delusions. Von Balthasar's Theo-Drama, in one stroke, combines the best of Eastern Orthodox theology of Trinitarian glory with Western theology's Christological sensitivity to human suffering. It is a firm foundation for a liturgical aesthetics that would see praise and lament as essential elements in the Church's liturgy.

A purely Trinitarian Theo-Drama, however, has little to say about the human side of the drama. How does the human drama of love and sex, birth and death, labor and rest, passage into adulthood, marriage, and old age, engage and participate in God's Theo-Drama? Indeed, how does the human art of dramatic form relate? For there is an anthropological correlate to the Trinity's inner life, the inner life of the human creature created in the image of God and given life by the breath of God. The Trinity's outer life is not the only window into its inner life, the human inner life is the other window, perhaps its most clear window. And that window achieves its greatest clarity in the liturgy's dramatic form, what we call a theodramatics.

Theodramatics attempts to address the human side of what von Balthasar calls the Theo-Drama. It attempts to relate the dramatic dimension of human life, the arts, and God's divine drama in ways that offer not only a theoretical liturgical aesthetics but also a guide to its practical enactment in liturgical celebrations. A theodramatics attempts to understand what can sum up and energize the inner meaning of a people's whole life so that it may become one with God's own life.

Von Balthasar gave us the basis for such a theodramatics in his notion of the dramatic horizon. Now the notion of the horizon has become commonplace in theology (and philosophy). Hans George Gadamer, the philosopher, and Karl Rahner, the theologian, are examples of two thinkers who have developed the image of a horizon in profound ways. The image of a horizon is fertile to the theologian because it is an apt image of mystery. Karl Rahner felt that the horizon was the only way to address the modern conviction that the physical world is all there is and, therefore, all we can know. Such a conviction leaves little room for a viable understanding of transcendence. Rahner, however, saw in the image of the horizon a way to describe the knowing of transcendent mystery to the modern mind. Human transcendental knowing of mystery can be compared to approaching a horizon. The horizon constantly recedes as we approach it. Moreover, it keeps ever before us a space open to explore, a space that nonetheless always keeps expanding. In this same way is human transcendental knowing of mystery. There is always "more" to be known even if what we come to know is finite.[13]

Rahner's description of mystery's transcendence as horizon is profound and, also, appealing. Nonetheless, Rahner's stress of horizon as an always receding line between heaven and earth speaks more to the coldly intellectual beauty that is the mark of the Thomistic tradition than to the sensible, moving beauty that marks a true aesthetic appreciation of mystery. What is ironic about Rahner's horizon is the example of a physical horizon to suggest a place beyond the physical. An alternative image to the physical horizon is the dramatic horizon mentioned above between audience and stage. Such a horizon rather than recede the meeting point between heaven and earth from our vision unites us to it. While a physical horizon invites contemplation, a dramatic horizon invites participation in its contemplation. Such is the power of dramatic form.

What is a dramatic horizon? Von Balthasar puts it succinctly:

> But for as long as theater has existed, in all its high periods—which were clearly characterized by something over and above the business side of things—people have asked more of drama than this. People have sought insight into the nature and meaning of existence things that cannot simply be read off from its immanent course but radiate from a background that explodes the beautiful and gripping play on the stage—which suddenly becomes inwardly relevant to the spectator—and that relates it to something that transcends it.[14]

Von Balthasar's notion of the dramatic horizon allows for a truly liturgical appropriation of dramatic form. For a dramatic horizon distinguishes between spectacle and drama, between mere theatre and insight into the human condition, between entertaining performance and salvific act. In the notion of dramatic horizon also lies the possibility of a theodramatics, a way to guide the *orthopoesis* of a liturgy, a way to guide the creativity of the arts into the exploration of the horizons that the liturgy now involved with the tragic sense of life offers the world.

Dramatic horizons in the liturgy transform the tragic sense of life. For such horizons take place in the liturgy under the presence of God, offered to us by the will of the Father, made present by the real presence of Christ, and given life through the gift of the Spirit. In such presence, horizons offer the promise of a beautiful whole to our lives in their individual and communal dimensions that is not only eminently valued and heartfully believed; it is sensibly felt. Dramatic horizons makes clear the liturgical meaning of Jesus' command: "Do this in memory of me." In this, he was asking us for more than a memory but a memory come alive and fully present through the gift of dramatic form, a gift to humanity from above, a gift that makes possible salvation as a sharing in the divine life not merely as an ecstasy that eschews suffering but a passion that enters the divine life precisely in our suffering. The art of dramatic forms that makes the anamnesis of Jesus' command the source of viable horizons that offer salvation through the sharing of God's inner life is the stuff of theodramatics.

"DO THIS IN MEMORY OF ME"

A playwright friend of mine, Fr. Harry Cronin, once said to me: "You know, Alex, when Jesus said 'Do this in memory of me,' he was asking us to put on a play." Many would shudder at such a suggestion. The translation of the Eucharist into a theatrical performance raises serious liturgical and theological objections. Indeed, the notion of anything theatrical in the Church has a long line of anathemas beginning with St. Augustine's identifying the City of Man with the Theatre. The Mass, after all, is more than a play. On the other hand, it has to be admitted, it is not unlike a play either. Theodramatics takes seriously the suggestion of Fr. Cronin above while making clear the difference between redemptive dramatic form and mere theatre.

As noted above, von Balthasar's notion of the dramatic horizon is the key to making this distinction. The dramatic horizon makes clear that the dramatic dimension of God's relationship with us on earth is not to be found solely in the immanent dimension of dramatic performance but in the revealing of a horizon, the meeting point where the transcendence of a view from heaven meets the immanence of a view from earth. In the liturgy, such a horizon demands more than being contemplated. Indeed, what makes such a horizon dramatic is its demand for participation in what is revealed. Moreover, what is revealed is also salvific. It addresses the tragic sense of life that our disjointed and broken lives bring to the liturgy and offers a foretaste of a life-giving wholeness that is a transcendental marvelous beauty. Indeed, it is a beauty that is alive, the Body of Christ.

Yet the question needs to be asked: Which are these horizons? Von Balthasar offers us three: death, struggle for the Good, and judgment.[15] Why these? Von Balthasar believes they are the ones that make dramatic action eminently meaningful by their ability to bear tremendous tension. As he puts it:

> Dramatic action is only meaningful within a situation that has two dimensions: one in which humans in their freedom clash and cooperate with one another with dialogue and diapraxis; the other (opened by the former) which locates the characters within the framework of humanity as a whole. Moreover, this second dimension raises two crucial questions: the individual's meaning within the totality and the totality's meaning within Being. The loss of these questions means the loss of dramatic tension.[16]

Thus, von Balthasar brings into the notion of dramatic form a more dynamic view of *orthodoxy*, right knowing, and *orthopraxis*, right action. Dramatic form involves *dialogue* and *diapraxis*. Dialogue and diapraxis may be seen as the dynamic equivalents of *orthodoxy* and *orthopraxis*. Such dynamic equivalents emphasize that knowing and acting exist in the context of a divine Work, and a beautiful Work at that. As such, dialogue and diapraxis make clear the dependent nature of knowing and acting on the totality of the Work in which they participate. It is for this reason that we offer the notion of the liturgy as *orthopoesis*. The liturgy places right knowing in the form of a dialogue and right action in the form of a *diapraxis* in such a way that they contribute to the felt presence of a divine Work at play in the lives brought to the liturgy for sanctification.

An *orthopoesis* brings to presence this divine Work, by doing a work, the work of making a sacred memory alive. Such a memory, however, is the memory of an individual, Jesus of Nazareth, Son of God and Son of Man. It is a memory, moreover, with a mission, the mission of the Lamb of God, a mission revealed in the liturgical address: "You who take away the sins of the world." In this mission the liturgical anamnesis of Christ must ground itself. It is here where the necessity of lament in the Church's liturgy finds its most theological persuasion. For to enter and make alive the memory of our Lord is to enter into the brokenness of the world that He took upon Himself to save. And to the extent that such a mission becomes alive in us as the Body of Christ, His memory becomes fully alive as well.

How does this mission become alive in us? It means taking a profound look at the human condition, the deep divisions within individual souls and in the midst of a community. It also means being moved by such a look to a way of life that fosters and cherishes justice. That way of life is the liturgical *habitus* that knows not only how to sing praises but also offer lament, to cry out with outrage at injustice, like a prophet, but also, like a saint, bear such injustices with sanctifying patience, prayer, and hope. Such insights are the work of a theodramatics, a dramatics applied toward the anamnesis of the One who bore the sins of the world. A theodramatics of anamnesis incorporates into the liturgy the dramatic horizons suggested in the Theo-Drama that is the Paschal Mystery. These dramatic horizons bring the world's joys and hopes, tragedies, and celebrations into an encounter with heaven through the liturgical anamnesis of our Lord's life, death, and resurrection. It is time now to take a deeper look at these horizons.

WHERE EARTH MEETS HEAVEN

As mentioned above, von Balthasar identified three dramatic horizons present in profound dramatic productions: death, the struggle for the Good, and judgment. I would another one, the struggle for one's role.

These horizons come into the liturgy by bringing the world's lament into the praise and thanksgiving of the liturgy. It is this encounter, the encounter between heaven and earth, that creates a marvelous tension that offers profound insight and transformative redemption. Horizons do not "solve" the world's problems. They grasp us, however, in our depths and instill us with a sanctifying tension that is capable of transforming our lives. There is no one place within the liturgy that such horizons can be placed. They take place in the reading of the scripture, the singing of a hymn, the preaching of a homily, as well as the prayers of the Church. Indeed, the entire liturgy can be a horizon.

The first of these horizons, death, is, perhaps, the most available. Drama has used the horizon of death in various ways. Death has been used as a means to interpret life. Death's immanence has been portrayed in drama as something carried with us even as we try to flee it. Death has also been used as a borderline across which God, angels, ghosts, and even demons encounter and engage us. Death has also been portrayed as atonement such as in the play, *Death of a Salesman*. Death has been used as a way to explore the meaning of justice as death has quite often meant the unmaking of power and of kings. More important, drama recognizes the mysterious connection between death and love. Love is not only that which death cannot conquer, death is that which makes love all the more desirable.[17]

What ought to catch our attention is how the horizon of death so aptly reveals the affinity of the world's suffering with our Lord's life, death, and resurrection. Films and plays that never mention a religious term or provide any religious content often use the dramatic tension inherent in the horizon of death. In doing so, however, the horizon connects worldly concerns to heavenly realities. In the horizon of death, indeed in all dramatic horizons, what appears to be secular and purely earthly concern encounters the heavenly mission of Jesus of Nazareth, the Christ of the Church. As such, a dramatic horizon is not only possible in the liturgy's anamnesis but indispensable. Moreover, dramatic horizons in the liturgy have the power to reveal our own individual missions on earth.

The next dramatic horizon is judgment. Perhaps the most popular dramatic device in plays and films is a trial. Such popularity stems from the fact that the horizon of judgment is the question of the meaning and the quality of life itself. It has close association with the horizon of death. Note how often social unrest begins at a funeral. This is because a person's death raises the question of the quality of life itself. Was life, with its joys and sufferings, ultimately worth living? Is life for those who continue to live worth living as well? Such questions raised at a death are questions that challenge the meaning of life and call for an answer.

Judgment, nonetheless, functions as a horizon in taking a look at how human decisions bring a community to the Good or not. Drama answers such queries by genre: tragedy, comedy, and tragi-comedy. Indeed, God abandoned by God on the Cross gives tragedy its ultimate example. Yet such divine tragedy can only avoid nihilism by a Christian understanding of the Paschal Mystery. In other words, judgment as a horizon in a theodramatics of the liturgy allows us to enter into the full experience of the tragic without despair. Judgment as a horizon often involves laughter. Laughter is as meaningful as weeping for it gives the sense of the quality of life as well. When judgment reveals that which lies beyond human competence, however, tragedy and comedy coincide. The award winning film *Life Is Beautiful* is a prime example.[18] In these forms, the dramatic horizon of judgment anticipates the Christian understanding of the Last Judgement.[19]

Von Balthasar also mentions the dramatic horizon that is the struggle for the Good. In classical ethical thought, the proper goal of decision-making is for the Good. In drama, however, there are only gradations of the Good. Dramatic tension occurs when the Good reveals itself only in the "trade-off" between two goods. Drama does not have its protagonists decide absolutely for the Good but to act toward union with the Good or act so as to give witness to the Good. This dramatic horizon gives perspective to liturgy's engagement with justice. Decisions that create injustice can and ought to be judged liturgically but via horizons that create union with what is Just or that give witness to what is Just. Liturgy's engagement with injustice is not an activism that eschews the ambiguities of human decisions but a creative dynamism toward a vision and union with the Just.

There is, in my opinion, another dramatic horizon that von Balthasar does not explicitly mention as such. It is the horizon that is the struggle of the individual with his and her role. One way to approach such a horizon is to note what every playwright has experienced. A good play allows its characters to develop. Characters in a play take on a life of their own even though that life depends ultimately on the author's creativity. Indeed, a playwright cannot write a mere script. It must be a script that can be performed. This sets the conditions for an actor who would attempt to play the part of a character in a play. The actor can be seen to be the center of two concentric spheres. One sphere comprises the reality embodied in the audience. The other sphere is the identity not directly accessible to the reality of the audience, an identity presented by the play itself. It is the actor's task to infuse the reality of the ordinary life of the audience with the aesthetic wholeness that is the dramatic play as a whole. When an actor plays his part well, the audience delights not only in the projection of what we already know of human living itself but also in the exciting anticipation of something further to be discovered, the promise of a possible solution of life's tragic sense.[20]

Having said this, it must be noted that an actor who would play a character in a play must struggle with his role. Indeed, if an actor is to give life and authenticity to the character he must play, then a struggle must take place within the actor himself to discover the nature of that character. Such a struggle, furthermore, must find the answer deep within the actor's own psyche. This struggle for identity, an identity that contributes to the unity of the play, is, I propose, another dramatic horizon worthy of the liturgy. For in this struggle for identity an insight into the meaning of the individual self emerges that cannot be simply read from the immanent course of an individual's daily life. In the struggle to play the role, the actor searches the audience's willingness to also struggle and to be willing to respond to the unfolding of the action even as the dramatic tension rises and threatens a deep transformation of the self. Indeed, in the dramatic horizon that is the struggle for the role, the spectator is struck by a strange fear: the self is called into question. This vulnerability reveals a marvelous innocence. One becomes open to the possibility of transformation of the self. Doubt and cynicism about the action in the play dissolve and innocence opens up in the mystery of this powerful dramatic horizon.

This is important in a theodramatics that proposes to be an anamnesis of our Lord's life, death, and resurrection for the role that each self must struggle with is the character that is the risen Lord Himself. The resurrection stories abound with such a struggle. Mary Magdalene did not at once recognize the risen Lord. The disciples at Emmaus also had problems. Thomas, my favorite character, only recognized him in the touching of His wounds. The biblical witness of the risen Lord is a witness to a struggle to grasp the identity of the risen Lord and, in doing so, revealing our role in the divine Script itself. Such a struggle calls for resources found only within the self's deepest depths and can only be performed out of a renewed innocence which allows the character that is played to shine through. In the mystery of a theodramatics, the characters we are asked to play and the self that we bring to the role happen to be one. They are to be found in the person of our Lord among the cast that make up the Body of Christ.

Thus four dramatic horizons contribute to the theodramatics that is the anamnesis of Christ's life, death, and resurrection. Through death, judgment, and struggle for the good and for the role, heaven meets earth and offers the promise of an aesthetic solution to the tragic sense of life. As such, it brings the world's lament and transforms it into Church Song. It takes a sacred memory and makes it a present, living reality. It takes an isolated self and weaves one into the marvelous community that is the Body of Christ. It offers not only a view of justice, but also union with the Just One. And, above all, it offers a praxis that is a struggle for a role whose main character is the Son in a divine Script written by the Father and directed by the Holy Spirit.

NOTES

1. I am thinking here of James Alison's treatment of this story in terms of Rene Girard's scapegoat theory. While I admire Alison's work and even more Girard's insightful treatment of human social psychology, I believe their emphasis on the sinful and violent forces at work in our humanity in this story misses a deeper and more nuanced interpretation. It is not only Cain's wickedness that is revealing of our humanity; it is also Abel's goodness. The contrast between farmer and shepherd is not the most illuminating here. What is revealing of what makes Abel and his offering "good" is what is lost in the loss of Abel's life, the joy and delight of a life lived in praise and thanksgiving. For Alison's work, the reader would profit by reading James Alison, *Raising Abel: The Recovery of Eschatological Imagination* (New York: Crossroad Publications, 1996).

2. Indeed, our ability to inflict suffering and injustice is said to de-humanize. On a more thorough treatment of the story of Cain and Abel as a lament see Sally A. Brown and Patrick D. Miller, *Lament: Reclaiming Practices in Pulpit, Pew, and Public Square* (Louisville, Ky.: Westminster John Knox Press, 2005), 18–24.

3. Miguel de Unamuno, Anthony Kerrigan, and Martin Nozick, *The Tragic Sense of Life in Men and Nations*, Bollingen Series, vol. 85 (Princeton, N.J.: Princeton University Press, 1972), 3–4.

4. The characterization of the act of knowing as a logical comparison comes from the work of the logician Charles Peirce. See Alex Garcia-Rivera, *The Community of the Beautiful: A Theological Aesthetics* (Collegeville, Minn.: Liturgical Press, 1999), ch. 3.

5. Rosemary Haughton, *The Drama of Salvation* (New York: Seabury Press, 1975), 48.

6. What is the future of liberation theology? An answer to this question will raise strong passions to those concerned with issues of justice and global poverty. One thing seems clear to us, however. The next step that liberation theology must take, if it is to remain a viable understanding of the Christian tradition, must be in the direction of a liberating understanding and praxis of the liturgy, a step in the direction that Rosemary Haughton points out in the suggestive sense of her term, the drama of salvation. Cf. Haughton, *Drama of Salvation*.

7. I am aware that orthodoxy is rightly translated "right praise" rather than "right knowing." Nonetheless, in recent usage, orthodoxy has come to mean "right knowing." Actually, its true meaning ought to humble those who champion "right knowing" as the mark of a loyal member of the Church. For being "orthodox" means knowing how to praise correctly. This is the task of an aesthetics not an inquisition.

8. Not everyone would agree with my assessment. I do want to make it clear that it is the critique of someone who cares deeply for the original insights of liberation theology and not the critique of someone who sees it as fundamentally flawed. Moreover, there is something of an intellectual outrage in my critique that such a beautiful vision has been allowed to be diminished by the theological community.

9. Pedro Luis Calderón de la Barca was a famous Spanish playwright of the fifteenth century. One of his most famous works was "El Gran Teatro del Mundo."

See Pedro Calderón de la Barca and Eugenio Frutos, *El Gran Teatro del Mundo* (Salamanca: Ediciones Anaya, 1958).

10. See for example his work on Nyssa, Hans Urs von Balthasar, *Presence and Thought: Essay on the Religious Philosophy of Gregory of Nyssa* (San Francisco, Calif.: Ignatius Press, 1995), and on Origen, Origen and Hans Urs von Balthasar, *Origen, Spirit and Fire: A Thematic Anthology of His Writings* (Washington, D.C.: Catholic University of America Press, 1984). For these works and others like it, Eastern Orthodox theologians have called von Balthasar one of their "own." Indeed, his most celebrated work *Herrlichkeit* or *The Glory of the Lord* has been called a theology of the icon.

11. Theologians have traditionally distinguished between the inner life and the outer life of the Trinity. The Trinitarian inner life or Immanent Trinity concerns the inner relationships between the three persons. The Trinitarian outer life or Economic Trinity concerns what German scholarship dubbed *Heilsgeshichte* or salvation history. The great Jesuit theologian Karl Rahner proposed what became a famous dictum: the Immanent Trinity and the Economic Trinity are for all practical purposes one. Speculation on the inner life of the Trinity alone is futile. What we know of the Trinity is through its outer life and this life must also be one with its inner life. Von Balthasar did not quite agree with this dictum. He boldly took a very Eastern (and unpopular in the West) approach of considering the inner life of the Trinity as the basis for understanding the outer life or salvation history. This reversal of view gave him a unique theology of history and of salvation. History, especially salvation history, is best seen in the dramatic way the three persons of the Trinity self-surrender to one another in the eternal processions or perichoresis of the Son, the Father, and the Holy Spirit. Cf. Hans Urs von Balthasar, *Theo-Drama: Theological Dramatic Theory*, translated by Graham Harrison (San Francisco, Calif.: Ignatius Press, 1988–1998), 5 vols.

12. Some great guides to the subtle and difficult reading of von Balthasar's Theo-Drama include Aidan Nichols, *No Bloodless Myth: A Guide Through Balthasar's Dramatics* (Edinburgh: T & T Clark, 2000); Christopher W. Steck, *The Ethical Thought of Hans Urs von Balthasar* (New York: Crossroad Publications, 2001).

13. See the discussion on Rahner's use of the horizon in Stephen Duffy, *The Graced Horizon: Nature and Grace in Modern Catholic Thought*, Theology and Life Series, vol. 37 (Collegeville, Minn.: Liturgical Press, 1992), 10.

14. Hans Urs von Balthasar, *Theo-Drama: Theological Dramatic Theory*, vol. 1, *Prolegomena*, translated by Graham Harrison (San Francisco, Calif.: Ignatius Press, 1988), 5 vols., 314.

15. von Balthasar, *Prolegomena*, 319ff.

16. von Balthasar, *Prolegomena*, 354–359.

17. These portrayals of death in drama were given by von Balthasar. Von Balthasar, *Prolegomena*, 361–369.

18. A review and description of the film can be found online at http://movie reviews.colossus.net/movies/l/life_beautiful.html.

19. Adrian Nichols gives a wonderful summary of these horizons in Nichols, *No Bloodless Myth*, 37. I have borrowed extensively from his presentation.

20. I take these insightful comments on the task of the actor and the nature of characters in a play from von Balthasar, cf. von Balthasar, *Prolegomena*, 279ff.

✝

Conclusion: Do This in Memory of Me

Thomas Scirghi

To begin this conclusion I ask the reader to indulge me in a brief fantasy. I imagine that someday, when we reach our final resting place in Heaven, we will have the opportunity to ask the Lord one burning question, a question that we have pondered for a long time. Of course, we will have all of eternity to ask all the questions we want, but upon first entering Heaven we have the opportunity to ask one burning question. So I imagine myself being escorted by St. Peter and presented to Jesus, meeting him face to face. Then I will pose my question, saying something like, "Lord Jesus Christ, Son of the living God, you are the savior of the world. Now, Lord, do you remember that night of your last supper, when you met with your friends, and you took a loaf of bread and said, 'This is my body.' Then you took a cup of wine and said, 'This is my blood.' Do you remember that, Lord?" And he will say, "Yes, Thomas, I remember that. Now what is your question?" Well Lord, after that you said 'Do this in memory of me.'[1] Lord, my question is: What did you mean by *this*?"

The fundamental reason we gather as a Christian community to celebrate the Eucharist, as discussed earlier, is in reverent response to the Lord's command, "Do this in memory of me." Here we want to ask, what did Jesus mean by the word "this"? Many Christians[2] understand it to mean the celebration of the Eucharist. It is obvious, however, that the first followers of Jesus elaborated upon the Supper scene of that evening. Clearly they followed His command to keep His memory through their action of gathering for the meal of bread and wine. But they also embellished the meal by adding a word service, reading from the books of the prophets and the letters of the apostles. Soon they added a dismissal rite,

173

a sending forth of the assembly in faith. Later they added an entrance rite, a mode of gathering and greeting.

Today Christians faithfully follow the Lord's command Sunday after Sunday. Yet the liturgy never has been a stagnant ritual. During two millennia of Christian history the liturgy has evolved to the current order in which we worship. Following the liturgical axiom of *semper reformanda*, we know that the liturgy is "always reforming." In all fidelity to the Lord, Christians are still trying to answer that question: What did he mean by "this"? The liturgy of the Eucharist functions as the paradigmatic symbol for Christians. And because it is a symbol it is polyvalent, that is to say rich with meaning; it cannot be restricted in its meaning; its meaning is never exhausted. If we wish to claim that we are indeed faithful to the Lord and his command, then the Supper must be seen in a richly symbolic way; "this" is not to be taken literally as if Jesus intended his disciples to re-enact an identical supper scene during the season of Passover. For clearly the liturgy of the Roman Catholic church today resembles that last supper but with much embellishment. A problem may arise when the embellishment overpowers the substance—when the performance overwhelms the sacrament—then we can forget the focus of our faith. It is necessary then, occasionally to return to the root of our worship and restore the vision of our church. We need to ask, on occasion, What did the Lord mean by "this"?

BETWEEN UNITY AND UNIFORMITY

Over time that question has been addressed usually through an understanding of the rubrics as formulated by the church's hierarchy. Especially in the throes of the Reformation, the Council of Trent sought to unify the church through a uniform liturgy, assuring that the Roman Liturgy would be celebrated in the same way throughout the world. Consequently the Council of Trent published a missal to be used by the universal church. Given the political situation at the time, it was thought necessary to celebrate a uniform worship and so to publish a uniform missal. This provided a means to unify the Roman Church at the time while challenging the teaching of the nascent Protestant churches. The need for unity led to the liturgy's uniformity.

The uniformity of the liturgy was a response to the abuses of the day. We can appreciate the call for uniformity when we consider the challenge to the Church's worship at the time of the Reformation. A special commission was organized by the Council of Trent to compile a list of abuses in the mass. One such abuse was superstition, causing a concern for the use of rites, prayers, and ceremonies that were not approved by the

Church and had not been in use by the faithful in worship.[3] Specifically, there was a problem with the multiplication of "votive masses," that is, masses offered for special intentions or occasions.[4] Some of these intentions became all too personal, even commercial, rather than spiritual. Erasmus, the sixteenth-century scholar and critic of the church, once remarked that "the content of so many votive masses approaches superstition."[5] Praying for special intentions carries a long respected tradition with it. But it is one thing to pray for an increase of peace in the world, or for the consolation of those who are suffering, or that someone may persevere in his or her vocation; it is another to pray for the success of one's own business or for a bountiful hunting expedition. The abuse lay in the expectation that the mass would bring about the desired results, as if it were a magical incantation, rather than entrusting the matter to the providence of the Lord. Certainly this is not what the Lord intended by the command "Do this in memory of me."

Besides these votive masses there was the problem of the malleability of the text. Prayers were added to the mass on a regular basis for special occasions and to honor certain individuals such as the saints of a particular region. Sometimes these prayers were not reviewed carefully by the local bishop and later some would be found to promote superstition or even heresy. The uniform missal ensured a degree of stability by no longer allowing alternative prayers. In its promulgation the pontiff stated strongly that nothing in the missal was ever to be changed.[6] In his words, "[I]t is desirable that in the church of God there be . . . one single rite for celebrating Mass." Also, "[S]o that the usages of the holy Roman Church, mother and teacher of all other churches, be adopted and observed by all. . . . We prescribe and order by this declaration, whose force is perpetual, that all the churches relinquish the use of their proper missals."[7]

The Council thought that a uniform missal would help to rein in the ecclesial and liturgical abuses and would remove superstitious matter from the celebration of the mass. The council members took as a model the religious orders. For example, the Dominicans and Franciscans used a uniform missal for their own liturgies and it was suggested that the secular clergy follow their custom. The purpose of a uniform missal, then, was in part to purge superstitions from the ritual of the mass. The use of standardized rubrics for all the churches affiliated with Rome would help with this purgation. The result was the Pius V Missal, named for the pope of the time. For Pope Pius V, the reform of the liturgy meant a *ressource-ment*, that is, "a return to the sources." The pope wished to return to a period beyond the liturgical innovations of the Middle Ages in order to rediscover the tradition of the early church. In this way he was quite innovative, foreshadowing the work of the liturgical reform movement. Unfortunately the missal did not achieve its purpose. Those who were commissioned by the Pope to draft the missal had little time to work; consequently, the final draft turned out to be a revision of the 1474 Missal of the Roman Curia, a revision that focused upon correcting and purging the perceived abuses.[8]

The publication of the Pius V Missal in 1570, aided by the invention of the printing press, did bring the desired unification to the Church. But this unification came at a substantial price for the development of the liturgy. Jungmann describes the price as follows.

> The Missal of Pius V was indeed a powerful dam holding back the waters or permitting them to flow through only in firm, well-built canals. At one blow all arbitrary meandering to one side or another was cut off, all floods prevented, and a safe, regular and useful flow assured. But the price paid was this, that the beautiful river valley now lay barren and the forces of further evolution were often channeled into the narrow bed of a very inadequate devotional life instead of a gathering strength for new forms of liturgical expression.[9]

The flowing river of *semper reformanda* was obstructed by the Pius V Missal.

Four centuries later the Catholic Church finds itself in similar circumstances. As we discussed in chapter one, the theme of "irreverence" is heard much within the current campaign to re-organize the liturgy. We hear of a number of "abuses" as counted by Cardinal Arrinze.[10] More recently, the bishops of the United States met to debate the language of the liturgy, insisting that the prayers should be more scripturally based and faithful to the Latin text.[11] Our present age raises the same concern for maintaining ecclesial tradition as the church is engaged in a new reform of the liturgy awaiting the publication of a new missal. In the midst of this renewal, the church still confronts the dichotomy of unity and uniformity.

Using the Scripture as our foundation, we hear the cry for unity from both the prophets and the apostles. And it was Jesus' prayer to his Father, in his final discourse: "I pray . . . so that they may all be one, as you, Father, are in me and I in you, that they also may be in us, that the world may believe that you sent me."[12] The striving for unity is the purpose of the followers of Jesus Christ. Union in Christ and with one another is the perennial goal for Christians. How we maintain that unity is a crucial issue for understanding the liturgy. It is important that the church be united and seen as one. The symbol of Christ's presence on earth is the united church. Perhaps, then, "this" refers to the unity to which all Christians are called, which is properly expressed in the liturgy of the Eucharist, the unity with each other through Jesus Christ.

THE LITURGICAL HABITUS: "TEACH US TO PRAY"

Here we want to propose that the *habitus* of the liturgy is the formation of the members of the assembly into a communion. We suggest that a liturgical *habitus* serves to dispose the assembly to *pray in communion*. The Eucharistic liturgy involves more than a gathering of Christians on Sunday praying side-by-side, but that they are praying in communion. This praying in communion is the goal of the liturgical *habitus*.

According to Prof. Garcia-Rivera, a *habitus* describes the pre-disposition to behave in a certain way. Reviewing his discussion of four thinkers on this subject, we learn that, according to Aristotle's observation of human behavior, a *habitus* is a propensity toward a kind of behavior, distinguishing one kind of animal from another. Also, this characteristic behavior is dynamic as it passes from one generation to the next, and adapts to new circumstances when necessary. Human beings differ from animals in that they transcend their characteristic behavior that allows them to choose to live the virtuous life. For humans, then, the *habitus* promotes the enhancement of human life. Thomas Aquinas wrote of "habits" as the path between full actuality and pure potentiality. John Locke opined that the *habitus* is more than a way to behave in the world; it is also a way to look at the world. And Jonathan Edwards spoke of the habits of the human being as "the sense of the heart," which propels the whole self in the pursuit of beauty. Since the *habitus* of liturgical worship propels the assembly toward praying in communion, we will consider these two points individually, first, the meaning of a prayerful disposition, and then, the assembly acting in communion.

When Jesus taught the disciples to pray, he did not mean to pray with words only. In reading Luke's account of this lesson, Jesus first recites a prayer that has come to be known as "The Lord's Prayer." Then he tells two brief parables, the first of which depicts a neighbor who comes knocking at midnight to borrow a loaf of bread; the second compares a father's generosity to his children with the overwhelming generosity of God the Father. Both parables teach a lesson of perseverance in prayer.[13] In learning how to pray, we learn what to say as well as how to pray, the content as well as the proper disposition.

Becoming a prayerful person means more than saying one's particular prayers at a set time every day. To be a prayerful person means to cultivate the *habitus* by which one receives and responds to the world through the context of a faith-filled personal relationship with God. One's personal prayer should help to dispose oneself to addressing the challenges of the day. Note the Gospel stories in which we find Jesus either complimenting or criticizing his disciples for their responses. He praises Peter for recognizing him as the Son of God, but chastises the disciples for being overwhelmed with fear during the storm at sea.[14] Thus the time spent in personal prayer—in meditation and reflection—should foster a personal disposition to "find God in all things," that is, to recognize the presence of God within the vicissitudes of daily life.

With this notion of "proper disposition" in mind, I was moved by a bishop's advice to the deacons he was about to ordain to the priesthood. He told them that he hoped they would learn how to *pray* the liturgy and not just to say it. I couldn't agree more. To be clear, learning to pray the liturgy cannot be learned from a manual, like memorizing and demonstrating the numerous rubrics from the General Instruction, nor can any teacher impart this directly. There is an old preacher's axiom that advises "preaching isn't taught; it's caught." The same can be said for learning to lead people in prayer: such leadership is caught rather than taught. In fact, couldn't the same be said of teaching art in general? A master may teach her technique, but she cannot teach her skill. This is something a student must acquire on her own. It is more a matter of developing a *habitus*. This is to say that for an appreciation of the liturgy we need to learn it "from the inside," it is a learning that comes from doing. With this learning comes the *habitus*, the transformed person, who is living the life of the liturgy outside of the worship space and outside of the one hour or so per week.

Let us consider first, the *habitus* of the presider, and then of the congregation. For the presider, the *habitus* is to pray the liturgy, and in doing so, to lead the people in prayer. Indeed this is much to ask of seminarians who are just learning to negotiate through the *Sacramentary*, flipping from section to section, and coordinating words with gestures. But without the *habitus* a presider will sound like a child just learning her prayers, more interested in saying the right words than in communicating their meaning. Indeed many adults can sound like children as they rattle off their prayers by rote.

When visiting the Camoldoli monastery at Big Sur, California, I was struck by the deliberately slow pace of praying used by the monks in choir. For a visitor, at first it feels uncomfortable, the pacing seems awkward. For example, instead of the usual immediate greeting and response such as "The Lord be with you . . . And also with you," here the congregation takes a long pause before responding. The purpose for the pause is to hear the blessing, to drink in its good news like savoring the first taste of a fine wine. What do we mean when we say "The Lord be with you"? A rapid-fire response, which leaves no time for reflection, reduces the blessing to a factual statement. No wonder some presiders feel inclined to say "good morning"; the proper liturgical greeting has lost its meaning.[15] Praying with the monks of Camoldoli allows one to hear the old words in a new way, and to savor the message. The manner in which we speak, not just the content of the speech, communicates much of the message. The manner of speaking helps to convey one's disposition.

This manner includes the communication of posture and gesture. For instance, where should the presider look when praying the Eucharistic Prayer? There are two points of focus during this prayer. For the most part the prayer is directed to God as we hear, for example, in the third Eucharistic Prayer, "Father, you are holy indeed, and all creation rightly gives you praise." But there are lines directed to the assembly as well, for example, "Let us proclaim the mystery of faith." So, when addressing God the presider could look upward, and when addressing the congregation, he might look at the people before him. An awareness of where one should look while praying could be a mark of the *habitus* in that the priest is no longer glued to the text or simply reciting the prayers, but interested in building the relationship between leader and assembly, and the church with God. It is also a recognition that the human body plays an important part in face-to-face communication. Not only speech, but posture as well, expresses our praise of God and solidarity with one another. To be sure, the goal of praying the liturgy, for most seminarians, probably will not be reached by graduation day; it will take some time, maybe years, to achieve this goal. It is a matter of becoming familiar with the liturgy to the point that the rubrics seem "second nature" to the young priest, and he will move through the mass the way a well-rehearsed actor moves through a play on stage. But first this will require much rehearsal and an appreciation for the way we worship. Eventually, it is hoped, he develops a "feel" for the worship, and soon prays the text rather than simply reads it. This is the beginning of the *habitus*.

For the congregation as well, the manner matters as much as the content. Sometimes a congregation may approach the liturgy as if it were a cerebral obligation, like college students cramming for an exam, interested only in spewing out the required information as quickly as possible. For example, as mentioned in chapter two, the Prayer of the Faithful is one specific exercise of the priesthood of the laity. Here the laity bring forth their petitions of prayer gathered from the people of God, locally and globally, concerns of the parish and of the world. Through the voice of the deacon or a lay person, these prayers are raised up to God in a similar way to the priest lifting up the prayer of the people throughout the liturgy, as when he says "Let us pray." And note that these petitions are prayers, not announcements. Often the Prayer of the Faithful is read as if it were another set of announcements, items of information rather than prayerful requests. The habitus of communal prayer calls for the proper words spoken in the proper tone of voice.

The *habitus* addresses more than a ritual performance. It is necessary for cultivating the proper disposition within communal prayer. The purpose of this disposition is to direct the faithful toward the transcendent, preparing them to encounter the Lord. The manner in which we pray together will either hasten or hinder our way. The *habitus* helps to keep us focused. The dynamic of this *habitus* is illustrated by the theology of the icon.

THE HABITUS AS AN ICON

The worshiping assembly is somewhat like an Orthodox icon painting in that the light of the divine should shine through the gathering. The Lord's command, "Do this in memory of me," creates a special kind of icon, one of dynamic presence. Here, we want to compare the liturgical gathering to an icon. Underlying the theology of the icon is the notion that light shines through the painting. Looking at an icon two qualities are noticed right away. First, notice that the figures in the painting are non-representational, this is to say that they suggest, more than resemble, the human form with their flat, two-dimensional look and expressionless faces.[16] The figures drawn in the icon do not look like anyone we know. A second observation is that the icon has no shadows. Compare this to a portrait in which the contrast of light and shadow adds depth to the picture, as well as indicating the point of perspective. The icon's lack of shadow suggests that the source of light emanates from behind the icon. The purpose for the non-representational figures and for the lack of shadows is to draw the viewer into and beyond the painting. Basil of Caesarea noted that the veneration of Christian images is directed to the archetype, that is the transcendental reality which they represent.[17] The icon is a dramatic window into the divine. The viewer does not focus on the figures but moves beyond them. The icon invites and directs the viewer into communion with God.

In their book *Art and Worship*, Christopher Irvine and Anne Dawtry discuss the purpose and process of icons. The purpose is to help the worshipers to focus themselves in a new way. For a little while they will set aside their earthly concerns and be transformed, drawn into a closer relationship with Christ himself. The process of painting an icon is a prayerful one that follows a set of rubrics. In their words, "The painter does not have a free hand (in the process) but must observe certain styles and forms laid down by the Orthodox Church, which are part of a sacred trust. . . . This has the effect of freeing the icon to help focus worship as the eye is not distracted by details of interpretation and expression imposed by the artist."[18] The painter serves as an interpreter of the message and so must follow a strict set of rules.[19]

A good leader of prayer stands before a congregation like an icon. To pray the liturgy means to lead the people in prayer, without calling undue attention to oneself, but enabling the congregation to focus on the divine. This is not to say that the priest is the only one capable of providing a window onto the divine realm. On the contrary, the congregation holds many holy people who provide this ability. But within the context of the liturgy the ordained minister is the one chosen to help the community focus together.

Further, icons are incarnational, as are Christians. Obviously the congregation cannot help but notice the man standing before them. They do not deny his appearance but look deeper into the mystery of the celebration, for the body is the symbol of the spirit. Recall the dialogue between Jesus and Philip during the Last Supper discourse. Philip says, "Master, show us the Father, and that will be enough for us." And Jesus said to him, "Whoever has seen me has seen the Father."[20] Jesus stands as an icon of the Father. As the Son of God took on human form to reveal the Father to humanity, and in turn to lead humanity to the Father, so the priest helps to mediate the way between the human and divine. We remember too the saying of St. Irenaeus: "For the glory of God is a living man; and the life of man consists in beholding God."[21] Ideally the liturgy shapes the life of the priest. This is the meaning of the presider as the *alter christus*. It is not a position of power. Rather, through an aesthetic understanding, the *alter christus* serves as an image of a memory come alive. The church is performing this worship now in memory of Christ. This makes the liturgy an encounter with mystery.[22]

Again, the people do not ignore the man standing before them, but if the liturgy works well, they will be drawn into something greater. They will not notice the leader of prayer as much as they will be caught up in the activity of praying. Lest this sound too ethereal or abstract, we could compare the presider to an actor on stage. Take, for example, the actor Kenneth Branagh, renowned for his portrayal of Shakespearean characters. Mr. Branagh's name, playing the lead role in *Hamlet*, will certainly draw people to the theater. Many in the audience will anticipate seeing him on stage. Yet, if the performance goes well, the audience will not notice Mr. Branagh so much as they will follow the story of Hamlet. A good performance by an actor becomes a window onto the character he portrays. Branagh's performance brings the character of Elizabethan culture to life and helps the audience to focus on Hamlet. In this way the presider is like an actor, moving the assembly from one realm to another, mediating the temporal and eternal.

In a very practical way this is the reason for the presider to beware of thoughtless improvising and to follow the Church's liturgy. Like the icon painter, he does not have a free hand in leading the Church's prayer. The congregation may be distracted by a barrage of self-referential remarks, or the attempts at humor which are unconnected to the message for the sake of a laugh, or the personal greetings that are not prayerful. (What does it mean when we follow the liturgical greeting "The Lord be with you" with the pedestrian "Good morning"?) The presider should help to enliven the liturgy, that is, to help bring it to life. However, too many personal or idiosyncratic remarks will stifle the liturgy, keeping us focused on the mundane rather than the divine. For this presider we want to say "Get out of the way and let the people pray." It must be admitted that many people find the liturgy boring. (Indeed, for some the phrase "liturgical celebration" has the ring of an oxymoron.) Consequently there is a certain distrust for the liturgy. Some presiders, along with their liturgy committees, wish to liven things up with comical priests and folksy greetings, among other things. We contend that it is not the liturgy which is boring, but the way in which it is celebrated. A Shakespearean drama is not boring in itself, but in the hands of an unskilled cast it will appear deadly dull. G. K. Chesterton once opined that it is not the case that Christianity has been tried and found wanting; rather, Christianity has been found difficult and left untried. The same may be said of Christian liturgy: some ministers find it difficult to express warmth and wisdom through the worship rites so they put aside the ritual book and turn the liturgy into a lounge act. Again the plea to get out of the way and let the people pray.

The image of the icon works for the preacher as well. Consider what constitutes an effective preacher. A preacher is truly effective when the people hear a holy person speak, that is, when the preacher is perceived to truly believe the message being preached. The congregation can presume the preacher holds a good understanding of the Scripture and of the tradition, and they will hope that the preacher possesses some skill in public speaking. However, neither intelligence nor eloquence will suffice in the pulpit. Credibility is key: preachers must indicate that they have integrated the sermon message into their lives, having endured the struggle and enjoyed the surprise of the Good News and made it their own. Then the faithful will perceive the preacher to be a holy person and be more readily disposed to an encounter with the Lord.

Those who are charged with leading the prayer of the church hold a special responsibility for transmitting the Christian tradition. They will serve the community faithfully if they allow themselves to become an icon of the Church, a window to the divine. Up until now we have discussed the ordained minister as the leader of prayer in terms of an icon. However all the baptized are called to serve a priestly role. How then does a lay person function as an icon of faith?

During the rite of baptism, the priest anoints the newly baptized and prays: "(God) now anoints you with the chrism of salvation, so that united with his people, you may remain forever a member of Christ who is Priest, Prophet and King."[23] As the ordained priest, with the help of the Holy

Spirit, serves to transform bread and wine into the Body and Blood of Jesus Christ, the lay priesthood works to transform the ordinary into the extraordinary, rendering Christ present to the world. In the words of the U.S. bishops, "All of the faithful are called to work toward the transformation of the world."[24] This call to transform the world follows the "sacramental principle," the belief that all created reality is imbued with the presence of God. The transubstantiation of the bread and wine reminds the Church of the transformation of all reality: nature is sacred because it is God's work. The non-ordained fulfill their priestly role by "elevating" the gifts they have received and revealing the divine through the mundane. The Sacrament of Marriage gives us a good example. The covenantal love promised by a bride and groom in matrimony gives the Christian community a glimpse of the covenant relationship that God established with humanity, a relationship that is indelible and unconditional. Human devotion is transformed into divine love when brought before the altar of the Lord. Similar to marriage, individual acts of forgiveness also enact a transformation of reality. A harmful action or a hurtful situation, becomes an opportunity for reconciliation and growth in God's mercy. A rift is repaired as victim and offender are once again made whole. With each act of forgiveness the community can hear an echo of Jesus' final request from the cross: "Father, forgive them, they know not what they do."[25] The couple in love and those who choose to forgive, do they not also become icons for the community? Their behavior is understood according to the Church's tradition to be a priestly action, one that reveals the presence of Christ. Once again, the ordinary is transformed into something extraordinary. Through them the community is given a glimpse of the divine and the dynamic presence of the liturgy extends beyond the worship service. Their actions of either unconditional love or healing forgiveness manifest a prayerful disposition through which shines the transcendent.

A painter of icons may, no doubt, find some discrepancy with using the icon as a model for presiding at the Church's liturgy. However, in an analogous way, a liturgist may learn from an iconographer. In the first place, worship activity draws the faithful into a dynamic presence. The gathering for worship is more than a town meeting presided over by the mayor. Worship provides the community with the distinct opportunity to encounter the Lord. Further, the icon painting is not merely a personal expression of the artist. There are rules to follow in order to properly interpret the significance of the icon so that the icon worshiper may enter into a prayerful experience. Similarly, a minister must respect the church's order of worship, as communal prayer is not a matter of self-expression. Rather, the prescribed order of worship provides the means by which the community may participate fully in the praise of God. Joined in this communion of praise, the divine presence shines through.

LIVING BEAUTY

According to the "Constitution on the Sacred Liturgy" (no. 11), in order for the sacred liturgy to be effective, the faithful must attend with the proper dispositions so that they may cooperate with divine grace. The faithful must participate knowingly, actively, and fruitfully. In a sense this instruction resembles the teaching of the "greatest commandment," that is, "to love the Lord with all one's heart, being, strength and mind."[26] A liturgical aesthetics promotes such a full participation in worship; a study of the theory and laws of the Church's ritual as well as an awareness of our purpose in praising God. This awareness is expressed in words, both spoken and sung, in symbols and sacraments, in gesture and silence. A liturgical aesthetics fosters a discipline by which we allow ourselves to be transformed by God through the ritual, then in turn we are charged to bring about the transformation of the world. It is more a matter of allowing the ritual to speak through the faithful rather than the faithful speaking the ritual. It is the way a good story overtakes the storyteller who then feels compelled to tell the story. As birds sing for enjoyment, storytellers tell the tale through which they recognize themselves. The liturgy of the Eucharist is the Christian story. And storytelling, similar to music and drama, is a living art; it lives only while it is being performed. "Storytelling lives only while the story is being told."[27] Like the concert pianist who breathes life into a classical score, and the actor reviving a popular script, the Christian assembly, in the presence of God, maintains the story of faith. In the telling and re-telling of this story, the creation and redemption of the world are revealed in new ways, and the members of the community attain a greater realization of who they are in union with one another and with the Son of God. The regular re-enactment of this theodrama keeps the story of Jesus Christ alive and He continues to breathe His Spirit upon His followers.[28]

The celebration of the liturgy gives the assembly a glimpse of the communion to which the Church strives. The liturgy serves as a reminder of that unity to which we are called. To illustrate this further we could imagine a family's celebration of Christmas, which often includes the taking of the family photograph. Those who engage in this annual ritual know it is no easy task. It is a great challenge to organize one's family, posing everyone properly to fit into the picture, shorter people up front, tall ones in back. The children fidget, wanting to get out of their Christmas suits and dresses and put on play clothes. They are uncomfortable squeezing next to each other, arms and legs touching. Adults run to and from the kitchen, fearing the food will overcook. Finally, everyone is posed, the photographer presses the automatic flash button, runs to take his spot with the family, and calls out a command to "smile." For a second frowns morph into smiles. The camera flashes. It's done. Several days later the picture is sent out for developing, and eventually returns to the home. Mom has it framed and mounted on the mantel piece. When friends come to visit they look admiringly at the picture and praise the parents, "My you have such a beautiful family. See how good they look and how they come together so nicely." And the parents say politely, through gritted teeth, "Yes, I know, they are wonderful."

Why do we re-enact this annual ritual? What is the purpose of displaying the family photo in the home? Isn't it partly a reminder of who we are? It is a way of saying, "This is us at our best." It is the way many of us would want to be remembered. If truth be told, we are not always like this—nicely dressed, well groomed, and arrayed in harmony—but this is the family's aspiration: to live in harmony.

The liturgy is something like the family photo. When the church is assembled for praise and thanksgiving to God it presents a picture of the Christian community at its best. For a moment—just an hour or so—the members gain a glimpse of what God intended for the Church, a life in harmony. In a sense the liturgical celebration provides a picture that the Church shows to God, as if to say, this is us at our best. Knowing full well that this is not the way they look all the time, but this is the goal to which they aspire in fidelity to the Lord. Moreover, the liturgy is more than a static photo; it is more of a dramatic performance, in which the assembly acts out its aspiration. Through the assigned roles of presider and congregation, through its script and ancient formulae, the people of God rehearse their roles as participants in the history of salvation. The liturgy shapes the life of the believers, guiding them toward the beautiful, that is, the glory of God.

The assembled community united in prayer and praise of God becomes a living icon, revealing the presence of Christ on earth. The liturgy is a living beauty through which we continue to ask the question, What did you mean by "this"?

NOTES

1. Matthew 26:26; Mark 14:22; Luke 22:19; 1 Corinthians 11:23.

2. Some Christian churches, especially those who do not celebrate the Eucharist regularly, may differ in their understanding of this passage.

3. For a full description of these abuses, see the essay by Reinold Thiesen, OSB, "Reform of Mass Liturgy and the Council of Trent," *Worship* 40 (1966): 565-583.

4. The word "votive" is derived from the Latin *votum* meaning a vow or a solemn promise to the gods. Thus a votive offering in general refers either to a commitment that has been vowed, or simply a wish or desire. In the Roman Catholic Church, votive masses are optional and may be used on weekdays in

ordinary time when no feast or other commemoration appears on the church's calendar. The current missal contains votive masses for the Trinity, the Blessed Virgin Mary, the Apostles, among others. Cf. Christopher Walsh, "Votive Masses," in *The New Westminster Dictionary of Liturgy and Worship*, ed. Paul F. Bradshaw (Louisville, Ky.: Westminster John Knox Press, 2002), 472.

   5. Walsh, "Votive Masses," 572. See also Owen Chadwick, *The Pelican History of the Church*, vol. 3, *The Reformation* (Harmondsworth: Penguin, 1972), 31–39.

   6. Robert Cabie, *History of the Mass*, translated by Lawrence Johnson (Portland, Ore.: Pastoral Press, 1992), 88. Note that there was some allowance for deviation. Those churches that could demonstrate that their particular practice or prayers were in use for two hundred years or more were permitted to retain that practice. Josef A. Jungmann, *The Mass of the Roman Rite: Its Origins and Development (Missarum Sollemnia)*, 2 vols. (Westminster, Md.: Christian Classics, 1986), 138.

   7. Pius V, promulgating the Tridentine Missal, in the Bull, *Quo primum tempore*, 19 July, 1570. Cabie, *History*, 87.

   8. Cabie, *History*, 88.

   9. Jungmann, *The Mass of the Roman Rite*, 140–141.

   10. In his instruction *Redemptionis Sacramentum* (On certain matters to be observed or to be avoided regarding the Most Holy Eucharist) Cardinal Arrinze observes: "[I]t is not possible to be silent about the *abuses*, even quite grave ones, against the nature of the Liturgy and the Sacraments as well as the tradition and the authority of the church, which in our day not infrequently plague liturgical celebrations in one ecclesial environment or another" (n. 4). (My emphasis.)

   11. This national meeting of the bishops took place on June 15, 2006, in Los Angeles. To read two opposing and well articulated viewpoints on this debate see Bishop Arthur Roche, "Translating the Order of Mass," *Origins: CNS Documentary Service* 36, no. 7 (June 29, 2006): 103, and Bishop Donald W. Trautman, "The Relationship of the Active Participation of the Assembly to Liturgical Traditions," *Worship* 8, no. 4 (July 2006): 290–310.

   12. John 17:20–21.

   13. Luke 11:5–13.

   14. Matthew 16:13–20. Mark 4:35–41.

   15. For a lively discussion on this problem see Thomas. Day, *Why Catholics Can't Sing: The Culture of Catholicism and the Triumph of Bad Taste* (New York: Crossroad Publications, 1990), 35–36.

   16. Paul Evdokimov and Stéphane Bigham, *The Art of the Icon: A Theology of Beauty* (Redondo Beach, Calif.: Oakwood Publications, 1990), 179–180; Donald K. McKim, *Westminster Dictionary of Theological Terms*, 1st ed. (Louisville, Ky.: Westminster John Knox Press, 1996), 136.

   17. Christopher Irvine and Anne Dawtry, *Art and Worship*, Pueblo Book (Collegeville, Minn.: Liturgical Press, 2002), 5. See also Gregory Woolfenden, "Icon," in *The New Westminster Dictionary of Liturgy and Worship*, ed. Paul F. Bradshaw (Louisville, Ky.: Westminster John Knox Press, 2002), 241.

   18. Irvine and Dawtry, *Art and Worship*, 68.

   19. "Icons," in *The Encyclopedia of Religion*, ed. Mircea Eliade and Charles J. Adams, vol. 7 (New York: Macmillan Collier Macmillan, 1987), 16 vols., 67–70.

   20. John 14:8–9.

21. Irenaeus, "Against Hereies," Book IV, chap. 20, no. 7. In *The Ante-Nicene Fathers*, vol. I, ed. The Rev. Alexander Roberts and James Donaldson (Grand Rapids, Mich.: Eerdmans, 1996), 490.

22. In the discussion of the priest as *alter christus*, we mean to emphasize the role of the priest with the community in worship, rather than the physical attributes of the presider resembling Jesus. We intend to remain focused on what "this" means.

23. "Christian Initiation of Adults," no. 228. *Rites*, vol. 1 (Collegeville, Minn.: Liturgical Press, 1990). For the teaching on the notion of the "priesthood of the laity," see *Decree on the Apostolate of the Laity* (*Apostolicam Actuositatem*), no. 10, and *Dogmatic Constitution on the Church* (*Lumen Gentium*), no. 33, in *The Documents of Vatican II*.

24. Catholic Church, *Co-Workers in the Vineyard of the Lord: A Resource for Guiding the Development of Lay Ecclesial Ministry* (Washington, D.C.: United States Conference of Catholic Bishops, 2005), 8.

25. Luke 23:33.

26. Luke 10:27.

27. Ruth Sawyer, *The Way of the Storyteller* (New York: Penguin Books, 1976), 29.

28. With the mention of the various arts here, it should be noted that a discussion of liturgical aesthetics would be incomplete without including the specific contribution of artists from various fields. In our course on Liturgical Aesthetics we invited several artists as guest lecturers: a playwright, a dancer, an author, an architect, a painter, a composer, and a film critic. There was not space enough to include the material from their lectures and class discussion in this book. Here we intended to explain our own theory of the relationship of beauty and worship. We hope to compile in a subsequent volume the conversations with the artists who graced our class.

✝

Bibliography

Abbott, Walter M., S.J. *The Documents of Vatican II.* New York: Herder and Herder Association Press, 1966.

Alison, James. *Raising Abel: The Recovery of Eschatological Imagination.* New York: Crossroad Publications, 1996.

Arrinze, Francis Cardinal. "Redemptionis Sacramentum: On Certain Matters to Be Observed or to Be Avoided Regarding the Most Holy Eucharist." *Congregation for Divine Worship and the Discipline of the Sacrament*, March 25, 2004.

Avila P., Rafael. *Worship and Politics.* Maryknoll, N.Y.: Orbis Books, 1981.

Bailey, Wilma A. *Music in Christian Worship: At the Service of the Liturgy.* Collegeville, Minn.: Liturgical Press, 2005.

Baldovin, John Francis, SJ. *Bread of Life, Cup of Salvation: Understanding the Mass.* Lanham, Md.: Rowman & Littlefield Publishers, 2003.

Balthasar, Hans Urs von. *The Glory of the Lord: A Theological Aesthetics.* Translated by Erasmo Leiva-Merikakis Riches and edited by Joseph Fessio and John Riches. San Francisco, Calif.: Ignatius Press, 1983–1989. 7 vols.

———. *Presence and Thought: Essay on the Religious Philosophy of Gregory of Nyssa.* San Francisco, Calif.: Ignatius Press, 1995.

———. *The Realm of Metaphysics in Antiquity.* Vol. 4 of *The Glory of the Lord: A Theological Aesthetics.* Translated by Brian McNeil et al. and edited by John Kenneth Riches. San Francisco, Calif.: Ignatius Press, 1989. 7 vols.

———. "Theology and Sanctity." In *The Word Made Flesh*, vol. 1, 181–209. San Francisco, Calif.: Ignatius Press, 1989.

Barton, John. "Amos." In *The New Interpreter's Study Bible*, 1286–1237. Nashville, Tenn.: Abingdon Press, 2003.

Berger, Teresa. "Lex Orandi—Lex Credendi—Lex Agendi: Auf dem Weg zu einer Okumenisch Konsensfahigen Verhaltnisbestimmung von Liturgie, Theologie, Ethik." *Archiv Fur Liturgiewissenschaft* 27 (1985): 425–432.

Berry, Wendell. "The Pleasures of Eating." In *What Are People for?* San Francisco, Calif.: North Point Press, 1990.

Bishop Arthur Roche. "Translating the Order of Mass." *Origins: CNS Documentary Service* 36, no. 7 (June 29, 2006).

Bishop Donald W. Trautman. "The Relationship of the Active Participation of the Assembly to Liturgical Traditions." *Worship* 8, no. 4 (July 2006): 290–310.

Bishop Roger Mahony. "The Eucharist and Social Justice." *Worship* 57 (1983): 52–61.

Brown, Frank Burch. "Christian Music: More Than Just Words." *Theology Today* 62 (2005): 223–229.

Brown, Raymond Edward. *The Gospel According to John (I–XII)*. Vol. 29 of *Anchor Bible*. New York: Doubleday & Company, 1981.

———. *An Introduction to the New Testament*. New York: Doubleday, 1997.

Brown, Sally A., and Patrick D. Miller. *Lament: Reclaiming Practices in Pulpit, Pew, and Public Square*. Louisville, Ky.: Westminster John Knox Press, 2005.

Brueggemann, Walter. *Finally Comes the Poet: Daring Speech for Proclamation*. Minneapolis, Minn.: Fortress Press, 1989.

Buber, Martin. *Good and Evil: Two Interpretations*. Upper Saddle River, N.J.: Prentice Hall, 1997.

Bump, Jerome. *Gerard Manley Hopkins*. Boston: Twayne Publishers, 1982.

Cabie, Robert. *History of the Mass*. Translated by Lawrence Johnson. Portland, Ore.: Pastoral Press, 1992.

Calderón de la Barca, Pedro, and Eugenio Frutos. *El Gran Teatro del Mundo*. Salamanca: Ediciones Anaya, 1958.

Casel, Odo. *The Mystery of Christian Worship, and Other Writings*. Westminster, Md.: Newman Press, 1962.

Catholic Church. *Built of Living Stones: Art, Architecture, and Worship*. Washington, D.C.: United States Catholic Conference, 2000.

———. *Co-Workers in the Vineyard of the Lord: A Resource for Guiding the Development of Lay Ecclesial Ministry*. Washington, D.C.: United States Conference of Catholic Bishops, 2005.

Catholic Church, National Conference of Catholic Bishops, Bishops' Committee on the Liturgy. *Environment and Art in Catholic Worship*. Washington, D.C.: National Conference of Catholic Bishops, 1978.

Chadwick, Owen. *The Reformation*. Vol. 3 of *The Pelican History of the Church*. Harmondsworth: Penguin, 1972.

Chauvet, Louis-Marie. *The Sacraments: The Word of God at the Mercy of the Body*. Collegeville, Minn.: Liturgical Press, 2001.

———. *Symbol and Sacrament: A Sacramental Reinterpretation of Christian Existence*. Collegeville, Minn.: Liturgical Press, 1993.

Childs, Brevard S. *The Book of Exodus; a Critical, Theological Commentary*. In *Old Testament Library*. Philadelphia: Westminster Press, 1974.

Cohen Stuart, G. H. *The Struggle in Man Between Good and Evil: An Inquiry Into the Origin of the Rabbinic Concept of Yetzer Hara*. Kampen: J.H. Kok, 1984.

"The Constitution on the Sacred Liturgy." In *The Documents of Vatican II*, edited by Walter M. Abbott. New York: Herder and Herder Association Press, 1966.

Day, Thomas. *Why Catholics Can't Sing: The Culture of Catholicism and the Triumph of Bad Taste*. New York: Crossroad Publications, 1990.

De lubac, Henri, O.P. *The Mystery of the Supernatural*. Milestones in Catholic Theology. New York: Crossroad Publications, 1998.

Dix, Gregory. *The Shape of the Liturgy*. London: Adam & Charles Black, 1993.

Dombrowski, Daniel A. *Divine Beauty: The Aesthetics of Charles Hartshorne*. In *The Vanderbilt Library of American Philosophy*. Nashville, Tenn.: Vanderbilt University Press, 2004.

Donahue, John, SJ. "Biblical Perspectives on Justice." In *The Faith That Does Justice: Examining the Christian Sources for Social Change*, edited by John C. Haughey. New York: Paulist Press, 1977.

Duffy, Stephen. *The Graced Horizon: Nature and Grace in Modern Catholic Thought*. Theology and Life Series, vol. 37. Collegeville, Minn.: Liturgical Press, 1992.

Edwards, Jonathan. *The Religious Affections*. Edinburgh: Banner of Truth Trust, 1986.

Evdokimov, Paul, and Stéphane Bigham. *The Art of the Icon: A Theology of Beauty*. Redondo Beach, Calif.: Oakwood Publications, 1990.

Fields, Stephens, SJ. "Balthasar and Rahner on the Spiritual Senses." *Theological Studies* 57, no. 2 (June 1996): 224–241.

Fitzmyer, Joseph A. *The Gospel According to Luke (I–IX)*. Vol. 28 of *Anchor Bible*. New York: Doubleday & Company, 1981.

Gamber, Klaus. *The Reform of the Roman Liturgy: Its Problems and Background*. San Juan Capistrano, Calif.: Una Voce Press, 1993.

Garcia-Rivera, Alejandro. "Light from Light: An Aesthetic Approach to the Science-and-Religion Dialogue." *Currents in Theology and Mission* 28, nos. 3–4 (June/August 2001): 273–278.

———. "A Tale of Two Altars: The Pilgrim Church of Vatican II." In *Pilgrimage; Concilium*, edited by Charles Duquoc and Virgil Elizondo. Maryknoll, N.Y.: Orbis Books, 1996, vol. 4, 123–135.

———. "The Whole and the Love of Difference." In *From the Heart of Our People: Latino/a Explorations in Catholic Systematic Theology*, edited by Orlando Espín and Miguel H. Díaz. Maryknoll, N.Y.: Orbis Books, 1999, viii, 271.

———. *A Wounded Innocence: Sketches for a Theology of Art*. Collegeville, Minn.: Liturgical Press, 2003.

Garcia-Rivera, Alex. *The Community of the Beautiful: A Theological Aesthetics*. Collegeville, Minn.: Liturgical Press, 1999.

———. "The Cosmic Frontier: Towards a Natural Anthropology." *CTNS Bulletin: The Center for the Theology and the Natural Sciences* 15, no. 4 (1995): 1–6.

Gilbert, Hugh, OSB. *Odo Casel: Prophet and Mystagogue*. http://mywebpages.com cast.net/enpeters/liturgy&sacraments_casel.htm. Accessed June 1, 2005.

Green, Daniel. "Gift of the Land." Unpublished work.

Hartshorne, Charles. *Born to Sing: An Interpretation and World Survey of Bird Song*. Bloomington: Indiana University Press, 1973.

———. *The Philosophy and Psychology of Sensation*. Port Washington, N.Y.: Kennikat Press, 1968.

———. *Wisdom as Moderation: A Philosophy of the Middle Way*. Albany, N.Y.: State University of New York Press, 1987.

Hick, John. *Evil and the God of Love.* London: Macmillan, 1966.

Hippolytus, and G. J. Cuming. *Hippolytus, a Text for Students.* Bramcote, Notts.: Grove Books, 1976.

Huesman, John E., SJ. "Exodus." In *The Jerome Biblical Commentary,* edited by Raymond Edward Brown, Joseph A. Fitzmyer, and Roland Edmund Murphy. Englewood Cliffs, N.J.: Prentice-Hall, 1968, 47–66.

Hyde, Lewis. *The Gift: Imagination and the Erotic Life of Property.* New York: Vintage Books, 1983.

"Icons." In *The Encyclopedia of Religion,* edited by Mircea Eliade and Charles J. Adams. New York: Macmillan Collier Macmillan, 1987, 16 vols., vol. 7, 67–70.

"Instruction on the Worship of the Eucharistic Mystery." In *Vatican Council II: More Postconciliar Documents,* edited by Austin Flannery, OP. Collegeville, Minn.: Liturgical Press, 1982.

Irvine, Christopher, and Anne Dawtry. *Art and Worship.* Collegeville, Minn.: Liturgical Press, 2002.

Irwin, Kevin W. *Models of the Eucharist.* New York: Paulist Press, 2005.

Iturbe, Borja. *Music and Theology of the Eucharist.* Unpublished manuscript.

Jasper, Ronald Claud Dudley, and G. J. Cuming. *Prayers of the Eucharist: Early and Reformed.* 3d ed. Collegeville, Minn.: Liturgical Press, 1990.

Johnson, Luke Timothy, and Daniel J. Harrington. *The Gospel of Luke.* Sacra Pagina, vol. 3. Collegeville, Minn.: Liturgical Press, 1991.

Joncas, Jan Michael. "Liturgy and Music." In *Handbook for Liturgical Studies,* edited by Anscar J. Chupungco. Collegeville, Minn.: Liturgical Press, 1997.

Jungmann, Josef A. *The Mass of the Roman Rite: Its Origins and Development (Missarum Sollemnia).* 2 vols. Westminster, Md.: Christian Classics, 1986.

Kasper, Walter Cardinal. *Sacrament of Unity: The Eucharist and the Church.* New York: Crossroad Publications, 2004.

Kaufmann, Walter Arnold. *Tragedy and Philosophy.* Garden City, N.Y.: Doubleday, 1968.

Kavanagh, Aidan. *On Liturgical Theology.* The Hale Memorial Lectures of Seabury-Western Theological Seminary, 1981. New York: Pueblo Publishing, 1984.

Kearney, Richard. *The Wake of Imagination: Ideas of Creativity in Western Culture.* London: Hutchinson, 1988.

King, P. J. "Amos." In *The Jerome Biblical Commentary,* edited by Raymond Edward Brown, Joseph A. Fitzmyer, and Roland Edmund Murphy. Englewood Cliffs, N.J.: Prentice-Hall, 1968.

Knight, Douglas A. "Idols, Idolatry." In *The Oxford Companion to the Bible,* edited by Bruce Manning Metzger and Michael David Coogan. New York: Oxford University Press, 2003.

LaVerdiere, Eugene. *The Eucharist in the New Testament and the Early Church.* Collegeville, Minn.: Liturgical Press, 1996.

"Leb." In *Theological Dictionary of the New Testament,* edited by Gerhard Kittel. Grand Rapids, Mich.: Eerdmans, 1964.

Lee, Sang Hyun. *The Philosophical Theology of Jonathan Edwards.* Expanded edition. Princeton, N.J.: Princeton University Press, 2000.

Lockwood, Lewis. *Beethoven: The Music and the Life.* New York: W.W. Norton, 2003.

Luther, Martin. "The Babylonian Captivity of the Church (1520)." Philadelphia, translated by Albert T. W. Steinhauser. In *Works of Martin Luther: With Introductions and Notes*, vol. 2. Philadelphia: Muhlenberg Press, 1943, 6 vols.

Mahony, Roger Cardinal. *Gather Faithfully Together: Guide for Sunday Mass*. Chicago, Ill.: Liturgy Training Publications, 1997.

Marion, Jean-Luc. *God without Being: Hors-Texte*. Paperback edition. *Religion and Postmodernism*. Chicago, Ill.: University of Chicago Press, 1995.

Maritain, Jacques. *Creative Intuition in Art and Poetry*. New York: World Publishing, 1968.

McIntosh, Mark Allen. *Mystical Theology: The Integrity of Spirituality and Theology*. Challenges in Contemporary Theology. Malden, Mass.: Blackwell, 1998.

McKim, Donald K. *Westminster Dictionary of Theological Terms*. 1st ed. Louisville, Ky.: Westminster John Knox Press, 1996.

Melloh, John. "Theology of Liturgical Time." In *The New Dictionary of Sacramental Worship*, edited by Peter E. Fink, 734–736. Collegeville, Minn.: Liturgical Press, 1990.

Merelman, Richard M. *Making Something of Ourselves: On Culture and Politics in the United States*. Berkeley: University of California Press, 1984.

Metzger, Marcel. "A Eucharistic Mission." In *The Eucharist*. Vol. III of *Handbook for Liturgical Studies*, edited by Anscar J. Chupungco, OSB. Collegeville, Minn.: Liturgical Press, 1997.

Mitchell, Nathan. "Present in the Sacraments." *Worship* 80, no. 4 (July 2006): 347–359.

Mitchell, Nathan D. "Other Voices, Other Rooms: The Future of Liturgical Language in Postmodern Cultures." *New Theology Review* 18, no. 4 (November 2005): 59–67.

Moyter, J. A. *The Message of the Exodus*. Downers Grove, Ill.: Intervarsity Press, 2005.

Murphy-O'Connor, Jerome. "The First Letter to the Corinthians." In *The New Jerome Biblical Commentary*, edited by Raymond Edward Brown, Joseph A. Fitzmyer, and Roland Edmund Murphy. Englewood Cliffs, N.J.: Prentice-Hall, 1990.

"Music in Christian Worship." 3rd ed. In *The Liturgy Documents: A Parish Resource*, edited by Elizabeth Hoffman and Catholic Church. Archdiocese of Chicago (Ill.). Liturgy Training Program. Chicago, Ill.: Liturgy Training Publications, 1991.

The New Interpreter's Study Bible: New Revised Standard Version with the Apocrypha. Nashville, Tenn.: Abingdon Press, 2003.

Nichols, Aidan. *No Bloodless Myth: A Guide Through Balthasar's Dramatics*. Edinburgh: T & T Clark, 2000.

"Nous." In *Theological Dictionary of the New Testament*, edited by Gerhard Kittel. Grand Rapids, Mich.: Eerdmans, 1964.

Ong, Walter J. *The Presence of the Word: Some Prolegomena for Cultural and Religious History*. New York: Simon & Schuster, 1970.

Origen, and Hans Urs von Balthasar. *Origen, Spirit and Fire: A Thematic Anthology of His Writings*. Washington, D.C.: Catholic University of America Press, 1984.

Osborne, Harold. "Revelatory Theories of Art." *The British Journal of Aesthetics* 4, no. 4 (October 1964): 332–347.

Parenti, Stefano. "Christian Initiation in the East." In *Sacraments and Sacramentals.* Vol. 4 of *Handbook for Liturgical Studies,* edited by Anscar J. Chupungco, OSB. Collegeville, Minn.: Liturgical Press, 2000, 5 vols., 175–187.

Phillips, L. Edward. "Ethics and Worship." In *The New Westminster Dictionary of Liturgy and Worship,* edited by Paul F. Bradshaw. Louisville, Ky.: Westminster John Knox Press, 2002.

Pickstock, Catherine. *After Writing: On the Liturgical Consummation of Philosophy.* Oxford: Blackwell Publishers, 1998.

Pinkus, Lucio Maria, OSH. "The Psychosociological Aspect of the Liturgy." In *Fundamental Liturgy.* Vol. 2 of *Handbook for Liturgical Studies,* edited by Anscar J. Chupungco, OSB. Collegeville, Minn.: Liturgical Press, 1997, 5 vols., 175–187.

Potter, Vincent G. *Charles S. Peirce on Norms & Ideals.* Amherst: University of Massachusetts Press, 1967.

Propp, William H. "Golden Calf." In *The Oxford Companion to the Bible,* edited by Bruce Manning Metzger and Michael David Coogan. New York: Oxford University Press, 2003.

Quasten, Johannes. *Music & Worship in Pagan & Christian Antiquity.* Washington, D.C.: National Association of Pastoral Musicians, 1983.

Rahner, Karl. *The Practice of Faith: A Handbook of Contemporary Spirituality.* New York: Crossroad Publications, 1983.

Ratzinger, Joseph. *A New Song for the Lord: Faith in Christ and Liturgy Today.* New York: Crossroad Publications, 1996.

———. *The Spirit of the Liturgy.* San Francisco, Calif.: Ignatius Press, 2000.

Rouet, Albert. *Liturgy and the Arts.* Collegeville, Minn.: Liturgical Press, 1997.

Saliers, Don. "Integrity of Sung Prayer." *Worship* 55, no. 4 (1981).

Saliers, Don E., E. Byron Anderson, and Bruce T. Morrill. *Liturgy and the Moral Self: Humanity at Full Stretch Before God: Essays in Honor of Don E. Saliers.* Collegeville, Minn.: Liturgical Press, 1998.

Sawicki, Marianne. *Seeing the Lord: Resurrection and Early Christian Practices.* Minneapolis, Minn.: Fortress Press, 1994.

Sawyer, Ruth. *The Way of the Storyteller.* New York: Penguin Books, 1976.

Schillebeeckx, E., OP. *Christ, the Sacrament of the Encounter with God.* Kansas City, Mo.: Sheed & Ward, 1963.

Schopenhauer, Arthur. *The World as Will and Representation.* New York: Dover Publications, 1966, 2 vols.

Steck, Christopher W. *The Ethical Thought of Hans Urs von Balthasar.* New York: Crossroad Publications, 2001.

Stuhlmueller, Carroll, CP. "The Gospel According to Luke." In *The Jerome Biblical Commentary,* edited by Raymond Edward Brown, Joseph A. Fitzmyer, and Roland Edmund Murphy. Englewood Cliffs, N.J.: Prentice-Hall, 1968.

Tatarkiewicz, Wladyslaw. "The Great Theory of Beauty & Its Decline." *Journal of Aesthetics and Art Criticism* 31, no. 2 (1972): 165–179.

Thiesen, Reinold, OSB. "Reform of Mass: Liturgy and the Council of Trent." *Worship* 40 (1966): 565–583.

Thompson, D'Arcy Wentworth. *On Growth and Form*. Cambridge: University Press, 1968, 2 vols.

Tillich, Paul. *Theology of Culture*. Edited by Robert C. Kimball. New York: Oxford University Press (imprint: Galaxy), 1964.

Tillich, Paul, and Michael F. Palmer. *Writings in the Philosophy of Culture*. Berlin: De Gruyter, 1990.

Turner, Denys. *The Darkness of God: Negativity in Christian Mysticism*. Cambridge: Cambridge University Press, 1995.

Unamuno, Miguel de, Anthony Kerrigan, and Martin Nozick. *The Tragic Sense of Life in Men and Nations*. Bollingen Series, vol. 85. Princeton, N.J.: Princeton University Press, 1972.

Unger, Roberto Mangabeira. *Passion: An Essay on Personality*. New York: Free Press Collier Macmillan, 1984.

United States Conference of Catholic Bishops. *The General Instruction of the Roman Missal*. Washington, D.C.: Committee on the Liturgy, 2003.

Viladesau, Richard. *Theology and the Arts: Encountering God Through Music, Art, and Rhetoric*. New York: Paulist Press, 2000.

von Balthasar, Hans Urs. *Prolegomena*. Vol. 1 of *Theo-Drama: Theological Dramatic Theory*. Translated by Graham Harrison. San Francisco, Calif.: Ignatius Press, 1988, 5 vols.

———. *Seeing the Form*. Vol. 1 of *The Glory of the Lord: A Theological Aesthetics*. Translated by Erasmo Leiva-Merikakis. Edited by Joseph Fession and John Riches. New York: Crossroad Publications, 1983, 7 vols.

Wainwright, Geoffrey. *Doxology the Praise of God in Worship, Doctrine, and Life: A Systematic Theology*. New York: Oxford University Press, 1980.

Walsh, Christopher. "Votive Masses." In *The New Westminster Dictionary of Liturgy and Worship*, edited by Paul F. Bradshaw. Louisville, Ky.: Westminster John Knox Press, 2002.

Wannenwetsch, Bernd. *Political Worship: Ethics for Christian Citizens*. Translated by Margaret Kohl. Oxford Studies in Theological Ethics. Oxford: Oxford University Press, 2004.

Weekly, Christopher S. "'Go to Love and Serve': The Concluding Rite (the Sending) of the Eucharist Ecumenically Observed." Thesis S.T.L., Jesuit School of Theology at Berkeley, 1999.

Westermann, Claus. *Creation*. Philadelphia: Fortress Press, 1976.

"Where Hunger is Found." *Origins* 35, no. 8 (July 7, 2005).

White, Morton Gabriel. *Science and Sentiment in America: Philosophical Thought from Jonathan Edwards to John Dewey*. London: Oxford University Press, 1973.

Wood, Susan K. *Sacramental Orders*. Lex Orandi Series. Collegeville, Minn.: Liturgical Press, 2000.

Woolfenden, Gregory. "Icon." In *The New Westminster Dictionary of Liturgy and Worship*, edited by Paul F. Bradshaw. Louisville, Ky.: Westminster John Knox Press, 2002.

Zajonc, Arthur. *Catching the Light: The Entwined History of Light and Mind*. Oxford: Oxford University Press, 1993.

Zenit News Agency. *Propositions of the Synod of the Eucharist*. http://www.zenit.org/english/visualizza.phtml?sid=79161. Accessed October 31, 2005.

✛
Index

About the Authors

Alejandro Garcia-Rivera is professor of systematic theology at the Jesuit School of Theology, Berkeley. He is the author of the award-winning *The Community of the Beautiful* and *A Wounded Innocence: Sketches for a Theology of Art*.

Thomas Scirghi is associate professor of liturgical theology at the Jesuit School of Theology, Berkeley. He regularly lectures on liturgical and sacramental theology.